Harnessing the Power of IoT-Enabled Machine Learning in Healthcare Applications

nova
science publishers

www.novapublishers.com

Medical Procedures, Testing and Technology

More information about this series can be found at
https://novapublishers.com/product-category/series/medical-procedures-testing-and-technology/

Computer Science, Technology and Applications

More information about this series can be found at
https://novapublishers.com/product-category/series/computer-science-technology-and-applications/

Mritunjay Rai
Ravindra Kumar Yadav
Neha Goel
Mahesh Kumar H. Kolekar
Editors

Harnessing the Power of IoT-Enabled Machine Learning in Healthcare Applications

nova
science publishers
www.novapublishers.com

DOI: https://doi.org/10.52305/MBEF3026

Library of Congress Cataloging-in-Publication Data

ISBN: 979-8-89530-626-0 (Hardcover)
ISBN: 979-8-89530-761-8 (eBook)

Published by Nova Science Publishers, Inc. † New York

Endorsement 1 – Academic Perspective

"This book offers a timely and comprehensive examination of the convergence between IoT and machine learning in healthcare. It brings together forward-thinking research that not only outlines current developments but also anticipates the future direction of intelligent health systems. A must-read for researchers, students, and policy-makers in health tech."

Professor (Dr.) Tanmoy Maity, IIT (ISM), Dhanbad, Jharkhand, India

Endorsement 2 – Industry Expert View

"Harnessing the Power of IoT-Enabled Machine Learning in Healthcare Applications captures the essence of digital health transformation. It skillfully balances academic depth with real-world relevance, making it an essential resource for engineers, clinicians, and healthcare innovators navigating the evolving tech landscape."

Dr. Chandan Kumar, Application Engineers-electronics, Arup India Pvt. Limited, Gurugram

Endorsement 3 – Clinical/Medical View

"As a healthcare professional, I found this book profoundly insightful. It translates complex technical advancements into tangible solutions that can improve patient care, diagnostics, and health outcomes. This volume bridges the gap between technology and clinical practice in a meaningful way."

Dr. Mohd. Danish Nadeem, Post-doc Fellow, IISc. Banglore

This book is dedicated to all those striving to create a smarter, safer, and more compassionate healthcare system through the convergence of technology and humanity. A special note of appreciation to our families, whose constant encouragement and patience have been our pillar of strength from the inception to the completion of this book.

Contents

Foreword

The global healthcare ecosystem stands at the threshold of a digital revolution. Rapid advancements in technology—particularly the integration of the Internet of Things (IoT) and Machine Learning (ML)—are transforming the way we diagnose, monitor, and treat patients. This convergence is ushering in an era of intelligent, connected, and personalized healthcare, where real-time data analytics, predictive modeling, and autonomous decision-making are no longer theoretical aspirations, but practical tools reshaping clinical practice.

Harnessing the Power of IoT-Enabled Machine Learning in Healthcare Applications is a timely and essential contribution to this rapidly evolving domain. This edited volume brings together an interdisciplinary group of researchers, engineers, data scientists, and healthcare professionals to explore the potential and challenges of IoT and ML in healthcare settings. From remote patient monitoring and predictive analytics to personalized medicine and smart hospitals, the chapters provide a comprehensive view of how these technologies are enhancing the quality, efficiency, and accessibility of healthcare services.

One of the most commendable aspects of this book is its balanced approach—celebrating the technological achievements while critically examining the challenges of data privacy, ethical implications, interoperability, and system integration. It offers valuable insights not only for academics and industry leaders, but also for clinicians, healthcare administrators, and policy-makers seeking to understand and leverage digital health solutions.

This book is more than a compilation of research—it is a forward-looking roadmap that reflects the future of healthcare: one where data-driven intelligence and human compassion work hand in hand to improve patient outcomes. I commend the editors and contributors for assembling such a thoughtful and impactful work. It will undoubtedly serve as a vital reference and catalyst for further innovation in smart healthcare systems.

Dr. Sameena Naaz,
University of Roehampton, London, United Kingdom

Preface

The healthcare sector is undergoing a transformative evolution driven by the convergence of two revolutionary technologies: the Internet of Things (IoT) and Machine Learning (ML). Together, these technologies are redefining how health data is collected, processed, and utilized to improve clinical outcomes, enhance patient engagement, and optimize healthcare delivery systems. The integration of IoT and ML has created a new frontier in smart healthcare, marked by remote monitoring, predictive diagnostics, personalized medicine, and efficient resource management.

This edited volume, *"Harnessing the Power of IoT-Enabled Machine Learning in Healthcare Applications,"* brings together pioneering research, technical insights, and practical applications that showcase the current advancements and future possibilities in this dynamic field. The chapters in this book delve into diverse areas such as heart disease prediction, smart hospitals, security and privacy in health data analytics, personalized healthcare systems, and patient-centric frameworks powered by AI and IoT.

The goal of this book is to serve as a comprehensive reference for academics, practitioners, industry professionals, and policy-makers interested in the transformative impact of IoT and ML on healthcare. It highlights both the immense potential and the complex challenges—ranging from data privacy and system interoperability to ethical considerations and regulatory compliance—that accompany these technologies.

By compiling interdisciplinary perspectives and cutting-edge developments, this book aims to inspire continued innovation and collaboration. It encourages stakeholders to explore novel frameworks, scalable solutions, and responsible deployment strategies to create a more efficient, accessible, and personalized healthcare ecosystem.

We extend our sincere gratitude to all the contributing authors, reviewers, and collaborators whose expertise and commitment made this volume possible. We hope that this work will act as a catalyst for further exploration and advancement in the field of intelligence.

Acknowledgments

We are deeply grateful to all those who contributed to the successful completion of this edited volume, *Harnessing the Power of IoT-Enabled Machine Learning in Healthcare Applications*. This work would not have been possible without the collective effort, support, and encouragement of many individuals and institutions.

First and foremost, we sincerely thank all the contributing authors for their insightful chapters and scholarly rigor. Their dedication to advancing research in the fields of healthcare, machine learning, and IoT has shaped this book into a meaningful and valuable academic resource.

We extend our appreciation to the reviewers and editorial advisors who offered critical feedback, ensuring the quality and integrity of the content. Their time, expertise, and constructive comments significantly enhanced the overall depth and coherence of this publication.

We also acknowledge the invaluable support of our respective academic and research institutions, which provided the infrastructure, encouragement, and intellectual environment necessary for the development of this project. To the tireless visionaries, researchers, clinicians, and engineers whose unwavering pursuit of innovation continues to reshape the landscape of modern healthcare.

We extend our heartfelt thanks to our institution, Shri Ramswaroop Memorial University (SRMU), Barabanki, for its unwavering support throughout this journey.

To the patients whose resilience inspires every line of inquiry and technological breakthrough.

Our heartfelt thanks go to Nova Science Publishers, Inc. for allowing us to collaborate on this important study, enabling us to explore and analyze diabetic foot ulcer management and its related complications. For their trust in this vision and for providing an excellent platform to share this work with the global research community.

Finally, we are thankful to our families and loved ones, whose patience, understanding, and encouragement have been a source of constant strength throughout this journey.

To everyone who contributed directly or indirectly—your support and collaboration are genuinely appreciated.

With warmest regards,
Editors

About the Editors

Dr. Mritunjay Rai works as an assistant professor in the Department of Electrical and Electronics Engineering, Shri Ramswaroop Memorial University, U.P., Barabanki, India. He received his Ph.D. from the IIT (ISM), Dhanbad, India, in Electrical Engineering with a specialization in image processing. Dr. Rai is an active researcher and has published several papers in SCI-indexed Q2 journals and at international and national conferences in his field. His areas of interest lie in image processing, medical image processing, health-care systems, artificial intelligence, machine learning, deep learning, IoT, communication, speech processing, and robotics and automation. He has contributed many chapters to books published by Intech Open Access, CRC, IGI Global, and Elsevier. He is an editor of books published by reputed publishers Wiley, AAP, NOVA, and IGI. Currently, he is actively working on various statistical models to improve the efficiency of surveillance systems.

Dr. R.K. Yadav is a professor and head of the department of electronics and communication engineering at RGIT, Ghaziabad. He has over 29 years of extensive experience in teaching and research, with expertise in the fields of microwave engineering, electromagnetic (EM) waves, and image processing. Dr. Yadav has authored more than 60 research papers published in reputed national and international journals, conferences, and symposiums. He has also authored a book on microwave engineering. His current research interests include microwave engineering, image processing, and integrated circuits. He is an active member of the IEEE.

Dr. Neha Goel currently works as a professor in the department of electronics and amp; communication engineering, RKGIT, Ghaziabad, India. She has a Ph.D. degree from SRM University, Chennai. She has 19 years of rich experience in teaching and research and development activities. Her areas of interest are VLSI design, CMOS design, Internet of Things, and machine learning. She has more than 20 published papers in Scopus Indexed Journals/ Conferences and 4 other reputed journals along with more than 25 international/ national conference papers presented. She also published 3 Indian patents, 1 patent grant, 4 published books, and 13 chapters. She has guided more than 42 B.Tech projects along with 4 M.Tech thesis projects. She has also attended various FDPs, workshops and seminars in various fields.

Senior Member, IEEE, *Dr. Maheshkumar H. Kolekar*, currently works as an associate professor in the Dept. of Electrical Eng. at the Indian Institute of Technology Patna, India. He received his Ph.D. degree in electronics and electrical communication engineering from IIT Kharagpur in 2007. From 2008 to 2009, he was a post-doctoral research fellow with the department of computer science, University of Missouri, and Columbia, USA where he worked on video surveillance systems. During May to July 2017, he worked as DAAD fellow in Technical University Berlin in the area of EEG signal analysis using machine learning and deep learning. He has authored a book titled, "Intelligent Video Surveillance Systems: An Algorithmic Approach," with CRC Press, Taylor and Francis Group, (2018). His name has appeared continuously for three years (2021, 2022, and 2023) in the top 2% of scientists in the world in the area of artificial intelligence and image processing, according to a list released by Stanford University, USA.

Introduction

The twenty-first century has witnessed a seismic shift in the way healthcare is delivered, managed, and experienced. At the heart of this transformation lies the convergence of two groundbreaking technologies: the Internet of Things (IoT) and Machine Learning (ML). Together, they are revolutionizing healthcare systems by enabling continuous monitoring, predictive diagnostics, personalized treatment, and real-time decision-making—capabilities that were once considered futuristic.

Harnessing the Power of IoT-Enabled Machine Learning in Healthcare Applications emerges as a comprehensive and timely response to the growing need for literature that examines this convergence through a multidisciplinary lens. It brings together researchers, technologists, medical practitioners, and data scientists to present a unified yet diverse examination of how IoT and ML are reshaping the future of healthcare.

The Rationale

The integration of IoT devices-such as wearable sensors, smart implants, and remote monitoring systems-with ML algorithms offers a powerful paradigm: connected intelligence. These systems can collect, analyze, and learn from vast quantities of health-related data, making healthcare more proactive, predictive, and personalized. However, this advancement also brings new challenges: data privacy, security vulnerabilities, ethical concerns, and the complexity of integrating heterogeneous systems within traditional clinical workflows.

This book aims to address both the opportunities and challenges inherent in this technological shift.

The Structure

The volume is organized into thematic chapters, each delving into a specific aspect of IoT and ML integration in healthcare:

- Foundational Concepts and evolving trends in medical IoT and machine learning.
- Practical Applications, such as heart disease prediction, remote monitoring, smart hospitals, and personalized medicine.
- System-Level Challenges, including data security, interoperability, latency, and trust in AI-driven decisions.
- Futuristic Perspectives, exploring emerging technologies like the Internet of Medical Things (IoMT), explainable AI, and ethical frameworks.

Each chapter is crafted to be informative yet accessible, offering theoretical grounding, technical insight, and practical relevance.

The Intended Audience

This book is intended for a wide audience including:

- Researchers and graduate students exploring the frontier of digital health.
- Healthcare professionals interested in leveraging intelligent technologies.
- Engineers and developers designing next-generation health solutions.
- Policy-makers and strategists shaping health innovation at institutional and national levels.

Looking Ahead

The journey toward intelligent, IoT-driven, machine learning–enabled healthcare is just beginning. As we stand at the intersection of technology and human well-being, this book invites readers to reflect on how innovation can serve humanity—not just through enhanced efficiency, but by delivering more responsive, ethical, and compassionate healthcare systems.

We hope this volume inspires further inquiry, collaboration, and action toward building a healthier, smarter future.

Editors

Chapter 1

IoT-Enabled Machine Learning in Healthcare: Transformations, Trends, and Future Directions

Prasenjit Maji[1,2,*]
Supriyo Maji[1,†]
Swagatalakshmi Ghosh[1,‡]
Swadhin Kumar Mondal[1,§]
and Hemanta Kumar Mondal[2,¶]
[1]Department of CSD, Dr. B. C. Roy Engineering College, Durgapur, WB, India
[2]Department of ECE, NIT Durgapur, WB, India

Abstract

Healthcare is among the industries that have evolved in the past few years due to the integration of machine learning (ML) algorithms and Internet of Things (IoT) technology. This chapter emphasizes IoT-enabled machine learning in healthcare and extensively assesses revolution and improvement in the domain in the last two decades. The chapter illustrates the potential advantages and consequences for enhancing patient outcomes, healthcare delivery, and resource usage while outlining significant trends, obstacles, and advancements in this field. Healthcare-enabled services and the innovative technologies that underpin them have become the focus of extensive research over the last ten years. The

* Corresponding Author's Email: maji.katm@gmail.com
† Corresponding Author's Email: akashmaji200680@gmail.com
‡ Corresponding Author's Email: swagatalakshmig35@gmail.com
§ Corresponding Author's Email: swadhinm50@gmail.com
¶ Corresponding Author's Email: hkmondal.ece@nitdgp.ac.in

In: Harnessing the Power of IoT-Enabled Machine Learning …
Editors: Mritunjay Rai, Ravindra Kumar Yadav, Neha Goel et al.
ISBN: 979-8-89530-626-0

delivery of top-notch medical services worldwide have transformed by integrating the IoT concept with medical equipment, sensors, and healthcare workers. Enhanced patient safety, lower healthcare costs, greater accessibility to care, and increased production and efficiency in the industry have all resulted from this integration. Recent studies show that IoT-based approaches have enormous potential for bettering healthcare outcomes. Machine learning-assisted techniques have recently become one of the most efficient data analysis techniques. This chapter illustrates developments in medical IoT, emphasizing healthcare services, supporting technology, and implementations that tackle different healthcare issues. It also investigated possible problems and concerns with the healthcare IoT system.

Consequently, by providing a thorough overview of the technology's various applications, this research is a significant resource for future academics interested in exploring and discovering fresh applications for IoT in healthcare. Although there are many benefits, there are drawbacks to using IoT-enabled machine learning in the healthcare industry. Since strict regulatory standards must protect sensitive information throughout the ongoing collection and analysis of health data, data safety is essential. To guarantee smooth communication, interoperability between various devices and healthcare systems is another crucial issue that calls for defined protocols. Furthermore, it's necessary to carefully analyse the ethical ramifications of automated decision-making and the scope of machine learning's utilization in clinical settings.

This chapter provides an in-depth analysis of the developments in IoT-enabled machine learning in the healthcare arena, emphasizing the enabling technologies, the scope of healthcare services they improve, and practical applications that tackle various healthcare issues. We offer future academics and practitioners a valuable resource by outlining the potential difficulties and opportunities related to this integration. It seeks to direct the investigation of fresh uses and advancements in machine learning and the Internet of Things, supporting the ongoing enhancement of healthcare offerings. Through this investigation, we highlight the crucial role that machine learning powered by the Internet of Things will play in reshaping healthcare and advancing the delivery of more effective, efficient, patient-centered care.

Keywords: remote monitoring, predictive analytics, data management, algorithm validation, data-driven healthcare solutions

1. Introduction

Access to healthcare is a fundamental pillar of modern society; however, the increasing demands on healthcare systems, driven by population growth and the rising prevalence of chronic diseases, are placing substantial pressure on existing resources. This strain is particularly evident in the growing need for hospital beds, healthcare professionals, and essential infrastructure. Innovative solutions are required to reduce the burden on healthcare systems while maintaining or enhancing patient care quality.

Recent research has IOT as a strategy for easing these burdens. Much of this chapter focuses on utilizing IoT for patient monitoring, particularly treating serious illnesses like Parkinson's and diabetes. Studies in this domain often involve comparing various sensor technologies, emphasizing communication efficiency. However, drawing a comprehensive framework from these individual studies proves challenging due to their narrow focus.

The proposed chapter presents a universal IoT-based healthcare model in response to the gap. This model integrates all critical components necessary for a comprehensive remote health monitoring system, marking a significant advancement as no end-to-end framework has been detailed in the existing literature. The chapter provides a detailed outline of a framework that combines cloud computing, various communication protocols (both short- and long-range), and a diverse array of sensors designed to monitor different health metrics [1].

This research distinguishes itself by providing an exhaustive examination of each component within IoT-based healthcare systems. It addresses the individual elements and their collective integration, offering a holistic view of how IoT can enhance healthcare delivery. A particular highlight of this study is its focus on Low Power Wide Area Networks (LPWANs), emphasizing their suitability for IoT applications in healthcare [2]. The chapter compares licensed-band standards, such as Narrowband IoT (NB-IoT), and unlicensed-band alternatives, evaluating their effectiveness and relevance in healthcare settings.

Furthermore, the chapter explores recent advancements in the proposed framework, including innovations in cloud computing, communication protocols, and sensor technologies. The study provides valuable insights into how IoT can be leveraged to improve healthcare systems by examining these developments. This comprehensive approach highlights the strengths and limitations of current technologies and identifies areas for future research and development [3].

In conclusion, this chapter offers a thorough and original contribution to IoT-based healthcare systems. Its focus on integrating all critical components into a cohesive model and an in-depth analysis of communication protocols and sensor technologies provides a valuable resource for researchers aiming to advance remote health monitoring and overall healthcare delivery.

2. Contribution of the Chapter

This chapter presents significant advancements in integrating IoT-enabled machine learning within healthcare. It begins with an in-depth analysis of how IoT and machine learning have been incorporated into healthcare over the past two decades. It highlights the technical innovations transforming resource management, patient outcomes, and healthcare delivery.

Additionally, the chapter introduces a comprehensive IoT-based healthcare model that integrates cloud computing, various sensors, and communication protocols. This model addresses a critical gap in the literature by providing a unified, end-to-end system for remote health monitoring. The study further explores the challenges and limitations of IoT implementation in healthcare, focusing on key issues such as data security, device interoperability, and ethical concerns. It also identifies future research directions, including developing Low Power Wide Area Networks (LPWANs) for healthcare applications.

These contributions serve as a valuable resource for practitioners and researchers striving to enhance IoT-based healthcare systems, paving the way for more efficient, secure, and ethical healthcare solutions.

3. Literature Review

Integrating the IoT into healthcare signifies a pivotal transformation in medical service delivery and management. IoT, categorized by a network of interrelated devices that exchange data, has become an effective tool for improving overall care quality, improving medical procedures, developing patient monitoring, optimizing healthcare operations, and elevating overall care quality [4].

3.1. Evolution and Impact of IoT in Healthcare

The trajectory of the applications in healthcare has progressed significantly, evolving from rudimentary telemedicine solutions to sophisticated remote monitoring and management systems. Initial implementations focused on essential data collection and transmission. Early devices like fitness trackers provided preliminary insights into patient activity and health metrics [5]. These early innovations laid the groundwork for a broader trend wherein IoT technologies began to reshape healthcare practices.

Advancements in sensor technology and real-time data analytics have considerably expanded the scope of IoT in healthcare. Contemporary IoT solutions encompass devices that monitor vital signs, manage chronic conditions, and deliver real-time health updates to patients and healthcare providers [6]. This development is particularly significant given the growing number of serious diseases like diabetes and cardiac arrest, which require regular monitoring and treatment [7, 8].

3.2. Applications and Innovations

Research has elucidated several key areas where IoT applications have made substantial progress. Chronic disease management is a prominent example. Studies, including those by [9], have demonstrated the efficacy of IoT-based systems in diabetes management through continuous glucose monitoring and insulin delivery. Similarly, advancements in Parkinson's disease management have been facilitated by IoT technologies, with devices capable of tracking motor symptoms and medication [10].

Another significant innovation is the IoT and cloud computing, which are attached. Because of this interaction, the massive amount of health data produced by IOT devices may be appropriately controlled. Extensive dataset analysis and machine learning algorithms for predictions are simplified by cloud-based platforms' growth and data storage and processing skills [11]. Such integration enhances predictive capabilities, allowing for timely and informed interventions.

3.3. Challenges and Limitations

Despite these advancements, several challenges continue to limit the widespread adoption of IoT in healthcare. Foremost among these are concerns regarding data security and privacy. Robust encryption and secure communication methods are essential for transmitting critical health information across networks to safeguard against data breaches and unauthorized access [12].

Additionally, the large volumes of data created by the devices present some management challenges. Effective data processing and analysis are crucial to ensure that healthcare systems can handle the influx of information without becoming overwhelmed. Research by [13] highlights the importance of developing efficient data management strategies to integrate IoT solutions seamlessly into existing healthcare workflows.

3.4. Future Directions

Future advancements in IoT applications for healthcare are expected to be significantly shaped by the development of Low Power Wide Area Networks (LPWANs). These technologies, such as Narrowband IoT (NB-IoT), offer enhanced connectivity and energy efficiency, making them ideal for smart devices that require extended battery life and wide-area coverage [14]. Comparative analyses of licensed-band and unlicensed-band standards are crucial for identifying the most appropriate communication protocols for diverse healthcare applications. These analyses will help optimize connectivity, reliability, and efficiency in IoT-enabled healthcare systems. The Table 1 shows the tabulated study of different methodologies from various researchers along with the key findings.

Future research should focus on designing comprehensive end-to-end IoT healthcare systems that seamlessly integrate all critical components, including data collection, transmission, analysis, and decision-making. Such holistic systems will overcome existing limitations and offer more robust, scalable, and efficient remote health monitoring and management solutions, ultimately enhancing patient care and system efficiency.

Table 1. Different studies and research related to healthcare with IOT enabled machine learning

Ref.	Methodology	Key-Findings
Singh 2019 [15]	Conducted an extensive review of existing literature on IoT applications in healthcare to understand current system architectures, technologies, and challenges.	Predictive analytics greatly increase the usefulness of IoT data by facilitating early identification of health problems, tailoring treatment plans to individual needs, and improving patient outcomes.
Tian et al. 2019 [16]	Reviewed existing literature and industry reports on emerging healthcare technologies, focusing on AI, IoT, block chain, 3D printing, and 5G networking.	Emerging technologies revolutionizing smart healthcare by enhancing diagnostic accuracy, enabling continuous monitoring, securing data, and supporting personalized and efficient care, while also addressing the challenges of integration and cost.
Vipin et al. 2021 [17]	Developed and tested an IoT healthcare monitoring system with Edge AI and optimized performance in smart city environments.	Enhances IoT healthcare monitoring systems in smart cities by using machine learning and real-time data processing available at an advantage.
Zhang et al. 2021 [18]	Developed and tested collaborative algorithms that integrate AI with IoT to enhance actual time tracking and managing systems by utilizing increased responses and data preparation.	Enhanced monitoring and control systems by improving real-time data analysis, predictive accuracy, and system responsiveness, leading to more effective and efficient management of complex environments.
Naskar et al. 2020 [19]	Conducted a review and analysis of machine learning applications across various medical fields, including diagnostics, imaging, and genomics, through literature, case studies, and performance evaluations.	Advances medical science by enhancing diagnostic accuracy, optimizing treatment plans, improving medical imaging analysis, personalizing genomics, and enabling real-time patient monitoring, thereby transforming various fields of healthcare.
Misra et al. 2021 [20]	Conducted the applicable use of various connected devices throughout the everyday healthcare IoT system usage application.	Reviewed the requirements, challenges and benefits of embracing digital devices in healthcare organizations.

4. Application and Usage

The Internet of Things (IoT) has emerged as a transformative force in healthcare, fundamentally changing medical services' delivery, monitoring, and management. Through the integration of sensors and connectivity in various medical devices, IoT enables real-time data collection, enhances patient monitoring, and streamlines healthcare processes. Its uses for medical purposes are complete and cover multiple fields that improve people's health, increase efficaciousness, and decrease costs. This brief overview highlights the importance and promise of IoT technology in healthcare by investigating its different applications and effects [21].

4.1. Online Medical Observation

By providing patients electronic devices and home-based sensors that continuously monitor vital signs including heart rate, blood pressure, glucose levels, and oxygen saturation, IoT technologies enable remote patient monitoring [22]. Real-time communication of information from these devices to healthcare medical professionals supports timely treatments and lowers the requirement for frequent visits to the clinic.

For instance, continuous glucose monitors for diabetic patients provide valuable data that helps in adjusting insulin doses and managing glucose levels effectively. Similarly, wearable heart monitors can detect arrhythmias and other cardiac abnormalities, prompting early treatment and potentially preventing severe complications.

4.2. Chronic Disease Management

The management of chronic diseases benefits significantly from IoT applications. Severe illness-specific devices and sensors monitoring the use of medications and symptoms, such as in cases involving allergies and chronic obstructive pulmonary disease, also referred to COPD. IoT-enabled smart inhalers, for instance, monitor use habits and alert users when their suppository is about to expire. Healthcare professionals can enhance patient adherence and outcomes by tailoring treatment plans, modifying prescription schedules, and providing personalized advice using data from these devices.

4.3. Elderly Care and Assisted Living

IoT has a profound impact on elderly care and assisted living environments. Sensors and smart devices installed in homes or care facilities observing the activities and comfort of elderly entities. Fall detection systems, for instance, use accelerometers and gyroscopes to identify falls and alert caregivers or emergency services. Additionally, smart home systems can track daily activities, medication adherence, and even provide reminders for appointments or medication, enhancing the quality of life for elderly individuals while ensuring their safety and independence.

4.4. Hospital and Facility Management

Within healthcare facilities, IoT is employed to streamline operations and improve efficiency. Medical equipment's real-time position is monitored by IoT-based solutions, guaranteeing that vital gadgets are available when needed. Resource management methods reduce time and reduce costs by detecting usage and maintenance. Furthermore, environmental sensors keep an eye on things like humidity, temperature, and air quality within developments to ensure that health and safety regulations are followed and enhance the general atmosphere for patients and employees.

4.5. Personalized Medicine

IoT enables the advancement of personalized medicine by providing detailed and continuous health data that supports individualized treatment plans. Integrating IoT with genomic data and electronic health records (EHRs) allows healthcare providers to adapt treatments based on a patient's exclusive genetic outline and real-time health status. For example, IoT devices can monitor responses to specific therapies and medications, allowing real-time adjustments to optimize therapeutic efficacy and reduce adverse effects.

4.6. Emergency Response and Disaster Management

IoT technologies offer immediate collection of information and communication, essential for emergency response and disaster management. Internet of Things gadgets may send vital health information to first responders in an emergency, enabling them to make informed decisions and administer the proper care. Wearable sensors, for example, can provide patients with real-time health data during problems, such as blood oxygen levels and heart rate, helping emergency responders concentrate on care and use facilities.

4.7. Research and Data Analytics

The extensive data produced by IoT devices offers a rich resource for research and data analytics. Researchers and healthcare providers can analyse trends, patterns, and outcomes to improve understanding of various health conditions and treatment responses. This data-driven approach supports evidence-based medicine and accelerates the development of new therapies and interventions. IoT-generated data also aids in the identification of public health trends and the assessment of healthcare system performance.

The application of IoT in healthcare offers a multitude of benefits, from enhanced patient monitoring and chronic disease management to improved facility operations and personalized medicine. As technology continues to advance, IoT's role in healthcare is likely to expand, further transforming how medical care is delivered and managed.

5. Working Principal and Methodology

In modern years, incorporating IoT and machine learning in healthcare has led to developing advanced, fully functioning health monitoring solutions. This project aims to create a comprehensive healthcare kit incorporating various sensors, including temperature, ECG, blood pressure, and oximeter sensors, to provide real-time health monitoring and insights. Leveraging an LSTM ML model, the kit filters and analyses data to deliver accurate, actionable health information. Supported by a user-friendly web application, this innovative system is designed to improve accessibility, particularly for users in remote areas, by reducing dependence on medical facilities and specialists.

5.1. System Design and Integration

The healthcare kit will integrate a comprehensive array of advanced sensors, designed to monitor a wide range of physiological parameters. Key sensors include:

- *Temperature Sensor:* Monitors body temperature to detect conditions such as fever, hypothermia, or temperature fluctuations indicative of infection or other health issues.
- *ECG Sensor:* Records the electrical activity of the heart to identify potential arrhythmias, ischemia, or other cardiac abnormalities, aiding in early diagnosis and management of heart-related conditions.
- *Blood Pressure Sensor:* Measures systolic and diastolic blood pressure to monitor cardiovascular health and detect conditions such as hypertension or hypotension.
- *Oximeter Sensor:* Determines blood oxygen saturation (SpO2) levels and pulse rate, providing insights into respiratory health, sleep disorders, or early signs of hypoxemia.
- *Respiratory Rate Sensor:* Tracks the rate of breathing to assess respiratory health and detect abnormalities such as apnea, dyspnea, or respiratory distress.
- *Glucose Sensor:* Continuously or intermittently measures blood glucose levels, assisting in the management of diabetes and monitoring for hypoglycaemia or hyperglycaemias.
- *Motion Sensor:* Monitors physical activity, posture, or mobility patterns to detect falls, inactivity, or changes in movement that may indicate underlying conditions.
- *pH Sensor:* Measures pH levels in bodily fluids (e.g., sweat, saliva, or blood) to monitor metabolic or hydration status.
- *Skin Conductance Sensor:* Measures skin conductance to assess stress levels or autonomic nervous system activity, useful in mental health monitoring.

Each sensor will be selected and calibrated for precision, reliability, and durability, ensuring consistent and accurate measurements under various conditions. The sensors will also be integrated with advanced data processing algorithms to enhance real-time monitoring, enabling personalized and proactive healthcare solutions. This robust sensor suite aims to provide a holistic view of the user's health, fostering better diagnosis, treatment, and preventive care.

The system includes a centralized processing unit to support the sensor integration and enable smooth data gathering from all sensors. This unit is designed to pre-process data by filtering noise, normalizing values, and ensuring compatibility across various sensor outputs. The data is securely transmitted to a cloud-based platform through reliable communication protocols, including Wi-Fi, Bluetooth, or LPWAN technologies, depending on the use case. The cloud platform uses machine learning algorithms to evaluate data in real-time, offering customized health recommendations and actionable insights for innovative healthcare settings. This cohesive integration ensures that the healthcare kit captures a wide range of physiological parameters, delivers accurate, real-time monitoring, and enhances the user experience through its robust and scalable architecture.

5.2. Gathering and Pre-Processing Data

Real-time gathering of information from the monitoring devices will take place. The pre-processing processes mentioned below will be used to guarantee the accuracy and use of the information that was previously obtained:

- Noise Reduction: Raw data often includes noise originating from various sources. To ensure data accuracy, an initial filtering process is employed, utilizing advanced digital signal processing techniques to eliminate extraneous noise effectively.
- Normalization: The data will be normalized to standardize different types of measurements, bringing them to a comparable scale. This ensures consistency and enhances the accuracy of subsequent analysis and processing.

5.3. LSTM Machine Learning Model

The heart of the system is the LSTM ML model, known for its ability to handle time-series data effectively. The methodology includes:

- *Data Training:* Historical health data from diverse populations will be used to train the LSTM model. The training process will focus on enabling the model to recognize patterns and anomalies in health data.
- *Real-Time Analysis:* Once trained, the current information collected by the sensors will be delivered to the model's usage.

- The LSTM's ability to remember long-term dependencies will help in filtering noise and identifying trends or irregularities in health metrics.
- *Anomaly Detection:* The model will flag deviations from normal patterns, which may indicate health issues. Alerts will be generated based on predefined thresholds and patterns learned during training.

5.4. Web Application Development

A web application will be developed to interface with the healthcare kit. Key features include:

- *Patient Database:* A secure, comprehensive database will store individual health data over time, allowing for longitudinal tracking.
- *Health Tracking:* Users will be able to view their health metrics, historical data, and trends through a user-friendly dashboard.
- *Alert System:* The application will generate and send alerts for detected risks or anomalies. These alerts will be actionable and provide recommendations for next steps, enhancing proactive health management.

5.5. Usability and Accessibility

Design Considerations: The healthcare kit will be designed with user-friendliness in mind:

- Intuitive Interface: The kit and web application will feature straightforward interfaces to accommodate users without medical backgrounds or technical expertise.
- Affordability: The kit will be manufactured in bulk to reduce costs, making it accessible to a broader audience.
- Minimal Training Required: Operation of the kit will be simplified to require minimal training. Clear instructions and visual aids will be provided to facilitate ease of use.

5.6. Remote Access

For users in remote locations with limited access to medical facilities or internet:

- Offline Functionality: Basic functionalities of the kit will be available offline, with critical alerts stored locally until the user can access the web application.
- Mobile Compatibility: The web application will be optimized for mobile devices to ensure access even in areas with limited computing resources.

5.7. Testing and Validation

Pilot Testing: Before full-scale deployment, the kit will undergo rigorous testing:

- Prototype Testing: Initial prototypes will be tested with a small group of users to identify and address any issues.
- Validation Studies: Clinical trials will be conducted to validate the efficiency of the sensors and the LSTM model.

5.8. Feedback Integration

User feedback from pilot testing will be used to refine and improve the kit's design and functionality, ensuring it meets user needs and expectations.

5.9. Deployment and Support

Following successful validation, the kit will enter mass production. Quality control processes will be implemented to ensure consistency and reliability.

Ongoing support will be provided to users, including:

- Customer Service: A support team will be available to address technical issues and user inquiries.

- Software Updates: Regular updates to the web application and LSTM model will be provided to enhance performance and security.

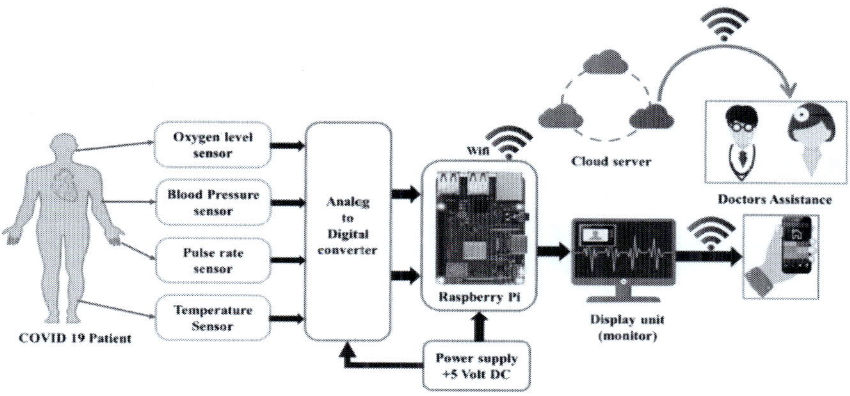

Figure 1. Work flow diagram of a health care application of a ML based IoT with Raspberry Pi.

This comprehensive methodology aims to deliver a user-friendly, cost-effective, and technologically advanced healthcare solution that enhances health monitoring and accessibility.

An all-in-one healthcare monitoring kit combining IoT and machine learning technologies offers a comprehensive solution for advanced health monitoring. This innovative approach integrates temperature, ECG, blood pressure, and oximeter sensors, streamlining health assessments and minimizing the need for multiple individual check-ups. This system reduces dependence on medical facilities and specialists by addressing the challenges patients face in remote areas, particularly during emergencies.

The kit leverages Long Short-Term Memory (LSTM) machine learning models to process and filter data, eliminate noise, and provide accurate real-time insights, enabling proactive healthcare management. A robust web application supports the system, allowing users to easily monitor health parameters and receive instant alerts for detected risks. Figure 1 illustrates the functioning of an IoT-based healthcare system implemented using Raspberry Pi and cloud-based machine learning for seamless data processing and analysis. The machine learning-based application, using an Arduino UNO and an AD8232 sensor, is illustrated in Figure 2. Additionally, the application is demonstrated running on a mobile device.

6. Detailed Discussion

Actual information gathered from the monitoring devices will be tested for the model's applications, significantly improving how medical services are delivered and managed. By embedding connectivity and smart sensors into medical devices, IoT offers transformative benefits across various dimensions of healthcare, ranging from patient monitoring to facility management. This discussion explores the implications of IoT applications in healthcare, addressing the advancements and challenges inherent in this evolving field.

6.1. Advancements in Patient Monitoring

Patient monitoring from a distance is a major use of IoT in healthcare. Vital signs which include heart rate, blood pressure, glucose levels, and oxygen saturation are continually monitored by Internet of Things (IoT)-enabled devices like wearable sensors and home-based monitors. These gadgets deliver real-time data to medical professionals, providing cause responses and reducing the number of meetings in person.

For example, continuous glucose monitors have transformed diabetes management by providing real-time glucose readings and enabling accurate insulin adjustments. Likewise, wearable heart monitors can detect arrhythmias and other cardiac issues early, facilitating prompt medical intervention.

6.2. Enhanced Chronic Disease Management

Chronic disease management has also seen considerable improvements due to IoT. Devices tailored for chronic conditions, such as smart inhalers for asthma or chronic obstructive pulmonary disease (COPD) monitors, offer features like medication adherence tracking and symptom monitoring. These devices help in customizing treatment plans based on real-time data, thereby improving patient adherence and outcomes. For example, smart inhalers equipped with IoT sensors remind patients to take their medication and track usage patterns, providing actionable insights for both patients and doctors,

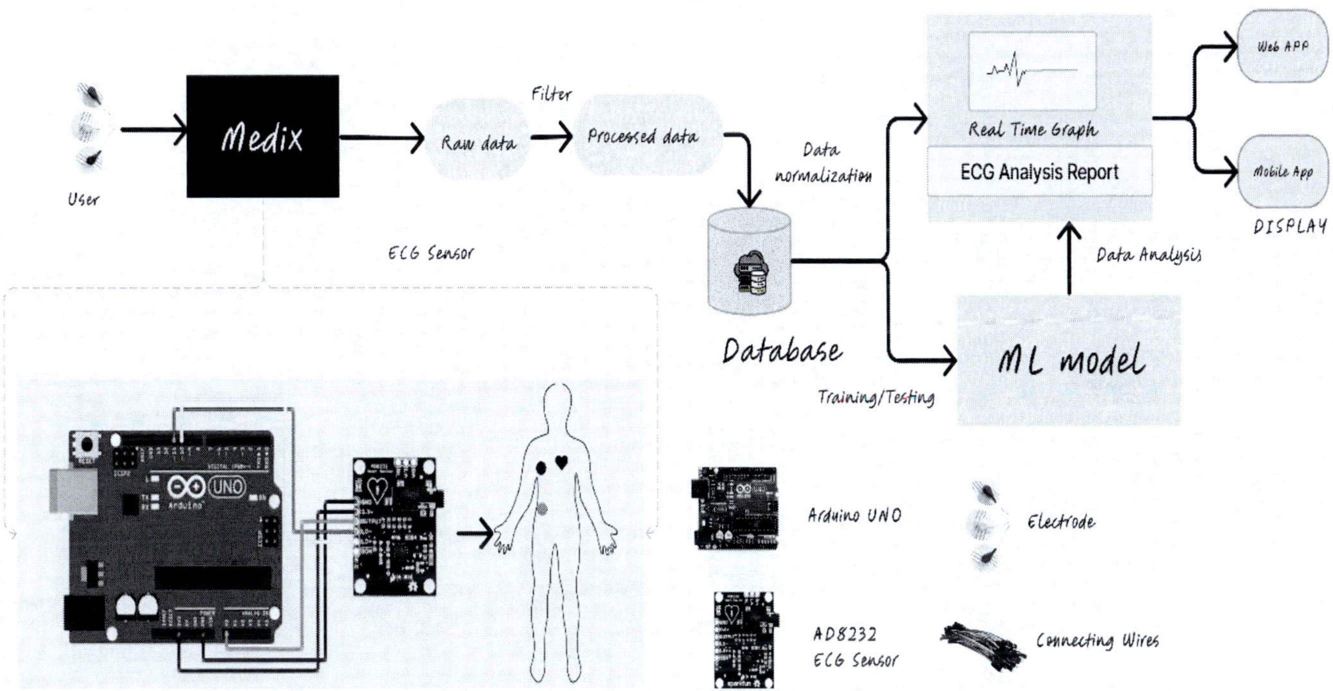

Figure 2. ML and IoT based health care application with Arduino and mobile app.

6.3. Impact on Elderly Care and Assisted Living

IoT has a profound impact on elderly care and assisted living. Smart home systems and sensors installed in residences or care facilities enhance the safety and quality of life for elderly individuals. Fall detection systems, utilizing accelerometers and gyroscopes, can notify caregivers or emergency services if a fall is detected, ensuring prompt assistance. Additionally, smart home technologies can monitor daily activities, medication adherence, and provide reminders for appointments, thereby supporting the independence of elderly individuals while ensuring their safety.

6.4. Optimization of Hospital and Facility Management

Within healthcare facilities, IoT contributes to operational efficiency through asset management and environmental monitoring. Real-time location tracking of medical equipment ensures that critical devices are readily available, minimizing delays and improving patient care. IoT systems also maintain monitoring on conditions in the environment like both temperatures and moisture, ensuring compliance with health and safety standards. This operational efficiency helps in reducing costs and improving the overall environment for both patients and staff.

6.5. Advancements in Personalized Medicine

IoT enhances personalized medicine by providing detailed, continuous health data that supports individualized treatment plans. Integrating IoT with genomic data and electronic health records (EHRs) allows for tailored treatments according to the biological history of an individual and real-time health status. This integration facilitates more precise and effective therapies, potentially improving treatment outcomes and reducing adverse effects.

6.6. Challenges and Future Directions

Despite the advancements, several challenges persist. Since transferring sensitive health information necessitates strong encryption and secure communication methods, data privacy and security remain significant problems. Additionally, integrating and interpreting the massive amount of data connected gadgets produce into current medical processes provides challenges. Further advances in Low Power Broad Area Networks (LPWANs), which include Narrowband IoT (NB-IoT), can improve IoT applications even more by providing more extended coverage and lower power consumption. Further studies must concentrate on creating complete IoT healthcare systems that flawlessly incorporate the necessary factors.

Many benefits come from IoT integration in healthcare, such as better ongoing health management, better patient monitoring, better care for older adults, and reduced management of facilities. The continued innovation in IoT technologies holds promise for further advancements in personalized medicine and overall healthcare efficiency [23].

Conclusion

The implementation and leadership of medical services have experienced a significant shift as a result of the Internet of Things (IoT) incorporation into the healthcare industry. IoT technology uses real-time data and networked devices to improve facility operations, chronic illness management, geriatric care, and patient monitoring. These developments tackle critical issues facing contemporary healthcare systems, improving operational management and efficiency of patient outcomes. Patient monitoring is one of the most prominent uses of IoT. IoT makes continuous tracking possible via wearable technology and home-based sensors, enabling real-time health data transfer. Technology like wearable heart rate monitors and continuous glucose monitoring make it easier to control chronic diseases and to intervene when needed. This constant observation reduces the need for frequent in-person meetings and improves the precision of healthcare requirements.

IoT devices offer tailored solutions in chronic disease management that track medication adherence and symptom patterns. Smart devices for diabetes and asthma enable personalized treatment plans, improving patient adherence and outcomes. This step increases the quality of life for individuals managing chronic conditions by ensuring treatments are effectively adjusted based on real-time data.

Elderly care has also benefited from IoT technologies. Smart home systems and sensors provide safety features such as fall detection and medication reminders, allowing elderly individuals to live while ensuring caregiver support is available when needed. These technologies not only enhance safety but also improve the quality of life for elderly individuals and reduce caregiver burden.

IoT optimizes operations within healthcare facilities through real-time medical equipment tracking and environmental monitoring. It leads to improved resource management, cost reductions, and operational efficiency. The ability to monitor conditions like temperature and humidity ensures compliance with health standards and contributes to a better environment for both patients and staff.

Despite these advancements, challenges remain, particularly concerning data privacy and security. The researcher will use effective encryption and communication protocols to secure sensitive health information. In addition, adequate processing of data and integration into established healthcare systems is necessary for managing the massive amounts of personal information generated through IoT hardware.

The development of Low Power Wide Area Networks (LPWANs), such as Narrowband IoT (NB-IoT), promises to further enhance IoT applications by offering extended coverage and lower power consumption. Future research should focus on creating integrated IoT systems that seamlessly connect all components of healthcare delivery, from data collection to analysis.

In conclusion, IoT has significantly advanced healthcare by improving patient monitoring, disease management, elderly care, and facility operations. While there remain problems with data security and management, modern technology can enhance healthcare systems' productivity and effectiveness, ultimately leading to better patient treatment and performance.

References

[1] Bhatia, H., S. N. Panda, and D. Nagpal. "*Internet of Things and Its Applications in Healthcare—A Survey*." In 2020 8th International Conference on Reliability, Infocom Technologies and Optimization (Trends and Future Directions) (ICRITO), 305–310. Noida, India, 2020.

[2] Tripathi, P., Kumar, N. Paroha, K. K. Rai, M. Panda, M. K. *"Applications of Deep Learning in Healthcare in the Framework of Industry 5.0,"* Infrastructure Possibilities and Human-Centered Approaches With Industry 5.0, IGI Global, 2024, doi: 10.4018/979-8-3693-0782-3.ch005.

[3] Badotra, S., D. Nagpal, S. N. Panda, S. Tanwar, and S. Bajaj. *"IoT-Enabled Healthcare Network with SDN."* In 2020 8th International Conference on Reliability,

Infocom Technologies and Optimization (Trends and Future Directions) (ICRITO), 38–42. Noida, India, 2020.

[4] Moher, David, Larissa Shamseer, Mike Clarke, Davina Ghersi, Alessandro Liberati, Mark Petticrew, Peter Shekelle, and Lesley A. Stewart. "Preferred Reporting Items for Systematic Review and Meta-Analysis Protocols (PRISMA-P) 2015 Statement." *Systematic Reviews* 4 (2015): 1.

[5] Patel, Mitesh S., David A. Asch, and Kevin G. Volpp. "Wearable Devices as Facilitators, Not Drivers, of Health Behavior Change." *Journal of the American Medical Association (JAMA)* 313, no. 5 (2012): 459–60. https://doi.org/10.1001/jama.2014.14781.

[6] Miorandi, Daniele, Sabrina Sicari, Francesco De Pellegrini, and Imrich Chlamtac. "Internet of Things: Vision, Applications and Research Challenges." *Ad Hoc Networks* 10, no. 7 (2012): 1497–1516. https://doi.org/10.1016/j.adhoc.2012.02.016.

[7] Rai, M., Maity, T., Sharma, R. *et al.* Early detection of foot ulceration in type II diabetic patient using registration method in infrared images and descriptive comparison with deep learning methods. *J Supercomput* 78, 13409–13426 (2022). https://doi.org/10.1007/s11227-022-04380-z.

[8] Rejeb, Abderahman, Karim Rejeb, Horst Treiblmaier, Andrea Appolloni, Salem Alghamdi, Yaser Alhasawi, and Mohammad Iranmanesh. "The Internet of Things (IoT) in Healthcare: Taking Stock and Moving Forward." *Internet of Things* 22 (2023): Article 100721. https://doi.org/10.1016/j.iot.2023.100721.

[9] Yang, Zhenzhen, Yutao Xing, and Yi Jin. "IoT-Enabled Glucose Monitoring and Insulin Delivery System for Diabetes Management." *Journal of Biomedical Informatics* 71 (2017): 58–65. https://doi.org/10.1016/j.jbi.2017.05.013.

[10] Ravi, Nishant, Rohit Dandekar, and Francesco Gregori. "IoT-Based Management of Parkinson's Disease Using Wearable Technology." *International Journal of Medical Informatics* 106 (2017): 49–62. https://doi.org/10.1016/j.ijmedinf.2017.07.005.

[11] Kansal, Gaurav, Trina Ghosh, and Prashant Gupta. "Integration of Cloud Computing with IoT for Enhanced Healthcare Solutions." *Journal of Cloud Computing* 9, no. 1 (2020): 22–35. https://doi.org/10.1186/s13677-020-00180-3.

[12] Zhang, Tingting, Yan Zhao, Wei Jia, and Miao-Yang Chen. "Collaborative Algorithms that Combine AI with IoT towards Monitoring and Control Systems." *Future Generation Computer Systems* 125 (2021): 677–686.

[13] Al-Emran, Mostafa, Shoaib Iqbal Malik, and Ali Tarhini. "A System for Secure Healthcare Data Management Using IoT Devices." *Journal of Healthcare Engineering* 2018 (2018): 1–12. https://doi.org/10.1155/2018/5402361.

[14] Khan, Muhammad Asif, Zeeshan Ullah, Muhammad Fawad Khan, and Muhammad Usman. "Low Power Wide Area Networks (LPWAN) in Healthcare: A Review and Outlook." *IEEE Access* 7 (2019): 102015–102031. https://doi.org/10.1109/ACCESS.2019.2930123.

[15] Singh, G. "IoT for Healthcare: System Architectures, Predictive Analytics and Future Challenges." In *Handbook of Multimedia Information Security: Techniques and Applications,* 753–773. Springer, 2019.

[16] Tian, S., W. Yang, J. Grange, "Smart Healthcare: Making Medical Care More Intelligent." *Global Health Journal* 3 (2019): 62–65.

[17] Vipin Kumar Rathi, Nikhil Kumar Rajput, Shubham Mishra, Bhavya Ahuja Grover, Prayag Tiwari, Amit Kumar Jaiswal, M. Shamim Hossain, An edge AI-enabled IoT healthcare monitoring system for smart cities, *Computers & Electrical Engineering,* Volume 96, Part B, 2021, 107524, ISSN 0045-7906,https://doi.org/10.1016/j.compeleceng.2021.107524.

[18] Zhang, Tingting, Yan Zhao, Wei Jia, and Miao-Yang Chen. "Collaborative Algorithms that Combine AI with IoT towards Monitoring and Control Systems." *Future Generation Computer Systems* 125 (2021): 677–686.

[19] Naskar, S., P. Dhruv, S. Mohanty, and S. Mukherjee. "Application of Machine Learning in Various Fields of Medical Science." In *Smart Healthcare Analytics in IoT Enabled Environment, edited by Pradeep Pattnaik, Smruti Ranjan Sarangi, and Sudip Misra.* Intelligent Systems Reference Library, vol. 178, Springer, 2020.

[20] Misra, Sudip, Arpan Mukherjee, and Anusree Roy. "Healthcare IoT." In *Introduction to IoT,* 293–305. Cambridge University Press, 2021.

[21] Gopal, Girish, Claudia Suter-Crazzolara, Luigi Toldo, and Werner Eberhardt. "Digital Transformation in Healthcare—Architectures of Present and Future Information Technologies." *Clinical Chemistry and Laboratory Medicine* 57 (2019): 328–335.

[22] Mittelstadt, Brent. "Ethics of the Health-Related Internet of Things: A Narrative Review." *Ethics and Information Technology* 19 (2017): 157–175.

[23] Jawad, Hussein H. M., Zaid B. Hassan, Bashar B. Zaidan, Faris H. M. Jawad, Dina H. M. Jawad, and Wadha H. D. Alredany. "A Systematic Literature Review of Enabling IoT in Healthcare: Motivations, Challenges, and Recommendations." *Electronics* 11 (2022): 3223.

Chapter 2

An Extensive Investigation of an IOT-Based Remote Monitoring System Enabled by Machine Learning in Advancing Heart Disease Prediction

Sandeep Bhatia[1,*]
Neha Goel[2,†]
Deepak Kumar[2,‡]
and Soniya Verma[3,§]
[1]School of Computing Science and Engineering, Galgotias University Greater Noida, Uttar Pradesh, India
[2]Department of ECE RKGIT, Ghaziabad, Uttar Pradesh, India
[3]Department of Humanities KIET Group of Institutions, Ghaziabad, Uttar Pradesh, India

Abstract

As technology develops, intelligent health monitoring systems gain popularity and importance. These days, physical infrastructure is being replaced by internet services in several industries, including healthcare. With the help of intelligent sensors and data collecting sources, the Internet of Things (IoT) has transformed communication. The IoT with Machine Learning (ML) capabilities in heart disease prediction offers several chances to enhance patient outcomes. Heart disease is becoming more common every day, which highlights the alarming and urgent need

* Corresponding Author's Email: sandeepbhatia1711@gmail.com
† Corresponding Author's Email: 17nehagoel@gmail.com
‡ Corresponding Author's Email: deepakkumarrkgit2013@gmail.com
§ Corresponding Author's Email: soniav134@gmail.com

In: Harnessing the Power of IoT-Enabled Machine Learning …
Editors: Mritunjay Rai, Ravindra Kumar Yadav, Neha Goel et al.
ISBN: 979-8-89530-626-0

for early detection of this ailment. Making a diagnosis of heart disease is a difficult and drawn-out procedure that calls for professional opinion. To appropriately classify and treat their patients, cardiologists must be able to diagnose and prognosticate cardiovascular illness with accuracy. ML algorithms are being employed in the healthcare industry more and more because of their ability to identify patterns in data. If diagnosticians employ ML to classify patients, there could be a decrease in incorrect heart illness diagnosis. The objective of this chapter is to proposed a machine-learning enabled IoT framework that can forecast the occurrence of heart disease based on certain parameters. This chapter employs a variety of ML techniques to examine the heart disease prediction. ML techniques like Randam Forest (RF), K-Nearest Neighbors (KNN), Support Vector Machines (SVM), and Naïve Bayes (NB) are extensively employed. Our research's main goal is to give a thorough understanding of the issues related to ML-enabled IoT in healthcare applications. The goal of this research is to remove the barriers standing in the way of fully utilizing ML-enabled IoT in healthcare applications in view of heart failure prediction, which will enhance patient outcomes, treatment personalization, and healthcare delivery. Through comprehension and resolution of these obstacles, we may facilitate the successful implementation of ML-enabled IoT in healthcare fields. Thus, this study provides a thorough overview of the use of ML and the IoT in the monitoring and prediction of heart disease. Considering heart failure prediction, the aim of this research is to eliminate the obstacles preventing the full use of ML-enabled IoT in healthcare applications, which will improve patient outcomes, treatment personalization, and healthcare delivery. By understanding and overcoming these challenges, we can help make the IoT with ML capabilities viable in the healthcare industry. As a result, this study offers a comprehensive review of how ML and the IoT are used to monitor and forecast cardiac disease.

Keywords: ML, IoT, healthcare applications, remote monitoring, heart disease, prediction

1. Introduction

As per World Health Organization (WHO), main causes of death worldwide happened due to heart disease, resulting in around 17.9 million deaths yearly, or 31% of all fatalities worldwide. Due to their episodic nature and reliance on patient-initiated healthcare visits, traditional monitoring approaches frequently fall short of the important needs of early identification and intervention in minimizing the burden of cardiac disease. This disparity emphasizes the requirement for more proactive and ongoing monitoring systems [1].

The world has been greatly impacted by the growing usage of smart devices and mobile technology in the health sector. The advantages of these technologies are being increasingly tapped into by medical professionals, leading to a notable enhancement in clinical settings health care. Heart disease is a global health concern since it is the primary cause of death worldwide. Patients, their families, and the governments of these countries have all faced severe socioeconomic repercussions as a result. Prediction algorithms that use risk stratification can effectively identify those who are more likely to acquire cardiovascular disease. After that, targeted therapies for this population, such statin use and dietary changes, can help lower that risk and support the prevention of primary heart disease [2, 3]. Advances in microelectronics, wireless networking, and wireless sensors have made it easier to address the social concerns and impending issues brought on by an aging population. India's population is growing steadily, and at the same time, the country's senior population is also growing. Hospitals are experiencing higher health maintenance expenditures because of innovative technological solutions. Moving health monitoring from hospital systems to the homes of the elderly is one practical solution to the issues. The elderly can remain in their homes for longer thanks to this solution, which makes quality healthcare more accessible. They can also become more independent while having their general health monitored more affordably [4].

The use of ML is critical in the healthcare industry. A wide spectrum of ailments may be identified, tracked, and forecasted with the use of ML [5]. The intersection of IoT and ML technology presents a revolutionary strategy for healthcare, namely for the prognosis and treatment of cardiac disease. Wearable technology can be used by IoT-based remote monitoring systems to continuously gather physiological data, which is then instantly sent to centralized servers for analysis. These massive data sets may be processed by ML algorithms, which can then be used to find patterns and provide highly accurate predictions about future heart disease episodes [6, 7]. This chapter aims to investigate the design and development of an IoT-based remote monitoring system that uses ML to improve cardiac disease prediction. Using intelligent data analysis and continuous, real-time monitoring, this system seeks to improve patient outcomes, decrease healthcare costs, and facilitate early diagnosis.

The design of the IoT-based remote monitoring system, data collecting and management procedures, ML algorithms for heart disease prediction, and system performance assessment are the main topics that this study will address. To show the system's usefulness and practical implementation, real-world case studies will also be looked at. The report also tackles the obstacles and constraints of creating such a system and recommends future topics for research.

This strategy, which combines IoT and ML technology, has the potential to completely transform the diagnosis and treatment of cardiac disease by providing a proactive, data-driven approach that can greatly enhance patient outcomes.

Advanced heart failure detection systems can completely transform patient care by offering proactive, individualized monitoring and management techniques through the combination of ML algorithms and IoT sensor data. Artificial intelligence is a component of ML, which is utilized in data science to solve a variety of issues. Predicting a result based on available data is a popular use of ML. To forecast the result, the machine first picks data from the known dataset and transfer to unknown dataset. One popular application of classification, an effective ML method, is prediction. While some categorization algorithms show limited accuracy, others predict with an acceptable level of accuracy [8]. The identification of cardiac disease using this method is not always accurate. It is both costly and challenging to analyse computationally. Extreme caution must be used when monitoring the patients' health state. Supporting optimal health and assisting with disease diagnosis, treatment, and recuperation are all made possible by healthcare. Following surgery or release, the patient's health needs to be closely watched to ensure a speedy recovery. The use of IoT and ML in healthcare is expanding quickly. A common healthcare application is remote healthcare monitoring, which assists medical professionals to keep an eye of illnesses in remote locations. Owing to the swift progress in technology, a plethora of wearable gadgets and health monitoring equipment are currently easily accessible in the market. Modern technologies like AI, ML, and IoT have greatly simplified the work of doctors. These technologies assist in determining the underlying causes of illness and apply modern algorithms [9].

In the field of clinical data analysis, cardiovascular disease prediction is thought to be one of the most crucial topics. In the healthcare sector, data volumes are enormous. Through data mining, the massive collection of unprocessed medical data is transformed into knowledge that can support forecasting and decision-making. Choosing the right set of important features is essential if you want to boost the prediction models' accuracy [10]. It is reasonable to say that the combination of IoT and ML will significantly impact the healthcare sector going beyond. Some of the potential benefits include the capacity to provide total transparency throughout the entire product consignment process, reduce the incidence of fraudulent operations, improve patient outcomes, and create a healthcare system that is patient-centered. As a result, the healthcare sector can guarantee that patients have the best care possible while reducing costs and maximizing effectiveness. It is essential to accept and integrate new technology as the healthcare industry develops to create a better, more effective, comprehensive, and efficient healthcare system [11].

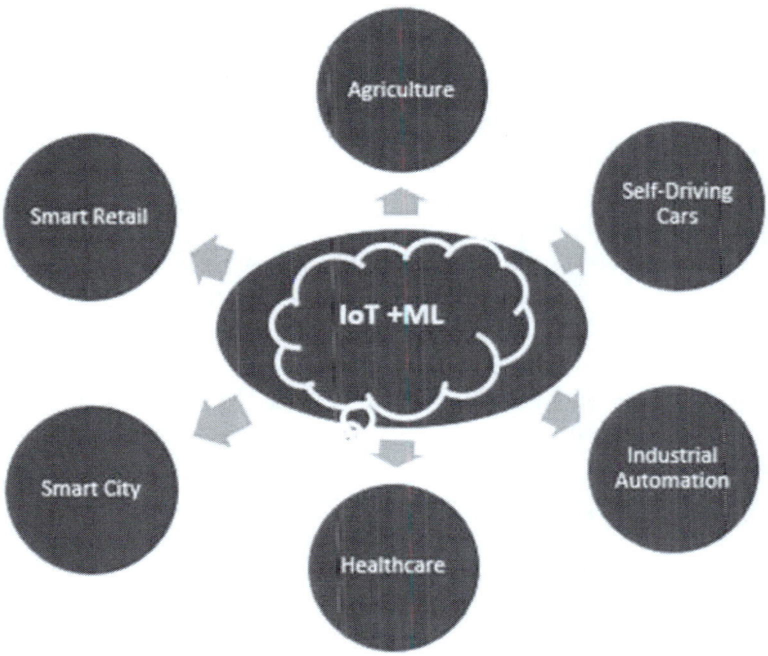

Figure 1. IoT based ML applications.

The different uses of IoT with ML in the fields of smart retail, self-driving cars, smart city, Industrial automation, healthcare, and smart agriculture are depicted in Figure 1. This chapter aims to present an IoT framework with ML capabilities that can predict the incidence of cardiac disease depending on specific characteristics. This chapter looks at the prediction of cardiac disease using a range of ML approaches. The primary objective of our research is to provide a comprehensive examination of the problems associated with ML-enabled IoT in healthcare applications. Considering heart failure prediction, the aim of this research is to eliminate the obstacles preventing the full use of ML-enabled IoT in healthcare applications, which will improve patient outcomes, treatment personalization, and healthcare delivery. By understanding and overcoming these challenges, we can help make the IoT with ML capabilities viable in the healthcare industry. As a result, this study offers a comprehensive review of how ML and the IoT are used to monitor and forecast cardiac disease.

1.1. Chapter Structure

The structure of the paper is as follows: Section 1 of the chapter provides an overview of IoT technology and ML applications in the healthcare sector. The review of the literature is found in Section 2. Various ML techniques to examine the heart disease prediction are covered in Section 3. The proposed machine-learning enabled IoT framework that can forecast the occurrence of heart disease based on certain parameters will be detailed in Section 4. The benefits of IoT remote monitoring system and ML over conventional technologies are covered in Section 5. In Section 6, a thorough analysis of the issues related to ML-enabled IoT in healthcare applications discussed under this section. Overview of the use of ML and the IoT in the monitoring and prediction of heart disease discussed in section 7.

The limitations and problems of IoT and ML associated with heart disease detection and prediction are covered in Section 8. Future directions for healthcare industry research are presented in Section 9. The conclusion is described in Section 10.

2. Literature Review

Bhatia et al. discussed how healthcare conditions being monitored with little human involvement with tools such as IoT-WSN-based systems. Numerous wireless protocols are now in use, such as Wi-MAX, LoRa WAN, RFID, MQTT, Zigbee, Sigfox, and BLE (Bluetooth low energy). LoRa WAN is a type of long-range, very efficient, and low power consumption wireless technology [12]. Bhatia et al. describe various wireless methods that can be preferred by the scientific community when sending data collected from any location to remote sites. Over the next 10 years, the healthcare sector will depend heavily on the superfast 5G connection to improve healthcare sector and quality with the least amount of labour. Intelligent healthcare may help patients become more informed and productive. With the advent of 5G, the nature of employment in healthcare sector will change dramatically. Flexible and effective solutions provided by the IoT-based WSN of the 5G network can help to enable smart IoT applications. They will make it easier for various autonomous agricultural equipment to operate automatically throughout crop cultivation phases including planting, ploughing, and management [13]. Goel et al., the ultimate objective is to enable the creation of unmanned farms while achieving safe, dependable, environmentally friendly, and energy-conserving operations [14].

Xian et al. discussed the concept of "Smart Guardian," an AI-based system created to forecast coronary heart disease (CHD), is presented [15]. The technology uses cutting-edge ML algorithms to evaluate physiological data that is gathered in real time from wearables with IoT capabilities. To improve the precision and dependability of heart disease forecasts, their study focuses on the integration of many AI technologies, such as deep learning and natural language processing. The study shows how artificial intelligence (AI) has the potential to revolutionize cardiac health monitoring by enabling continuous, real-time data processing and warning production, thereby offering a proactive approach to illness prevention and management.

Ganai et al. discussed the integration of IoT technology into cyber security measures in the healthcare industry is thoroughly analysed in the study. The authors list and go over the cyber security issues that the spread of IoT devices in healthcare settings has brought about. These difficulties include IoT device vulnerabilities, data privacy issues, problems with regulatory compliance, and the possibility of malevolent cyberattacks that target healthcare infrastructure [16].

Bhatia et al. discussed an extensive analysis of IoT dependability and its related metrics. A conceptual framework for IoT dependability is presented in this chapter, along with definitions of important terms and elements including fault tolerance, resilience, and system availability. It addresses how security, scalability, performance, and dependability interact in IoT deployments and emphasises the necessity of comprehensive strategies to guarantee stable and trustworthy IoT systems [17].

Tuli et al. introduces "HealthFog," which is a smart healthcare system that combines deep learning and ensemble learning to automatically diagnose cardiac problems in environments that combine fog computing with the IoT. To improve the effectiveness and responsiveness of healthcare services, the system combines fog computing with IoT devices for real-time data processing. Their study demonstrates important developments in the implementation of smart healthcare systems by highlighting the potential of fog computing to lower latency and increase the precision of heart disease diagnosis [18].

Bhatia et al. describe the creation and study of an IoT-based smart agricultural system that can support heterogeneous nodes is presented in the work. The article addresses how IoT technology supports smart agricultural techniques including environmental sensing, crop monitoring, and precision farming. It investigates the integration of IoT sensors, actuators, and communication networks to build intelligent agricultural systems that can gather, process, and act on real-time data [19].

Jaiswal et al. discussed the integration of drone technology with intelligent irrigation systems for agricultural purposes is examined in the study. The article addresses drone technology's use in agriculture, emphasising its use in precision farming, insect identification, and crop monitoring. It investigates how data on crop health, soil moisture content, and environmental factors may be gathered using drones fitted with sensors and imaging equipment to improve irrigation techniques. The system's components and functionalities are outlined in the study, which proposes a drone automation framework for smart irrigation. It talks about how irrigation choices may be automated using drones, IoT sensors, cloud computing platforms, and data analytics algorithms gathered from the field in real time [20].

Umrao et al. illustrate the application of precision agricultural methods made possible by IoT technology. Various IoT applications are covered in the study, such as crop monitoring, insect control, irrigation optimization, and soil nutrient management [21].

Al-Makhadmeh et al. show how well IoT technologies and cutting-edge ML methods work together to create a reliable and live health monitoring system [22]. Bhatia et al. discussed the method for improving stock market trading tactics is the incorporation of ML techniques with technical indicators in algorithmic trading. Traders can improve their trading decisions and obtain more accurate market projections by utilizing the predictive power of ML models. Subsequent studies ought to concentrate on enhancing the resilience of the model, integrating supplementary data sources, and investigating sophisticated ML methods like reinforcement learning [23].

Ramkumar et al. shows how well IoT and deep learning work together to produce precise and timely predictions, which may enhance patient outcomes and allow for proactive healthcare treatments [24]. Bhatia et al. discussed the applications of ML in Zomato food delivery services. The applications of ML for locating customer and provide services has been discussed [25]. Chaithra et al. highlights ML's potential to increase diagnostic precision and encourages the application of these methods in clinical settings to enhance patient outcomes [26]. Bhatia et al. discussed ML algorithms that can be used in driver drowsiness detection and remote monitoring [27]. Bhatia et al. discussed ML algorithms that can be used in weather forecasting and shows how important steps can be taken to overcome the disaster situations [28]. Bhatia et al. discussed ML algorithms that can be used in animal remote monitoring and caring [29]. Goel et al. describe the techniques for managing safe smart devices that prioritize energy efficiency. The author also investigates several ways to improve smart device energy efficiency without sacrificing security. The study emphasizes how crucial it is to balance power efficiency and security when designing IoT devices [30]. Gautam et al. describe the planning and execution of an automated system that, in response to traffic circumstances, dynamically modifies traffic signals and activates speed breakers. This study demonstrates how IoT and ML may be used to build traffic infrastructure that is more intelligent and responsive [31]. Bhatia et al. compares the MAC, SMAC, and TMAC protocols in wireless sensor networks with an emphasis on their performance metrics and design requirements. Their analysis focuses on the advantages and disadvantages of each protocol, offering insightful information for choosing the best one in accordance with application needs [32]. Madan et al. highlights how crucial it is to maximize network longevity and energy efficiency in wireless sensor networks. a wildland safety fire alarm system with LoRaWAN capability that is intended to improve early wildfire detection and response, as covered in this study. Their research shows how the system can instantly monitor the surrounding environment and notify authorities and locals of any changes, enhancing safety and lowering the possibility of fire-related damages. This study highlights how LoRaWAN technology may be used to create scalable and efficient environmental monitoring systems [33]. Bhatia et al. introduce an image processing and IoT-based automatic seat identification system for smart transportation. The system's accurate real-time seat availability identification seeks to increase customer convenience and transportation efficiency. Their study demonstrates how cutting-edge imaging methods can be used with IoT infrastructure [34].

Bhatia et al. developed an autonomous mobile rescue robot that can identify live human beings in disaster settings. To find survivors amidst debris and devastation, the system combines sensors and autonomous navigation algorithms. Their study demonstrates how robotic technology might enhance the efficacy and efficiency of search and rescue missions, potentially saving lives in dire circumstances [35]. Nancy et al. shows how cutting-edge AI approaches may be effectively integrated with IoT and cloud computing to enable precise, real-time health monitoring and early diagnosis [36]. Bhatia et al. discussed LPG leakage detection using robots carry with specific sensors and can be monitored from remote location through IoT [37]. The Table 1 below highlights the IoT-based ML state-of-the-art work comparison in heart disease prediction.

Table 1. Different methodologies along with their objectives and advantages

Reference	Methodology and Objectives	Advantages
[2]	Hybrid deep learning for congestive heart failure detection in IoT.	Automatic detection, leveraging IoT data.
[3]	ML for automated coronary artery disease diagnosis.	Accurate diagnosis, potential for early intervention.
[4]	IoT and ML for health monitoring and heart attack prediction.	Real-time monitoring, proactive health management.
[6]	IoT-based smart health monitoring system.	Remote monitoring capability, continuous health tracking.
[7]	Deep CNN model for heartbeat classification.	High accuracy in heartbeat classification.
[8]	Ensemble classification for heart disease risk prediction.	Improved prediction accuracy through ensemble techniques.
[9]	Heart disease prediction in remote health monitoring based on IoT-cloud.	Secure data handling, scalable cloud infrastructure.
[10]	Data mining-based heart disease prediction.	Identification of significant features, interpretable models.
[11]	Review of ML techniques in heart disease prediction.	Comprehensive overview, synthesis of existing methods.
[18]	Ensemble DL for automatic diagnosis of heart diseases in IoT and fog computing.	Robust diagnosis, efficiency in fog computing environments.

3. Overview of Various ML Techniques to Examine the Heart Disease Prediction

Under this section, we are highlighting some of the ML algorithms to predict heart disease prediction.

3.1. KNN

When utilizing (KNN), the method searches the dataset for K close instances. The program will then use its output to evaluate the variable y of the inspection that needs to be predicted. For separating two observations, the Euclidean distance formula is:

$$d(x_i, y_i) = \sqrt{(x_{i,1} - y_i, 1)^2 + \cdots + (x_{i,m} - y_{i,m})^2} \quad (1)$$

For such a distance function, the Euclidean distance is often an acceptable choice if the data is numerical. Our new data point's attribute values are x_(i,1) through x_(i,m). The suggested work can calculate the distance d(x_i,y_i) between any two data points, y_i and x.

3.2. RF

Random Forest (RF) is a variant of the Decision Tree (DT) technique. Decision trees have significant volatility and little bias, hence the variance component of the model is decreased by averaging them. By averaging the forecast, samples that are unknown can be created.

$$I = \frac{1}{N} \sum_{n=1}^{N} f(x) \quad (2)$$

Where uncertainty is,

$$\sigma = \sqrt{\frac{\sum_{n=1}^{N} (f(x) - f)^2}{N-1}} \quad (3)$$

Finding the best branch for your forest is made easier by the formula, which determines each node's degree of divergence from the estimated actual value. In this case, f(x) denotes the decision tree's output, while f stands for the value of the data point that is being assessed at a particular node.

3.3. SVM

SVMs use the hyperplane to increase the boundary line between training set classes to categorize data. Hyperplanes are expressed using the following formula:

$$f(x) = a^T x + c \tag{4}$$

In this formula a denoted to dimensional coefficient, and c demoted to offset in this case.

3.4. NB

One way that Bayes' Theorem stands out is that it considers consecutive events in which prior knowledge affects the initial probability. These possibilities are referred to as "posterior probability" and "prior probability." Prior probability, also referred to as marginal probability, is the first chance of an event occurring in isolation. The posterior probability is the likelihood that something will occur after a data point.

The NB approach, which is extensively employed, relies on the mathematical utilization of Bayes' theorem.

$$P(A|B) = \frac{P(A|B)P(A)}{P(B)} \tag{5}$$

The above Bayes theorem states that the dependent feature vectors, $x_1$through y_j, and the supplied class variable, y, are related.

$$P(y|x_1, \ldots\ldots y_j) = \frac{P(x_1, \ldots\ldots y_j|y)P(y)}{P(x_1, \ldots\ldots y_j)} \tag{6}$$

3.5. CNN

When analyzing grid-based input data, such as photographs, CNN excels. Binary representations of visual data are what make up digital images. Color and brightness values are assigned to pixels and they are arranged in a grid. Figure 2 shows the suggested architectural design.

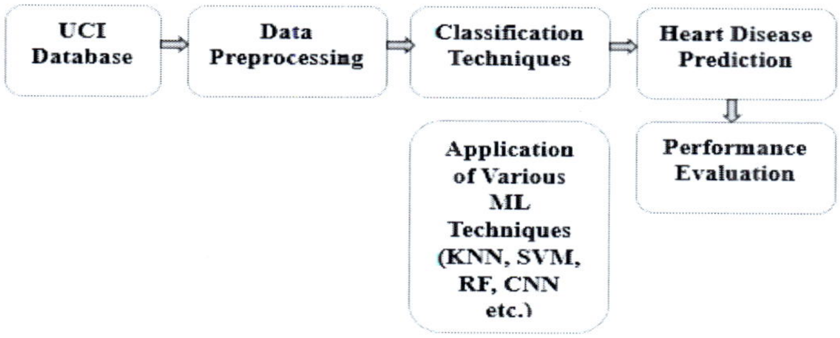

Figure 2. Proposed architecture of CNN based.

We will compute the accuracy standard deviation and average using-

$$\text{Accuracy} = \frac{\text{TP+TN}}{\text{TP+FP+FN+TN}} \quad (7)$$

This statistic calculates the proportion of successfully detected positive data points relative to all positive data points, based on intuition. A higher TPR lowers the number of overlooked good data signals. FPR/Fallout:

$$\text{FRP} = \frac{\text{FP}}{\text{FP+TN}} \quad (8)$$

$$\text{Precision} = \frac{\text{TP}}{\text{TP+FP}} \quad (9)$$

The recall is calculated by dividing the number of projected positive samples by the total number of samples that were positive.

Recall can be used to determine the proportion of optimistic predictions that came true. Below is the formula.

$$\text{Recall} = \frac{\text{TP}}{\text{TP+FN}} \quad (10)$$

Result metrics like the F-score consider memory and accuracy. This article defines it as the harmonic mean of memory and accuracy. Below is the F-score, F1 score, or F-measure equation.

$$\text{F1 Score} = \frac{2*(\text{Precision}*\text{Recall})}{(\text{Precision}+\text{Recall}} \tag{11}$$

4. Proposed Architecture of IoT-Based Remote Monitoring System Enabled by ML in Advancing Heart Disease Prediction

The proposed architecture, which consists of three stages, for an IoT-based remote monitoring system that advances cardiac disease prediction through ML is shown in Figure 3. The initial phase involves gathering patient data pertaining to cardiac disease. The second stage consists of a cloud layer that will store data relating to patients. The third level is data analytics, which is the application of ML algorithms to process and extract information from data. Lastly, medical staff will receive all pertinent data so they can take appropriate future action.

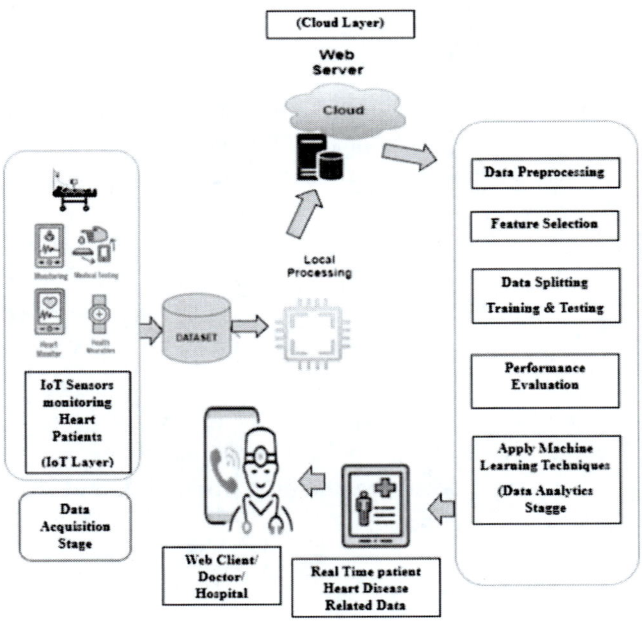

Figure 3. Proposed architecture of IoT-based remote monitoring system enabled by ML in advancing heart disease prediction.

5. Benefits of IoT Remote Monitoring System and ML over Conventional Technologies

Combining ML with IoT remote monitoring systems is a big step forward from traditional technology and has many applications in many industries. The improved real-time monitoring and data collection capabilities are two of the main benefits. IoT devices can continuously gather data from various sources, providing a more comprehensive and accurate view of the operating environment [38]. This constant data flow makes real-time monitoring possible, which lowers maintenance costs and downtime by enabling quick issue diagnosis and resolution. Furthermore, massive amounts of data may be analysed by ML algorithms, which can spot patterns and abnormalities that conventional approaches might be lacking [39].

With proactive maintenance and process optimization made possible by these predictive analytics capabilities, efficiency is further increased and expenses are decreased.

Furthermore, a greater level of automation and astute decision-making are made possible by IoT and ML. Without human involvement, automated systems may react to data-driven insights, guaranteeing quicker and more precise replies. IoT sensors, for instance, may track environmental factors and machinery performance in the manufacturing industry, and ML models can anticipate possible faults, enabling prompt maintenance before a breakdown happens. This increases output while extending the life of the machinery [40].

In the field of healthcare, ML algorithms use data from remote monitoring via IoT devices to identify early indicators of a patient's declining health, allowing for prompt medical intervention. IoT systems' scalability and adaptability also provide them a major advantage over traditional technology. IoT networks are easily expandable, allowing for the addition of new sensors and devices as needed without needing significant reconfiguration. Scalability like this is very useful in dynamic contexts with changing conditions and needs, like expanding businesses. Furthermore, by incorporating ML, these systems can develop and get better over time as fresh data is fed into algorithms that increase in precision and efficiency [41].

All things considered, the marriage of ML and IoT remote monitoring systems changes conventional procedures by increasing their intelligence, effectiveness, and responsiveness. This technological synergy pushes industries toward a more connected and data-driven future by streamlining processes, cutting costs, and creating new opportunities for innovation and growth [42]. Table 2 demonstrates how IoT and ML, in contrast to conventional approaches, improve operational capabilities, efficiency, and cost-effectiveness, resulting in a more sophisticated and adaptable technological environment.

Table 2. Highlights the IoT remote monitoring and ML benefits in contrast to conventional technologies

Benefit	IoT Remote Monitoring & ML	Conventional Technologies
Data Collection	Continuous, real-time data from multiple sources	Periodic, manual data collection
Data Analysis	Advanced analytics, pattern recognition, predictive analytics	Basic statistical analysis, manual interpretation
Response Time	Immediate, automated responses based on real-time data	Delayed, manual responses
Maintenance	Predictive maintenance based on data insights	Reactive maintenance after failures
Cost Efficiency	Reduced downtime and maintenance costs through optimization	Higher costs due to inefficiencies and unplanned downtime
Scalability	Easily expandable and adaptable to new devices and sensors	Limited by infrastructure and manual processes
Decision-Making	Automated, data-driven decisions	Human-dependent, slower decision-making
System Flexibility	High, with adaptable and upgradable systems	Low, with rigid and fixed systems
Operational Efficiency	Enhanced through continuous monitoring and automation	Limited by manual and periodic checks
Predictive Capabilities	High, with ML predicting future trends and failures	Low, reliant on historical data and human judgment
Real-Time Monitoring	Continuous, real-time visibility into system status	Sporadic, based on scheduled checks
Equipment Lifespan	Extended through timely maintenance and optimization	Reduced due to lack of predictive maintenance
Innovation Potential	High, fostering new applications and improvements	Low, limited by conventional technology constraints
User Intervention	Minimal, with automated processes and alerts	High, requiring manual intervention and oversight
Accuracy and Precision	High, with precise data analytics and ML models	Variable, dependent on human accuracy and periodic checks.

6. Issues Related to ML-Enabled IoT in Healthcare Applications

While incorporating ML into IoT-enabled healthcare applications have many advantages, there are several important concerns that need to be resolved to guarantee a secure and efficient deployment. Data security and privacy are among the top issues. The use of IoT devices creates a great deal of personal health information, and healthcare data is extremely sensitive. Given the growing sophistication of cyberattacks, it is crucial but difficult to ensure that this data is processed, stored, and transported securely. Data breaches are another possibility that could result in identity theft or improper use of patient information due to illegal access to patient data [43].

The accuracy and dependability of ML algorithms is another important concern. Although ML has the potential to greatly improve diagnostic and predictive capacities, the algorithms behind ML must be thoroughly examined and verified to prevent mistakes that can result in inaccurate diagnosis or treatment suggestions. It is imperative that the data used to train these algorithms be of a high quality, as inadequate or biased data might lead to models that are not well-suited to a variety of patient populations, therefore aggravating health inequities [44].

A major obstacle is also interoperability. It might be challenging to integrate diverse IoT devices and guarantee smooth data transmission because healthcare systems and equipment frequently employ disparate standards and protocols. The full promise of ML-enabled IoT in healthcare cannot be achieved without efficient interoperability, as disjointed systems impede thorough data analysis and coordinated care.

Furthermore, there will be a significant infrastructure and training investment required for the implementation of these cutting-edge technologies. ML-enabled IoT systems can be expensive and time-consuming to utilize, so healthcare providers need to be prepared with the right resources and expertise. Strong regulatory structures are also required to direct the ethical and safe application of these technologies. It is imperative for regulatory agencies to keep up with the swift progress of technology to establish unambiguous norms and standards that safeguard patient safety and promote innovation.

Lastly, the broad use of ML-enabled IoT in healthcare depends on patient acceptance and confidence. Patients may be hesitant to entrust their health management to automated systems because of concern for machine faults or a loss of human interaction. To foster acceptance and foster confidence, it is imperative to inform patients about the advantages and drawbacks of these technologies and to maintain transparency in their use [45].

In conclusion, while ML-enabled IoT in healthcare has a lot of potential, its ethical and effective application depends on resolving concerns about patient trust, infrastructure investment, data privacy, algorithm accuracy, interoperability, and regulatory guidance.

7. Overview of the Use of ML and the IoT in the Monitoring and Prediction of Heart Disease

With previously unheard-of possibilities for early detection, ongoing monitoring, and individualized therapy, the convergence of ML (ML) and the IoT is transforming the monitoring and prediction of heart disease. Wearable sensors and smartwatches are examples of IoT devices that continuously send teal time data. This enormous volume of information gives a patient a full picture of their cardiovascular health throughout time, far more thorough than typical monthly medical check-ups. This data is analysed by ML algorithms to find trends and abnormalities that might point to the beginning or development of cardiac disease.

These algorithms use past data to forecast possible cardiac problems before they are serious, enabling earlier treatment and improved condition control.

Offering individualized healthcare is one of this method's main advantages. Based on each patient's particular data, ML models can customize forecasts and suggestions, considering variables like age, lifestyle, and genetic susceptibility. As therapies may be tailored to each patient's unique demands, this level of personalization improves the efficacy of interventions and the accuracy of predictions. Furthermore, constant observation made possible by IoT devices guarantees that any alterations in a patient's state are quickly identified, permitting rapid medical intervention, and lowering the possibility of serious consequences.

Furthermore, remote monitoring is made easier by the combination of ML and IoT, which is especially helpful for patients who live in rural places or have limited access to medical institutions. By monitoring patients' health remotely and offering guidance and treatment adjustments in lieu of regular in-person visits, healthcare practitioners can enhance patient convenience and curtail expenses. This remote capability comes in particularly handy when face-to-face consultations are difficult, such during pandemics.

Notwithstanding its promise, there are drawbacks to using ML and IoT for heart disease monitoring and prediction. These include issues with data privacy, the necessity for strong and trustworthy algorithms, and the demand for the smooth integration of several systems and devices.

In general, the combination of IoT and ML for cardiac disease represents a breakthrough in healthcare, providing improved patient outcomes and quality of life through ongoing monitoring, tailored treatment, and improved prediction capacities.

8. Limitations and Problems of IoT and ML Associated with Heart Disease Detection and Prediction

Although there is great potential for the detection and prediction of cardiac disease through the combination of IoT and ML (ML), there are several issues that need to be resolved to guarantee the efficacy and dependability of this approach.

8.1. Security and Privacy of Data

Security and privacy of data are among the main issues. Sensitive health data that is constantly being collected by IoT devices may be subject to data breaches and cyberattacks if it is not properly secured. With the sophistication of cyber threats on the rise, it is imperative but difficult to guarantee the confidentiality and integrity of this data. Identity theft and improper use of personal health information are just two serious ethical and legal ramifications that can result from breaches of patient data.

8.2. Integrity and Quality of Data

The accuracy of ML predictions can be impacted by the wide variations in data quality that IoT devices acquire. Unreliable results may result from inconsistent data caused by device malfunction, inadequate calibration, or user error. Furthermore, it can be difficult to integrate data from multiple devices, each of which may be utilizing a different set of standards and protocols. This can lead to incomplete or erroneous datasets, which can impair the effectiveness of ML algorithms.

8.3. Algorithm Accuracy and Prejudice

Another crucial concern with ML algorithms is their dependability. To guarantee that these algorithms produce precise and trustworthy forecasts, they must undergo extensive training and validation. However, the models may yield skewed findings, worsening health disparities, if the training data is biased or not representative of various patient populations.

8.4. Regulatory and Ethical Difficulties

IoT and ML technologies are developing faster than legal frameworks, which creates a gap that puts patient safety and ethical standards at risk. To ensure that these technologies are used safely and ethically in healthcare, clear rules and norms must be in place. It is imperative for regulatory authorities to stay up with technology changes to offer sufficient supervision and guidance.

8.5. Problems with Interoperability

One of the biggest obstacles still facing IoT devices and healthcare systems is interoperability. IoT and ML cannot reach their full potential without smooth integration. Different systems may result in data silos, which compromise the efficacy of predictive analytics and make it challenging to obtain an accurate data.

8.6. Cost and Infrastructure

A significant infrastructure investment is necessary for the implementation of IoT and ML solutions. This investment includes robust data storage systems, dependable internet access, and sophisticated processing power. To use these technologies efficiently, healthcare providers also require training, which may be expensive and time-consuming. These expenditures may be prohibitive for smaller healthcare facilities and those operating in low-resource environments, which would restrict the widespread use of these cutting-edge instruments.

8.7. Acceptance and Trust by Patients

Lastly, the effective application of IoT and ML in the detection and prediction of cardiac disease depends on patient acceptance and trust. Concerns about accuracy, privacy, and the apparent lack of human touch in healthcare may make patients reluctant to rely only on automated systems for managing their health. Encouraging patient involvement and compliance requires honest communication about the advantages, drawbacks, and safety measures of these technologies to establish confidence. Even though IoT and ML provide substantial improvements in the identification and prognosis of cardiac disease, these issues and constraints must be resolved for IoT and ML to be successfully and morally applied in the medical field. The key to maximizing the promise of these cutting-edge technologies is ensuring data privacy, enhancing data quality, improving algorithm reliability, resolving interoperability challenges, providing sufficient infrastructure, and building patient trust.

9. Future Directions for the Healthcare Industry Using IoT and ML

The following are some crucial future paths:

9.1. Individualized Medical Care

Precision Healthcare: As IoT devices continue to collect enormous volumes of unique health data, more precise and customized treatment regimens will be possible. Precision medicine is possible because to ML algorithms that can evaluate this data and customize therapies based on the individual genetic composition, way of life, and surroundings of each patient.

9.2. Preventive Healthcare

Fitness, nutrition, and lifestyle aspects will be tracked by IoT devices, which will be used more and more for preventive healthcare. By analysing this data, ML can offer individualized advice for preserving health and averting illnesses. By swiftly evaluating complicated datasets and revealing insights that would be challenging to find manually, ML (ML) helps expedite this study.

9.3. Electronic Health Records (EHRs) Integration

Future technologies will guarantee smooth data integration, giving patients a complete picture of their medical history, across IoT devices and EHRs. Care continuity and more informed clinical decision-making will be made easier by this integration.

9.4. Investigation and Creation

Medical research can be expedited by utilizing the massive amounts of data gathered from IoT devices to discover novel illness markers, comprehend epidemiological patterns, and create innovative treatments.

9.5. Enhanced Privacy and Security of Data

Proficient Security Procedures: The focus on creating cutting-edge security procedures to safeguard private health information will increase as IoT and ML are used in healthcare. Data security and privacy will be greatly enhanced by developments in blockchain and encryption technology.

9.6. Cooperation and Industry Standards Standardization

To fully realize the promise of IoT and ML, efforts will be directed at standardizing protocols and guaranteeing compatibility between various devices and systems. It will be crucial for technology companies, healthcare providers, and regulatory agencies to work together.

In conclusion, major breakthroughs in customized medicine, predictive analytics, remote monitoring, operational efficiency, preventative care, and medical research are expected.

Conclusion

Heart disease is a major global health concern that accounts for a disproportionately high death toll. Clinical data analysed methodically can identify coronary artery disease, heart attacks, and other conditions that could save lives. It is commonly acknowledged that cardiovascular disease has a high death rate. Patients with cardiac issues can have a far better prognosis by stopping the progression of heart failure with an early and accurate diagnosis. Over time, plaque accumulation results in heart disease. Most of the plaque, which partially obstructs coronary artery blood flow, is composed of calcium, fibrin, and cholesterol. To improve the prediction of cardiac illness occurrence in categorization scenarios, this research introduces deep learning and ML methodologies. The thorough analysis of a ML-enabled IoT remote monitoring system demonstrates ML's revolutionary potential in improving heart disease prognosis. These systems offer a full and dynamic picture of a patient's cardiovascular health by continuously and real-time gathering data from wearable sensors and other Internet of Nevertheless, there are certain difficulties in applying ML and IoT to the prediction of cardiac disease. To guarantee the system's efficacy and broad acceptance, concerns including data privacy, algorithm dependability, interoperability, and the requirement for a substantial infrastructure investment must be addressed. To prevent breaches of sensitive patient information, data security must be ensured. To prevent diagnostic errors and provide fair treatment for a variety of populations, ML models that are impartial and trustworthy are important. Furthermore, thorough data analysis and efficient patient care depend on the smooth integration of diverse IoT devices and healthcare systems. Heart disease can be detected earlier and with greater accuracy with the help of ML algorithms that use this massive amount of data to find patterns and anomalies that traditional monitoring techniques would overlook. The movement toward telehealth is supported by the integration of predictive analytics and remote monitoring, which increases access to healthcare, particularly in underserved or remote locations. The UCI dataset is used in this study to assess the accuracy of the CNN, KNN, SVM, RF, and NB cardiac prediction models that are trained. With an accuracy rate of 92%, the CNN algorithm was shown to be the most effective in predicting cardiac issues. The creation of frameworks that not only satisfy the technology requirements of the healthcare industry but also maintain the highest standards of patient confidentiality and data security should remain a top priority for future research projects. By doing this, we open the door for a healthcare ecosystem that values individual empowerment and well-being in addition to innovation, guaranteeing that technological breakthroughs will really improve patient care and overall health outcomes.

Improving data privacy protocols, strengthening ML algorithms' openness and resilience, and promoting interoperability standards ought to be the main goals for the future. Building a supporting ecosystem for these cutting-edge technologies would require cooperation between regulators, healthcare providers, and technology companies. Furthermore, trust-building and IoT-based monitoring system adoption depend heavily on patient education and involvement.

In conclusion, ML-enabled IoT-based remote monitoring systems have a great deal of potential to transform the diagnosis and treatment of heart disease. These technologies can result in more proactive, individualized, and effective healthcare by overcoming present limits and emphasizing innovation and collaboration. Ultimately, this will improve the quality of life for patients who have or are at risk of cardiac disease.

References

[1] World Health Organization. (n.d.). Cardiovascular diseases (CVDs). Retrieved from https://www.who.int/news-room/fact-sheets/detail/cardiovascular-diseases-(cvds).

[2] Ning, W., S. Li, D. Wei, L. Z. Guo, and H. Chen, "Automatic Detection of Congestive Heart Failure Based on a Hybrid Deep Learning Algorithm in the Internet of Medical Things," *IEEE IoT Journal,* vol. 8, no. 16, pp. 12550–12558, 2021, doi: 10.1109/JIOT.2020.3023105.

[3] Gill, K. S., A. Sharma, V. Anand, and S. Gupta, "An Automated Coronary Artery Disease Diagnosis System using ML," International Conference on Automation, Computing and Renewable Systems, *ICACRS 2022 - Proceedings,* no. Icacrs, pp. 1173–1178, 2022, doi: 10.1109/ICACRS55517.2022.10029195.

[4] Tripathi, P., Kumar, N. Paroha, K. K. Rai, M. Panda, M. K. "Applications of Deep Learning in Healthcare in the Framework of Industry 5.0," Infrastructure Possibilities and Human-Centered Approaches With Industry 5.0, IGI Global, 2024, doi: 10.4018/979-8-3693-0782-3.ch005.

[5] Park, A. and A. Iwasaki, "Type I and Type III Interferons – Induction, Signaling, Evasion, and Application to Combat COVID-19," *Cell Host and Microbe,* vol. 27, no. 6, pp. 870–878, 2020, doi: 10.1016/j.chom.2020.05.008.

[6] Kumar, P. M., & Raj, P. H. (2016). IoT based smart health monitoring system. *Journal of Network Communications and Emerging Technologies (JNCET),* 6(3), 37-42.

[7] Acharya, U. R., Oh, S. L., Hagiwara, Y., Tan, J. H., & Adam, M. (2017). A deep convolutional neural network model to classify heartbeats. *Computers in Biology and Medicine,* 89, 389-396.

[8] Latha, C. B. C., & Jeeva, S. C. (2019). Improving the accuracy of prediction of heart disease risk based on ensemble classification techniques. *Informatics in Medicine Unlocked,* 16, 100203.

[9] Patro, S. P., & Padhy, N. (2023). A Secure IoT-Cloud Based Remote Health Monitoring for Heart Disease Prediction Using ML and Deep Learning Techniques. *Engineering Proceedings*, 56(1), 241.

[10] Amin, M. S., Chiam, Y. K., & Varathan, K. D. (2019). Identification of significant features and data mining techniques in predicting heart disease. *Telematics and Informatics,* 36, 82-93.

[11] Chaithra, C. S., Siddesha, S., Aradhya, V. N., & Niranjan, S. K. (2024). A Review of ML Techniques Used in the Prediction of Heart Disease. *Revue d'Intelligence Artificielle,* 38(1).

[12] Bhatia, S., Jaffery, Z. A., &Mehfuz, S. (2023, January). A Comparative Study of Wireless Communication Protocols for use in Smart Farming Framework Development. In *2023 3rd International Conference on Intelligent Communication and Computational Techniques (ICCT)* (pp. 1-7). IEEE.

[13] Bhatia, S., Mallikarjuna, B., Gautam, D., Gupta, U., Kumar, S., & Verma, S. (2023, March). The Future IoT: The Current Generation 5G and Next Generation 6G and 7G Technologies. In *2023 International Conference on Device Intelligence, Computing and Communication Technologies, (DICCT)* (pp. 212-217). IEEE.

[14] Bhatia, S., Jaffery, Z. A., Mehfuz, S., & Goel, N. (2023). Integration of WSN and IoT: Wireless Networks Architecture and Protocols–A Way to Smart Agriculture. In *the Handbook of Research on ML-Enabled IoT for Smart Applications Across Industries* (pp. 435-455). IGI Global.

[15] Xian, L., & Xu, J. Smart Guardian: An AI-Based Coronary Heart Disease Prediction System, Focusing on Your Cardiac Health!. Available at SSRN 4713171.

[16] Rai, M., Maity, T., Sharma, R. et al. Early detection of foot ulceration in type II diabetic patient using registration method in infrared images and descriptive comparison with deep learning methods. *J Supercomput* 78, 13409–13426 (2022). https://doi.org/10.1007/s11227-022-04380-z.

[17] Bhatia, S., Goel, N., Ahlawat, V., Naib, B. B., & Singh, K. (2023). A Comprehensive Review of IoT Reliability and Its Measures: Perspective Analysis. *Handbook of Research on ML-Enabled IoT for Smart Applications Across Industries,* 365-384.

[18] Tuli, S., Basumatary, N., Gill, S. S., Kahani, M., Arya, R. C., Wander, G. S., & Buyya, R. (2020). HealthFog: An ensemble deep learning based Smart Healthcare

System for Automatic Diagnosis of Heart Diseases in integrated IoT and fog computing environments. *Future Generation Computer Systems,* 104, 187-200.

[19] Bhatia, S., Jaffery, Z. A., &Mehfuz, S. (2023, May). Development and Analysis of IoT based Smart Agriculture System for Heterogeneous Nodes. In *2023 International Conference on Recent Advances in Electrical, Electronics & Digital Healthcare Technologies (REEDCON)* (pp. 62-67). IEEE.

[20] Jaiswal, P., Rajput, N., Kumar, R., Bhatia, S., & Kumar, R. (2022, June). Drone Automation with Smart Irrigation. In *Futuristic Sustainable Energy & Technology: Proceedings of the International Conference on Futuristic Sustainable Energy & Technology (ICFSE, 2021),* 19-20 September, 2021 (p. 467). CRC Press.

[21] Umrao, R., Srivastava, R., Shama, S., Kumar, D., & Bhatia, S. (2022, June). Precision Farming System using IoT. In *Futuristic Sustainable Energy & Technology: Proceedings of the International Conference on Futuristic Sustainable Energy & Technology (ICFSE, 2021),* 19-20 September, 2021 (p. 477). CRC Press.

[22] Al-Makhadmeh, Z., & Tolba, A. (2019). Utilizing IoT wearable medical device for heart disease prediction using higher order Boltzmann model: A classification approach. *Measurement,* 147, 106815.

[23] Bhatia, S., Mallikarjun, B., Naib, B. B., & Goel, A. K. (2023, September). Algo-Indicator Based Trading in Stock Market. In *2023 4th International Conference on Smart Electronics and Communication (ICOSEC)* (pp. 1730-1734). IEEE.

[24] Ramkumar, G., Seetha, J., Priyadarshini, R., Gopila, M., & Saranya, G. (2023). IoT-based patient monitoring system for predicting heart disease using deep learning. Measurement, 218, 113235.prediction using higher order Boltzmann model: A classification approach. *Measurement,* 147, 106815.

[25] Bhatia, S., Arya, C., Verma, S., Gautam, D., Naib, B. B., & Kumar, A. (2023, July). Predict Success of a Zomato Restaurant using ML. In *2023 World Conference on Communication & Computing (WCONF)* (pp. 1-7). IEEE.

[26] Chaithra, C. S., Siddesha, S., Aradhya, V. N., & Niranjan, S. K. (2024). A Review of ML Techniques Used in the Prediction of Heart Disease. *Revue d'Intelligence Artificielle,* 38(1).

[27] Bhatia, S., Naib, B. B., Goel, A. K., Kumar, L., & Singh, K. (2023, June). Drowsy Driver Alert System Using OpenCV. In *2023 3rd International Conference on Pervasive Computing and Social Networking (ICPCSN)* (pp. 614-619). IEEE.

[28] Bhatia, S., Naib, B. B., Goel, N., Agarwal, B., Mallikarjun, B., & Arvindhan, M. (2024, February). A New Era in Weather Forecasting: Harnessing the Potential of ML. In *2024 IEEE International Conference on Computing, Power, and Communication Technologies (IC2PCT)* (Vol. 5, pp. 1355-1361). IEEE.

[29] Bhatia, S., Mallikarjun, B., Goel, N., Dandeva, D., Sharma, N., & Naib, B. B. (2024). Detection of Posture Using MS-IoT-Based Solution to Provide Timely Treatment. In *Using ML to Detect Emotions and Predict Human Psychology* (pp. 209-244). IGI Global.

[30] Goel, N., Bhatia, S., & Rana, P. (2023, November). Secure Smart Devices Control with Low Power Consumption. In *2023 3rd International Conference on Advancement in Electronics & Communication Engineering (AECE)* (pp. 83-87). IEEE.

[31] Gautam, D., Bhatia, S., Neha, P., & Naib, B. B. (2023, September). IoT Based Automatic Traffic Light and Speed Breaker System. In *2023 3rd International Conference on Innovative Sustainable Computational Technologies* (CISCT) (pp. 1-6). IEEE.

[32] Bhatia, S., Bhadauria, R. V. S., Mehrotra, K., Malik, J., Goel, A. K., & Naib, B. B. (2023, July). A Comparative Analysis and Design Criteria of MAC, SMAC, and TMAC Protocols in Wireless Sensor Network. In *2023 14th International Conference on Computing Communication and Networking Technologies (ICCCNT)* (pp. 1-6). IEEE.

[33] Madan, K., Gautam, D., Bhatia, S., & Kashyap, S. (2023, July). LoRaWAN Enabled Wildland Safety Fire Alert System. In *2023 14th International Conference on Computing Communication and Networking Technologies (ICCCNT)* (pp. 1-7). IEEE.

[34] Bhatia, S., Gautam, D., Kumar, S., & Verma, S. (2023, January). Automatic Seat Identification System in Smart Transport using IoT and Image Processing. In *2023 3rd International Conference on Intelligent Communication and Computational Techniques (ICCT)* (pp. 1-6). IEEE.

[35] Bhatia, S., Dhillon, H. S., & Kumar, N. (2011, December). Alive human body detection system using an autonomous mobile rescue robot. In *2011 Annual IEEE India Conference* (pp. 1-5). IEEE.

[36] Nancy, A. A., Ravindran, D., Raj Vincent, P. D., Srinivasan, K., & Gutierrez Reina, D. (2022). Iot-cloud-based smart healthcare monitoring system for heart disease prediction via deep learning. *Electronics,* 11(15), 2292.

[37] Bhatia, S., Ahlawat, V., & Verma, S. (2022). An IoT Based Framework of LPG Real Time Gas Leakage Detection and Controlling. *Proceedings of the Advancement in Electronics & Communication Engineering.*

[38] Bhatia, S., Verma, S., Singh, N., Saxena, I., & Verma, I. (2022). IOT and ai based women's safety night patrolling robot. *Social Science Research Network electronic library,* 2022, e4158918-e4158918.

[39] Bhatia, S., Ahlawat, V., & Verma, S. (2022). An IoT Enabled Smart Garbage Management System for Effective Waste Utilization Strategy in Cities. *Proceedings of the Advancement in Electronics & Communication Engineering.*

[40] Bhatia, S., Sharma, P., Verma, S., Ansari, M. T., Kumar, U., & Singh, S. P. (2022). Automatic Window Curtain System. *Proceedings of the Advancement in Electronics & Communication Engineering.*

[41] Mallikarjuna, B., Bhatia, S., Goel, N., & Naib, B. B. (2025). Blood bank mobile application of IoT-based android studio for COVID-19. In *Applied Data Science and Smart Systems* (pp. 76-81). CRC Press.

[42] Mallikarjuna, B., Bhatia, S., Goel, A. K., Gautam, D., Naib, B. B., & Kumar, S. (2025). Analysis of soil moisture using Raspberry Pi based on IoT. In *Applied Data Science and Smart Systems* (pp. 194-201). CRC Press.

[43] Bhatia, S., Ashraf, G., Naib, B. B., & Gautam, D. (2023, November). An Intelligent Credit Card Fraud Detection Using a Classification Algorithm. In *International Conference on Innovations in Data Analytics* (pp. 129-142). Singapore: Springer Nature Singapore.

[44] Jeet, V., Dhillon, H. S., & Bhatia, S. (2015, April). Radio frequency home appliance control based on head tracking and voice control for disabled person. In *2015 Fifth International Conference on Communication Systems and Network Technologies* (pp. 559-563). IEEE.

[45] Bhatia, S., Gautam, D., Tomar, R., Bhandari, M., & Chaubey, S. (2022). IoT Enabled Smart Irrigation Techniques with Leaf Disease Detection. *Proceedings of the Advancement in Electronics & Communication Engineering.*

Chapter 3

The Integration of IoT and Machine Learning in Healthcare

D. Menaka*
K. S. Subhashini
and S. Kalyani
Department of ECE, Sri Venkateswara College of Engineering Sriperumbudur, India

Abstract

The healthcare industry could undergo a significant transformation as a result of the confluence of machine learning (ML) and internet of things (IoT) technology. This could lead to proactive and individualized patient care, effective resource allocation, and data-driven. While IoT is involved in the gathering of resources and data, ML approaches handle data analysis, data expansion, learning, and decision-making based on input data. Combining these two technologies can greatly benefit the clinical sector by creating an environment that is responsive and interconnected, which will benefit patients and healthcare workers by offering a variety of services. The creation of smart apps for medical applications, such as wearable modules, smart capsules, and sensory-based units to assist medical professionals in gathering data, form the basis of IoT devices. By assessing and identifying multiple variances in a patient's health state, ML models can offer alternate diagnosis procedures and ultimately enhance the patient's health outcome. This chapter explores the integration of ML algorithms with IoT devices in healthcare contexts, highlighting the symbiotic link between these two paradigms. It delves into the various applications of ML in processing

* Corresponding Author's Email: menaka@svce.ac.in

In: Harnessing the Power of IoT-Enabled Machine Learning …
Editors: Mritunjay Rai, Ravindra Kumar Yadav, Neha Goel et al.
ISBN: 979-8-89530-626-0

vast streams of IoT-generated healthcare data, including predictive analytics for disease diagnosis, anomaly detection for remote patient monitoring, and optimization of healthcare operations. The Internet of Medical Things (IoMT) is a next-generation bioanalytical tool that integrates network-linked biomedical devices with a software application to improve human health, emerging in the same age. In this chapter, the role of AI and IoMT in enhancing the functionality, detection precision, decision-making capability, and assessment of related hazards created for cutting-edge biomedical applications are also addressed. Thus it provides insights into the revolutionary potential of merging ML and IoT to reform healthcare delivery and enhance patient outcomes through real-world case studies and future prospects. A detailed comparative analysis of various methodologies in terms of advantages, challenges and applications has been addressed which will aid healthcare practitioners, and future researchers by providing insightful information about recent developments in smart healthcare. Furthermore, the challenges and opportunities inherent in this integration, such as ensuring data privacy and security, addressing interoperability issues, and fostering collaboration among stakeholders are examined. In summary, the application of IoT and ML in healthcare has a great potential as it can incorporate novel methods such as explainable AI, federated learning, and context-aware health monitoring systems which will enhance the system's responsiveness, accuracy, and patient-centeredness, ultimately leading to better patient outcomes and care quality.

Keywords: machine learning, internet of things, predictive analysis, healthcare

1. Introduction to ML

ML is a subset of artificial intelligence that allows computers to identify patterns in data and draw conclusions from them with little assistance from humans. Computers that employ ML are provided patterns and data rather than instructions, enabling them to draw their own conclusions. It focuses on creating algorithms that can examine and decipher patterns in data in order to generate predictions or judgments that are well-informed. Massively parallel data processing, object detection in photos, email screening, and other applications are all made possible by ML algorithms. Computer programs that automatically check emails for spam, recognize objects in photos, and manage massive volumes of data use ML systems. Research on ML in healthcare, which has many potential applications, is making headway in the field of precision medicine. Patient data is becoming more accessible, which means that ML will become increasingly important for healthcare professionals and health systems to interpret medical data. Through improved image analysis and personalized medicine with customized therapies and faster drug discovery, ML is transforming the healthcare sector and also increasing the hospital management's operational efficiency. ML is also essential for remote monitoring through wearables and virtual assistants, which improves patient outcomes, especially for managing chronic diseases. Nevertheless, there are obstacles to ML adoption that must be properly addressed, such as worries about data privacy and the possibility of algorithmic bias.

1.1. Types of ML

There are three categories for ML as given in Figure 1.

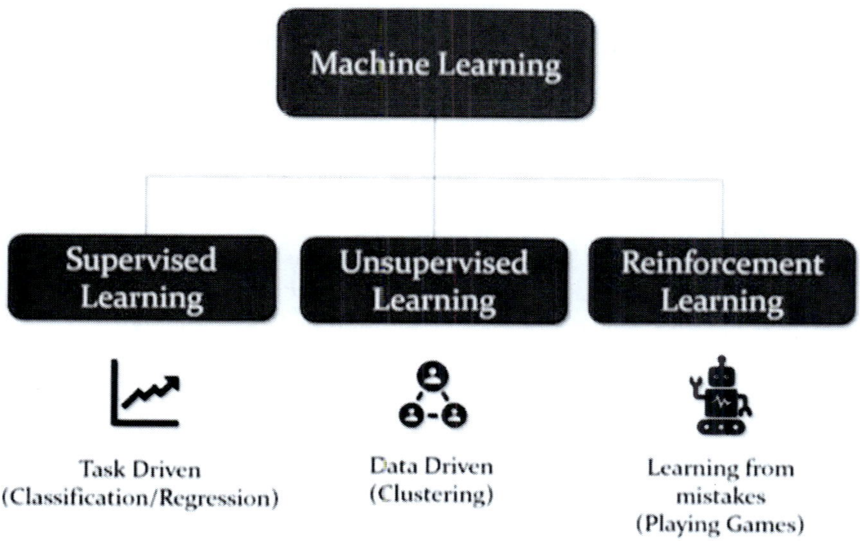

Figure 1. Types of ML.

- *Supervised Learning:* In this type of learning, the algorithm picks up the knowledge from labeled data, in which every sample has the right response marked on it. By using input features as a basis, the model is trained to predict the outcomes. The objective of supervised learning is to discover the rules that govern the mapping between a given set of inputs and outputs. For instance, the weather forecast might be one of the inputs and the beachgoers would be the result. The objective of supervised learning is to acquire the mapping that explains the connection between beach visitor volume and temperature. The model is trained to predict outcomes using the input attributes as a foundation. Giving labeled data from prior input and output pairings to a model during the learning process is known as "supervised" learning.

- *Unsupervised Learning:* Without explicit direction, algorithms can recognize patterns and structures in unlabeled data. Common techniques include clustering and dimensionality reduction. Without explicit guidance, algorithms can recognize patterns and structures in unlabeled data. Dimensionality reduction and grouping are common strategies. Unsupervised learning examples are limited to input data. Sorting different colored coins into different heaps is a practical example of unsupervised learning. By simply seeing a coin's color or other characteristic, one may determine which coins are connected to each other and group them into the proper categories.
- *Reinforcement Learning:* In this, the algorithm learns through trial & error and feedback in the form of rewards or punishments based on their actions. To maximize the cumulative benefits, they gradually refine their decision-making. Game theory offers an ideal environment rich in data, making it a prominent area of research.. Reward-motivated behaviors can be trained with game scores, which are perfect reward signals. To shorten the total amount of training time, time can also be accelerated in a simulated game setting.

1.2. Healthcare

"A state of complete emotional, mental, and physical well-being" is the way the World Health Organization (WHO) defined health in the early days. People can lead happy and peaceful lives by adopting a healthy lifestyle. The term wellness is typically used to refer to an ongoing condition of improved well-being. Therefore, the purpose of healthcare is to maintain a person's health in the major domains of life. Thus, addressing the population growth, declining birthrate, aging populations, and socially unequal resource usage are the top priorities for all governments in the present days.

1.2.1. Healthcare and the Role of ML

Due to their ability to interpret the massive amounts of healthcare data generated every day in electronic health records, ML algorithms are particularly helpful to the healthcare industry. By utilizing ML approaches, such as ML algorithms, it is feasible to find patterns and insights in medical data that would be impossible to identify manually [1]. With the increasing use of ML in healthcare, healthcare professionals now have the opportunity to take a more predictive approach to precision medicine, which can result in a more unified system with better patient outcomes, better care delivery, and more efficient patient-based procedures.

The three domains where ML is most commonly used by healthcare professionals are medical billing automation, clinical practice standards development inside the health systems, and clinical decision assistance. ML in healthcare as shown in Figure 2 have several notable high-level applications in research and treatment. At the point of service in the electronic health record, primary care physicians can receive clinical decision support from deep learning-generated medical data in clinical workflows that can automatically identify complex patterns.

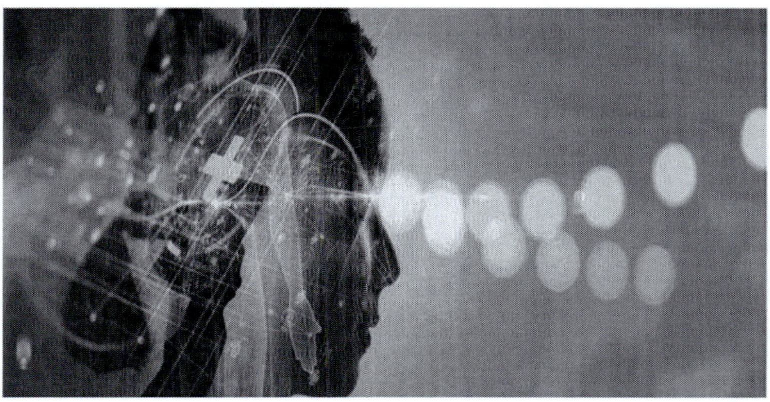

Figure 2. ML in healthcare.

Approximately 80% of healthcare data was locked in the electronic health record systems during the recent past and was unstructured. These are text or data files that need to be examined by a human in order to extract patient information. Using a variety of natural language processing tools, these texts are now converted into more valuable and analyzable data without requiring human participation with the penetration of ML and AI.

1.3. Benefits of ML for Healthcare Providers

1.3.1. Improving Diagnosis

Healthcare professionals can use ML to develop more sophisticated diagnostic tools for examining medical images. For instance, a ML system can look for patterns that indicate a given illness by using pattern recognition in medical imaging (such as X-rays or MRI scans). This type of ML technique may help doctors diagnose patients more quickly and precisely, which could enhance patients' health.

1.3.2. Developing New Treatments/Drug Discovery/Clinical Trials

A deep learning model can also be used by pharmaceutical companies and healthcare institutions to extract relevant information from the data that could aid in drug discovery, the development of new medications, and the invention of creative illness remedies. For example, ML could be applied to medical research and clinical trial data to determine the side effects of the previously unknown drugs. Results from these clinical trials could improve patient care, drug development and the safety and effectiveness of medical procedures.

1.3.3. Reducing Costs

The implementation of ML technologies has the potential to enhance healthcare efficiency and lower costs for healthcare organizations. ML could be used to develop better algorithms for managing patient data or booking appointments. This type of ML could reduce the amount of time and money wasted on tedious tasks within the healthcare systems.

1.3.4. Data Security and Privacy

Patient data security is critical given the growing digitization of health records. Real-time cybersecurity threat detection and response is one way that ML may improve data security. Patient data is thus protected as ML algorithms are able to recognize unusual trends that can point to a data breach.

1.3.5. Improving Care

ML can be used in healthcare by medical professionals to improve patient care. Deep learning algorithms, for example, might be used by the healthcare industry to develop systems that proactively monitor patients and alert medical devices or electronic health records when a patient's state changes. Using ML to collect data may make it easier to ensure that patients receive the right care at the right time. Though its applications are still in the early stages of development, ML is already having a significant impact on the healthcare industry. The global market size for AI in healthcare is estimated to increase from 20.9 billion USD to 148.4 billion by the year 2029 as shown in Figure 3. The Capital Annual Growth Rate (CAGR) is expected to rise to 48.1% during the forecast period. Future healthcare will rely more on ML as we attempt to make sense of the increasing amount of data.

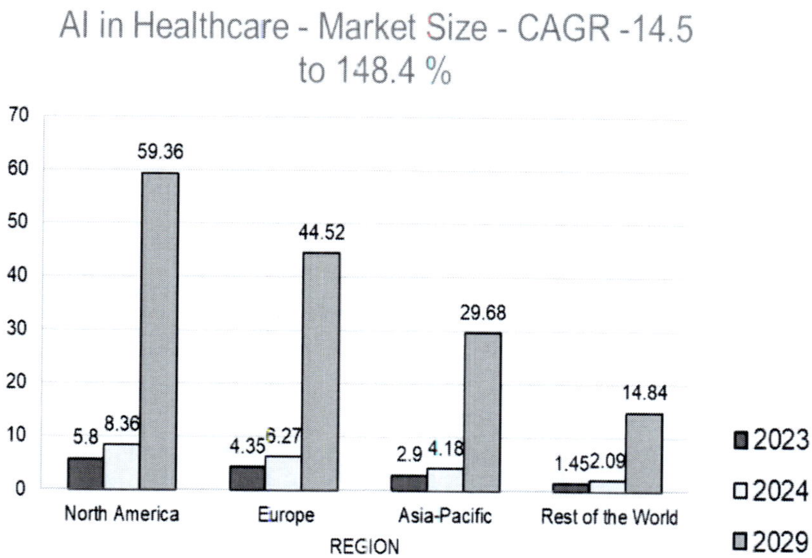

Figure 3. Market size of AI in healthcare.

1.4. ML Applications in the Healthcare Industry

Developing algorithms that can analyze and decipher data patterns to produce precise evaluations or projections is the primary goal. The healthcare business depends heavily on ML and deep learning (DL) for several reasons [2–3].

1.4.1. Personalized Care

Large datasets can be analyzed by ML algorithms to find patterns and predict individual patient outcomes. This enables medical practitioners to tailor therapy to each patient's specific needs, increasing treatment effectiveness and lowering adverse effects.

1.4.2. Medical Imaging

To assist radiologists in more rapidly and accurately identifying anomalies, ML algorithms can be used to evaluate medical images such as CT, MRI, and X-rays. These pictures depict fractures and malignancies, for example. This could lead to early sickness diagnosis and treatment.

1.4.3. Predictive Analytics

ML models are able to predict a variety of patient health outcomes, including the chance of a readmission, the course of an illness, or the effectiveness of a certain medication. This enables the effective use of resources and the implementation of preventive measures, which ultimately lead to better patient outcomes and reduced healthcare costs.

1.4.4. Drug Development and Discovery

ML algorithms can be used to evaluate genetic and molecular data in order to identify potential new drugs, predict how well they will work, and enhance the design of existing drugs. This speeds up the process of finding and developing novel drugs and cures as well as introducing them more swiftly.

1.4.5. Clinical Decision Support

Medical staff can receive evidence-based recommendations and insights from ML algorithms at the point of care. Through the integration of patient data, medical literature, and best practices, these technologies can assist the doctors in making more informed decisions that will improve the patient's safety and treatment quality.

1.4.6. Healthcare Operations and Efficiency

By forecasting patient admissions, resource usage, and personnel requirements, ML (ML) can improve hospital and healthcare system operations. In addition, it can aid in revenue cycle management, fraud detection, and administrative process optimization, all of which can reduce costs and increase productivity [4].

1.4.7. Remote Monitoring and Telemedicine

Wearable technology with ML capabilities as well as remote monitoring systems may gather and evaluate patient data continually, enabling the early identification of health problems and prompt intervention. Furthermore, ML algorithms can improve access to healthcare, particularly in areas with limited resources, by enabling remote consultations and diagnostics.

1.4.8. Population Health Management

ML can evaluate population-level health data to locate hotspots for disease, risk factors, and trends in health. Utilizing this data, public health policies, preventative measures, and targeted treatments can be created to enhance community health. In general, ML has the potential to transform healthcare by providing more precise diagnoses, personalized therapies, and proactive care delivery, which eventually improves patient outcomes and makes the healthcare system more effective [5, 6].

2. Introduction to IoT

The primary goal of the IoT is to more effectively and transparently link smart items to the internet. As a result, data is exchanged throughout all entities, increasing the security of user information. IoT is stated as "a self-configured dynamic global network infrastructure with standards and interoperable communication protocols where physical and virtual "things" have identities, physical attributes, and virtual personalities, and are seamlessly integrated into the information infrastructure." IoT comprises of three main components: (i) global network that links smart objects through extended Internet technologies, (ii) set of supporting technologies required to make this vision a reality (such as RFIDs, sensor/actuators, machine-to-machine communication devices, etc.), and (iii) collection of services and applications that use these technologies to create new business and market opportunities. IoT technology's core uses include monitoring the environment, tracking items from far-off locations and providing a real-time solution in a global setting (both indoor and outdoor). Identification, Sensing, Communication, Computation, Services, and Semantic are the six primary components of IoT that allow its operation and services to be comprehended [7].

- *Identification:* The first and most important element of the IoT is to recognize the details of the user whenever he/she demands.
- *Sensing:* It is a process of collecting information from various devices and storing that information for further processing. The market is seeing a large introduction of sensors to help with this process. The demand, sensing method, measurement attribute, conversion process, and application location all influence the choice of a sensor.
- *Communication:* It is essential to establish communication between various objects to share information in the IoT. This can be achieved through different communication protocols ranging from short range to long range such as UWB, RFID, NFC, Bluetooth, LTE etc.
- *Computation:* The raw input data from the sensors are processed and stored for future references. For processing the data various processing units, hardware and software components are employed with which the computation capability of the IoT can be determined. Most of the IoT applications rely on real-time operating systems.
- *Services:* IoT services go into one of two categories: i) identity-based services, which use devices' identities. ii) information aggregation services to gather, handle, and send sensor data to IoT applications ex. smart healthcare systems, smart education etc. iii) collaborative-aware services to decide and act according to the received information ex. smart home, intelligent transport system etc. iv) ubiquitous services which aim to offer services to people everywhere, such as in smart cities that enhance people's quality of life by offering a range of services.
- *Semantic:* It involves gathering data from every IoT device and providing users with services as and when needed.

2.1. IoT in Healthcare

The IoT revolutionizes healthcare by enhancing patient care and significantly reducing costs. It enables real-time monitoring and data collection, improving response times and patient outcomes. By automating the administrative tasks and routine procedures like vital sign monitoring and medication dispensing [8], IoT streamlines the operations, reduces errors, and decreases the labor costs. Its early detection capabilities helps to prevent costly complications and minimize hospitalizations, substantially lowering overall healthcare expenses.

The Global IoT in healthcare market is expected to increase from USD 127.7 billion in 2023 to USD 289.2 billion by 2028 at a CAGR of 17.8% over the next 5 years. The market will be driven by advancements in medical equipment, enhanced healthcare infrastructure, and digital transformations in the healthcare sector as shown in Figure 4.

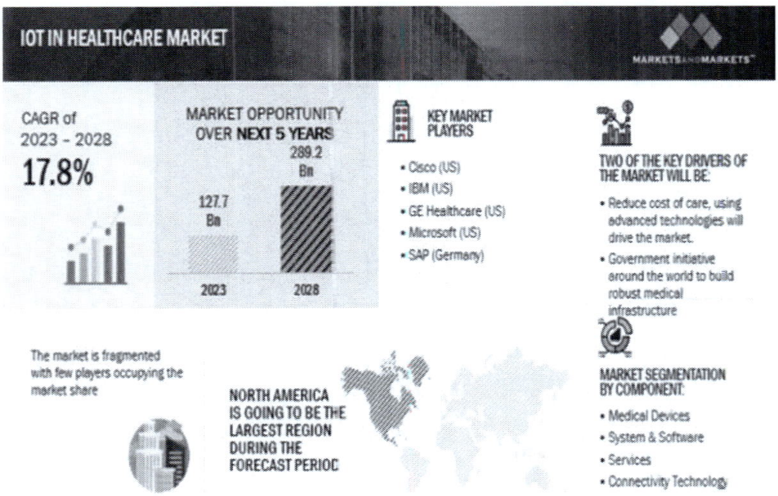

Figure 4. Market research on IoT in healthcare.

IoT also gives patients the ability to take an active role in managing their healthcare. Medical records can be accessed through patient portals, while wearable technology and smartphone apps let people track their health information. Real-time data sharing and virtual consultations are made possible via telemedicine and remote monitoring. Direct communication with healthcare providers is made possible via secure messaging platforms, which promotes greater participation and better health outcomes. But proper training and education are necessary to ensure that users can fully benefit from these new technologies.

The management of healthcare and services, particularly in hospitals, have been enhanced by recent developments in IoT systems, allowing for more efficient and rapid access to patient treatment and diagnostic data. Hospital management system functionalities have been improvised as a result of several academics' investigations into the implications of IoT integration in the healthcare management space [9, 10]. Even though the government prioritizes healthcare, a few issues in the industry have emerged as more prominent, such as:

- Inability to effectively respond to emergencies.
- Significant shortages of medical personnel and institutional resources, particularly in rural areas.
- Insufficient capabilities for disease prevention and early detection.

2.1.1. Overview of IoT Technologies in Healthcare

The IoT is revolutionizing healthcare by creating a network of interconnected devices that collect, analyze, and transmit medical data [11].

2.1.1.1. Wearable Devices

Smartwatches, fitness trackers, and even smart clothing can monitor heart rate, blood pressure, blood sugar, and other wearable that monitor vital signs, physical activity, and sleep patterns [12, 13]. These devices can alert users and healthcare providers to potential health issues.

2.1.1.2. Implanted Devices

Pacemakers, blood glucose monitors, and insulin pumps can transmit data wirelessly.

2.1.1.3. Sensors

Incorporated into pills, bandages, or the environment, these sensors track vitals, medication adherence, and even room temperature. IoT has numerous and diverse applications as illustrated in Figure 5.

2.1.1.4. Remote Patient Monitoring

- IoT devices allow continuous monitoring of patients with chronic conditions from their homes.
- This reduces hospital readmissions and improves quality of life for patients.

2.1.1.5. Medication Management

- Smart pills and connected dispensers help ensure patients take the right medication at the right time.
- These systems can alert caregivers if doses are missed.

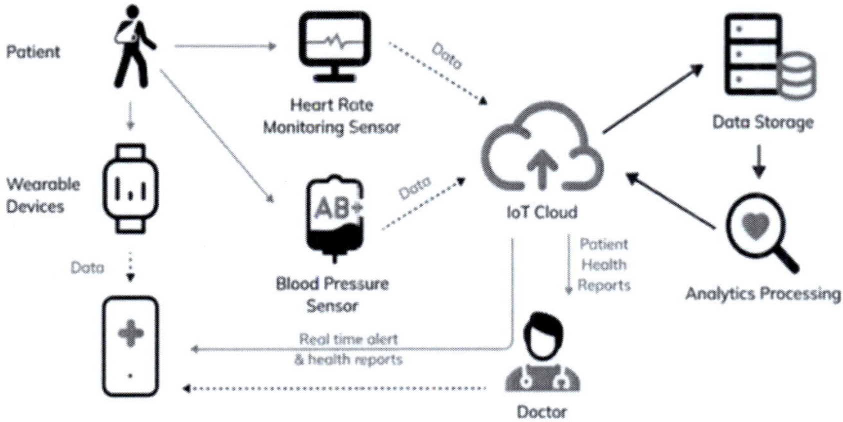

Figure 5. IoT in healthcare.

2.1.1.6. Asset Tracking

RFID tags and other IoT sensors help hospitals track equipment, reducing losses and improving efficiency.

2.1.1.7. Environmental Monitoring

- IoT sensors monitor temperature, humidity, and air quality in healthcare facilities [14].
- This helps maintain optimal conditions for patients and sensitive medical equipment.

2.1.1.8. Smart Hospital Rooms

Connected devices adjust lighting, temperature, and entertainment based on patient preferences and needs [15].

2.1.1.9. Telemedicine

IoT enables remote consultations and diagnoses through video calls and data sharing.

2.1.1.10. Real-Time Location Systems

Track the location of patients, staff, and equipment within healthcare facilities.

2.1.1.11. Predictive Maintenance

IoT sensors on medical equipment can predict when maintenance is needed, reducing downtime.

2.1.1.12. Data Analytics

The enormous amount of data collected by IoT devices can be analyzed to improve treatments and identify trends.

2.1.1.13. Benefits

- *Reduced costs:* Fewer hospital visits and readmissions lead to overall cost savings.
- *Improved patient outcomes:* Early detection and better treatment plans can lead to better health [16].
- *Empowered patients:* Patients can take a more active role in managing their health.
- *Enhanced healthcare delivery:* Telemedicine and remote care become more efficient.

2.1.1.14. Challenges

- *Data security and privacy:* Protecting sensitive health data is crucial [17].
- *Device interoperability:* Ensuring different devices can communicate seamlessly is important.
- *Cost of implementation:* Setting up and maintaining an IoT network can be expensive.
- *Data overload and analysis:* Managing and interpreting large amounts of data requires new tools.

2.1.2. Healthcare Technologies

Generally, healthcare IoT is used for mobile medical applications and as wearable devices which help to capture the health data of the patients [18, 19]. In the hospitals, IoT is used to keep track of the location and records of medical equipment, staff and patients. Some of the technologies applied to IoT-based healthcare systems are as listed below.

2.1.2.1. Cloud Computing

It facilitates widespread access to various resources, offers services on request over the network by integrating cloud computing with IoT-based healthcare technologies [20].

2.1.2.2. Grid Computing

With the help of various biomedical sensor nodes, it is possible to continuously monitor patients at remote places through this technology. Nowadays, small wearable devices can continuously monitor vital signs such as blood pressure, temperature, Electrocardiogram (ECG), Electromyogram (EMG), oxygen saturation with which the patients' health conditions can always be kept under observations as illustrated in Figure 6.

2.1.2.3. Big Data

The input data from the medical sensors are stored, analyzed and used for efficient diagnosis and prognosis of health.

2.1.2.4. Networks

It offers short-range communications, such as WPANs, WBANs, WLANs, WSNs and long-range communications, e.g., any type of cellular network in the healthcare environment. For low-power medical sensor devices, UWB, BLE, NFC and RFID technologies are used [21].

2.1.2.5. Augmented Reality

Augmented reality will have a major impact in the healthcare sector in the near future by offering surgical assistance and improving the efficiency of various processes in healthcare organizations.

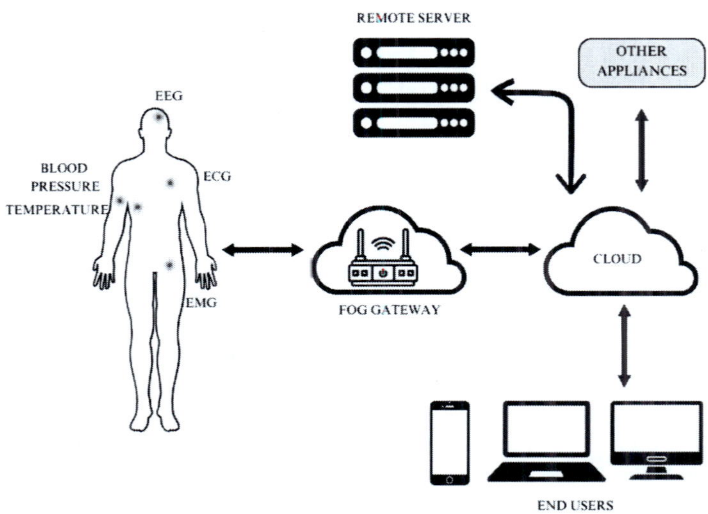

Figure 6. IoT based healthcare system.

2.3. Applications of IoT in Healthcare Systems

The IoT-enabled healthcare ecosystem consists of four primary components. The primary component, which houses patients and medical professionals, is the hospital. Secondly, wearable or embedded medical body sensors which are used for real time monitoring of the health conditions of patients especially those who are at home. It is followed by the application software to retrieve, process and transform the sensor readings into useful information. Finally, ambient assisted living devices with IoT capabilities are provided to out-patients to manage their well-being. As a result, IoT-enabled healthcare systems improve patient wellbeing and give us the vital resources and knowledge required for the general population to receive the best possible healthcare—a concept sometimes referred to as "smart healthcare."

From a technological perspective, the IoT and sensors are essential components because they streamline the healthcare system and are thus directly tied to the needs of the user or patient. The applications in healthcare systems are listed below:

2.3.1. IoT Enabled Smart Ambulance System

Ambulance services can be significantly impacted by traffic jams, which are among the major challenges faced by roadways in India. As a consequence, the patient's life may become crucial.

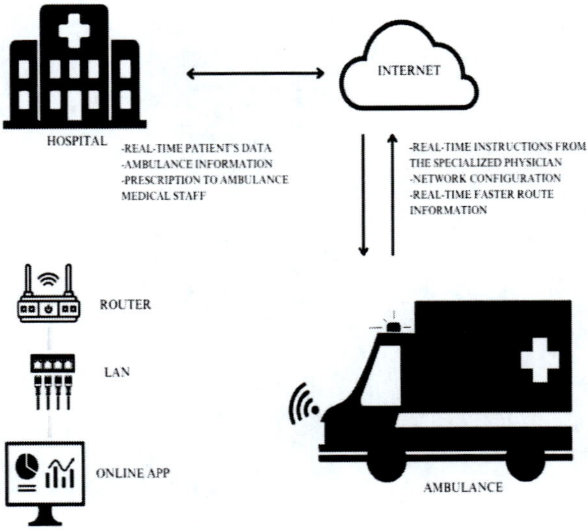

Figure 7. IoT enabled smart ambulance system.

IoT enabled smart ambulances are provided with sensors like heart rate sensor, blood pressure, ECG to monitor the vital signs of the patient and readings will be transmitted to the hospital's database simultaneously. Accordingly, based on the vitals, the remote medical team will plan, ensuring that patients are attended to on time. Additionally, the system is designed so that when an ambulance approaches within a short range, the traffic signal automatically turns green. The communication between smart ambulances and traffic signals can be done by cloud computing. Red Ninja created the Life First Emergency Traffic Control (LiFE) algorithm, which modifies the traffic signal pattern for ambulances in an emergency as illustrated in Figure 7.

2.3.2. IoT Enabled Home Care Services

Quio, a connected health startup, collaborates with hospitals, health plans, and clinicians to create and implement programs that improve patient outcomes and promote medication adherence. Their technology makes it easier for patients to take their prescribed medications on time every day. As the population grows, IoT-enabled healthcare systems can turn homes into hospitals, enabling all hospital care services to be delivered as home care. This could assist in tracking the drug's efficacy and real-time medication adjustments in case the patient needs them. Sensors installed throughout the house monitor every movement of the patient and wirelessly transmit the data to the attending physician. The physician reviews the patient's report and provides prescriptions based on the information gathered from the home. This IoT-connected, home-based service has proven to be a highly effective solution during the COVID-19 pandemic.

2.3.3. Smart Watches

Smart watches were initially utilized for amusement and other purposes. However, it has evolved into one of the most potent medical instruments as a result of the producers' creation of numerous uses. Smartwatches were initially designed for entertainment and general use. Over time, they have transformed into advanced medical devices due to the development of various health-focused applications by manufacturers For instance, the Apple Watch Series 4 comes with an app to identify atrial fibrillation (AFib), a heart ailment that can result in a stroke, blood clot, etc. Asthma and other respiratory conditions can be tracked with the Apple Watch Series 6 function. In a similar vein, Fitbit and Samsung Galaxy have given their wearables blood pressure and ECG sensors. These watches also come with other health-related features including tracking, tracking, step counts, sleep cycles, movement reminders, medication reminders, and running. This application is particularly helpful for elderly individuals in monitoring their health conditions and identifying any falls, unusual movements, or periods of inactivity following sudden changes in them. The patient's location is then sent to emerency services in a message.

Some smart watches are equipped with glucometers for monitoring the glucose level of the patients. Long-term elevated blood sugar levels are common in diabetic people. Therefore, keeping an eye on those individuals' blood sugar levels helps identify their pattern of blood glucose fluctuations and helps them with everyday tasks like eating, drinking, and taking medication. Real-time glucose measurement methods are also suggested, with the data being uploaded to a server and sent to concerned doctors for additional analysis. Thus, the IoT facilitates data sharing between the physician and the patient.

2.3.4. Advanced Metering Infrastructure (AMI)

Hospitals, healthcare facilities, and any related infrastructure must have a constant power supply during pandemic emergencies. The AMI handles this function since smart grids are made up of sensors and transducers that track the amount of electricity that is supplied and demanded. The Advanced Metering Infrastructure (AMI) performs this function by utilizing sensors and transducers in smart grids to monitor electricity supply and demand. Numerous smart meters make up an AMI in a smart grid, and they are all connected to the internet via the IoT. A meter's reading is transmitted to the power providers' main server as soon as it is gathered. The meter reading is instantly transmitted to the power provider's central server as soon as it is collected.

2.3.5. Smart Wheelchair

A smart wheelchair is integrated with numerous sensors, assistive technologies, and computers that work together to provide users with disabilities—such as impairments, handicaps, and permanent injuries—the freedom and security to move around. Over the past few years, a lot of work has gone into integrating different technologies to create an autonomous wheelchair that employs voice recognition technology to operate the wheelchair and ML principles to navigate. The mobility of the wheelchair, the user's location, the surroundings, and other factors are used to detect the patient's data, which are then shared with the relevant medical team.

2.4. IoT Healthcare Architecture and Components

A comprehensive review of IoT healthcare architecture and its key components are given below. The layered structure of IoT healthcare systems, the essential elements at each layer, the challenges and opportunities in implementing these systems are discussed. The architecture of IoT healthcare systems is designed to collect, transmit, process, and analyze vast amounts of health-related data from various sources.

2.4.1. IoT Healthcare Architecture

The four main levels of an IoT healthcare architecture are the perception layer, network layer, middleware layer, and application layer, as described in [22].

2.4.1.1. Perception Layer

This layer comprises sensors and actuators that interact directly with the patient or environment. Key components include:

- Wearable devices (e.g., smartwatches, fitness trackers)
- Implantable sensors
- Environmental sensors (temperature, humidity, air quality)
- Medical equipment with IoT capabilities

2.4.1.2. Network Layer

The network layer facilitates data transmission from the perception layer to higher layers. It includes:

- Short-range communication protocols (Bluetooth, ZigBee, NFC)
- Long-range communication technologies (Wi-Fi, cellular networks, LoRaWAN)
- Gateway devices for protocol translation and data aggregation.

2.4.1.3. Middleware Layer

This layer manages data and ensures interoperability between diverse devices and platforms. Components include:

- Data preprocessing and filtering mechanisms
- Device management systems
- Service management platforms

2.4.1.4. Application Layer

The application layer processes data and presents actionable insights. It encompasses:

- Cloud computing infrastructure
- Big data analytics platforms
- ML and AI algorithms
- User interfaces for healthcare providers and patients

2.4.2. Key Components

The key components in the IoT systems are illustrated in Figure 8.

2.4.2.1. Sensors and Wearables

These devices gather ambient data as well as physiological data, such as blood pressure, glucose levels, and heart rate. More advanced and less invasive sensor technology has been made possible by advancements in miniaturization and battery technology.

2.4.2.2. Gateways

Gateways serve as intermediaries between sensors and cloud platforms. They perform critical functions such as protocol translation, data aggregation, and edge computing. Reduced latency and bandwidth requirements can be achieved by utilizing edge computing in gateways.

2.4.2.3. Cloud Infrastructure

Cloud platforms provide scalable storage and computing resources [23]. They often incorporate services for data analytics, ML, and integration with existing healthcare IT systems. Ensuring compliance with healthcare regulations (e.g., HIPAA) is crucial for cloud-based healthcare solutions.

2.4.2.4. Analytics and AI

To extract valuable insights from the massive volumes of data gathered, advanced analytics including AI and ML algorithms are necessary. These technologies enable predictive analytics, personalized treatment recommendations, and early disease detection.

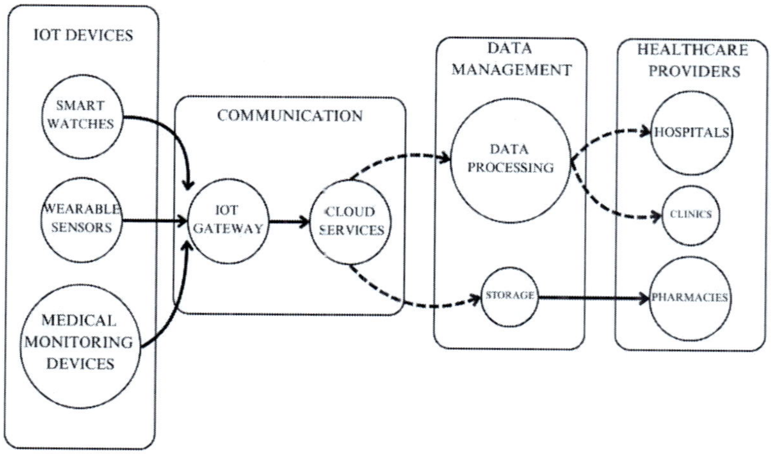

Figure 8. Key components in IoT systems.

The architecture of IoT Healthcare with applications is shown in Figure 9.

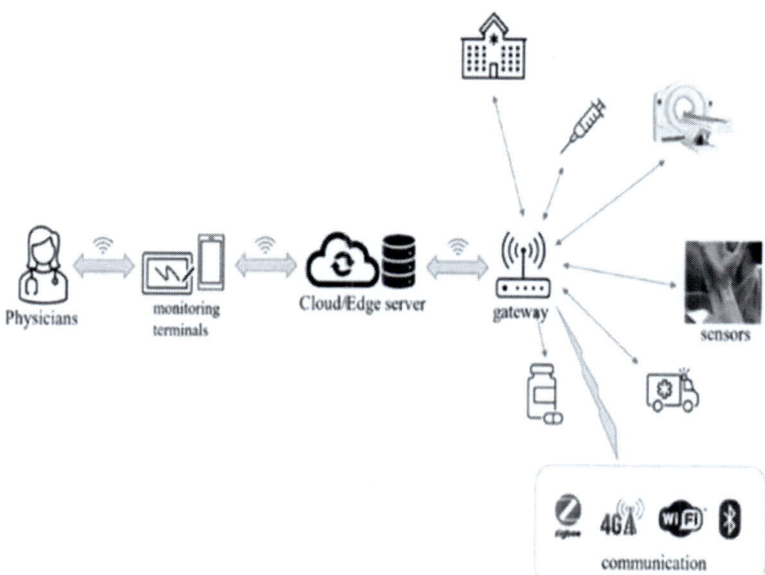

Figure 9. IoT healthcare architecture with applications.

2.4.3. Challenges and Opportunities

2.4.3.1. Interoperability

Interoperability in IoT healthcare systems is severely hampered by the variety of devices and protocols. These problems are intended to be addressed by standardization initiatives like the Fast Healthcare Interoperability Resources (FHIR) standard.

2.4.3.2. Security and Privacy

It is imperative to provide strong encryption, access control, and data anonymization methods. Blockchain technology has the potential to improve IoT healthcare systems' data security and privacy [25].

2.4.3.3. Data Quality and Reliability

Ensuring the dependability and correctness of the data gathered from diverse sources are crucial in making informed clinical decisions. Developing robust data validation and error detection mechanisms is an ongoing challenge.

2.4.3.4. Scalability

As IoT healthcare systems grow, managing the increasing volume of data and devices becomes more complex. Developing scalable architectures that can handle this growth while maintaining performance is a key area of research. Thus, the IoT healthcare architecture provides a framework for transforming healthcare delivery through continuous monitoring, data-driven insights, and personalized care. As the field evolves, addressing challenges related to interoperability, security, and scalability will be crucial. To fully grasp the promise of this technology in enhancing patient outcomes and healthcare efficiency, future research should concentrate on creating more resilient, effective, and secure IoT healthcare systems.

2.4.4. Benefits of an IoT-Based Healthcare Infrastructure

Error-free diagnostic data collected and processed by IoT devices can make better treatments possible. Patients' faith and confidence in the medical staff and hospital infrastructure are enhanced when they receive high-quality care. Additionally, the internet enables people to access real-time, affordable medical advice anytime and from anywhere. Constant monitoring, made possible by embedded camera sensor devices, contributes to the upkeep and security of healthcare facilities through smart healthcare [26]. Moreover, it allows the elderly to manage serious health conditions without the need for frequent hospital visits for examinations by physicians or nurses.

2.4.5. Challenges in Smart Healthcare

The section is divided into two subsections, domain-specific issues and open research challenges, to address the research problems. Examining current research across various healthcare fields is essential for identifying the domain-specific challenges addressed within them. The main problems with applying ML approaches to IoT-based smart healthcare are outlined in terms of open research challenges. The subject of smart healthcare has advanced significantly as a result of the collaboration between IoT and ML. However, due to the intrinsic difficulties of each field separately and the complications that result from integrating these two sectors, there are still many challenges to be resolved. The open research issues around ML and IoT-based smart healthcare systems are given below.

- Resource Constraints
- Real-time Learning
- Continuous Learning
- Data Synchronization
- Interoperability
- Security and Privacy Ethical challenges
- Distinguishing True and False Signals

2.5. Integration of ML and IoT

The amalgamation of IoT with ML offers a groundbreaking method for analyzing data and making decisions. This chapter explores the applications, advantages, difficulties, and potential ramifications of this synergy as it digs into the conceptual underpinning for fusing IoT and ML. This chapter also attempts to provide a thorough knowledge of the possibility of combining these two technologies by studying the role of ML in the IoT and vice versa, as well as suggesting solutions for seamless integration.

As a subfield of artificial intelligence, ML focuses on creating algorithms that let computers learn from data and make predictions or judgments. To improve the functionality of IoT devices, ML algorithms can be included into them. For example, ML-enabled smart home appliances may recognize human preferences and modify settings appropriately. Healthcare, transportation, and manufacturing are just a few industries that use ML in the IoT. These industries can improve operations through anomaly detection and predictive maintenance. The benefits of integrating ML in IoT systems are manifold, including improved efficiency, enhanced data analysis, and predictive capabilities that enable proactive decision-making.

IoT, on the other hand, refers to the process of connecting gadgets to the internet so they can exchange and gather data. When it comes to ML, the IoT is essential for supplying the data required for developing and implementing ML algorithms. In order to train ML models, sensors, cameras, and other data sources are gathered via IoT devices.

However, there are drawbacks to using IoT data in ML models, including problems with data security, privacy, and quality. Notwithstanding these drawbacks, the massive volume of data produced by IoT devices is a useful tool for raising the precision and potency of ML algorithms.

There is a lot of promise for data analysis and decision-making processes when ML and the IoT are combined [27]. By integrating the data collection and transmission capabilities of IoT devices with the predictive abilities of ML, enterprises can gain valuable insights to optimize processes and improve customer experiences. To achieve seamless integration, strategies such as developing edge computing solutions to process data locally on IoT devices, implementing federated learning techniques to train models on distributed data, and ensuring data security and privacy are essential. In the future, the convergence of IoT and ML will propel developments in fields like precision agriculture, smart cities, and driverless cars, completely changing the way data is gathered, processed, and used across a range of sectors.

To sum up, combining ML with the IoT is a revolutionary way to use data to improve operational effectiveness and decision-making. Organizations may fully utilize these technologies by comprehending the role that ML plays in the IoT and vice versa, as well as the opportunities and problems that come with integrating these two fields. The proposed conceptual framework provides a roadmap for effectively integrating ML algorithms into IoT devices, paving the way for future advancements and innovations in data analytics and automation. As the synergy between ML and IoT continues to evolve, the possibilities for driving growth and innovation across industries are limitless. Table 1 compares different methodologies in terms of their functionality, advantages, challenges, and applications, helping to understand how IoT and ML are being integrated into healthcare systems.

Table 1. Comparison of different methodologies in integrating ML and IoT for the healthcare applications

Methodology	Description	Advantages	Challenges	Applications
Hybrid Edge-Cloud AI	Combines edge computing for real-time decision-making with cloud computing for more complex tasks.	• Optimized resource utilization • Balance between real-time processing and complex analytics	• Higher complexity in system architecture • Potential synchronization issues between edge and cloud	Smart hospital management systems integrating real-time alerts with long-term analysis.
On-device ML	ML models run directly on resource-constrained IoT devices, often using lightweight frameworks.	• Low latency • Enhanced privacy • Independence from constant internet connectivity	• Limited model complexity • Potential for reduced accuracy	Smart inhalers predicting and preventing asthma attacks.
Federated Learning	Distributed ML models trained across decentralized IoT devices without sharing raw data, preserving privacy.	• Enhanced privacy • Utilizes decentralized data • Personalized models	• Communication overhead • Complexity in managing and aggregating model updates	Collaborative learning models for chronic disease management across different hospitals.
Explainable AI (XAI)	AI models integrated with IoT systems provide transparent and interpretable insights, aiding clinical decision-making.	• Increased trust and adoption • Improved understanding of model decisions	• Complexity in model interpretation • Potential trade-off between explainability and accuracy	Diagnostic tools explaining abnormal heart rhythms detected by wearable devices.
Blockchain-integrated IoT	Uses blockchain for secure and decentralized management of health data collected by IoT devices.	• Enhanced data integrity • Tamper-proof records • Improved patient control over data	• High computational cost • Scalability issues • Complexity in implementation	Secure sharing of electronic health records (EHRs) across healthcare institutions.

Table 1. (Continued)

Methodology	Description	Advantages	Challenges	Applications
Adaptive IoT Systems	IoT devices use adaptive ML models that evolve based on real-time patient data, offering personalized healthcare.	• Personalized care • Continuous model improvement • Better handling of dynamic conditions	• Complexity in continuous learning • Potential for model drift	Insulin pumps adapting to real-time glucose levels and patient behavior.
Multi-modal Data Fusion	ML models integrate data from various IoT devices (e.g., sensors, EHRs, imaging) to provide comprehensive health insights.	• Holistic patient view • Improved diagnostic accuracy • Enhanced decision-making	• Data integration complexity • Handling heterogeneous data types	Integrated systems combining wearable data, imaging, and patient history for diagnostics.
Real-time Feedback Loops	IoT devices use ML to provide immediate feedback or interventions based on continuous data analysis.	• Proactive healthcare • Immediate response to health events • Improved patient engagement	• Potential for over-reliance on automated systems • Need for robust real-time processing	Mental health apps providing real-time mindfulness exercises based on stress detection.

2.6. Future Directions

In this section, the future direction of IoT and ML systems have been discussed.

- *Advancements in AI and IoT:* Continuous breakthroughs in IoT, AI, and ML will spur innovations in healthcare by facilitating the development of more complex prediction models, tailored interventions, and remote monitoring features.
- *Ethical and Regulatory Considerations:* For ML and IoT technologies to be deployed responsibly in the healthcare industry, it will be essential to address the ethical issues, guarantee algorithmic fairness, and adhere to data privacy and security standards.

2.6.1. Developing Lightweight and Energy Efficient Solution

Issues related to smart healthcare, like excessive energy use and absence of a workable resource management plan, are critical. As most of the currently available solutions lack these features, developing a unique, lightweight, and energy-efficient ML based data aggregation method is essential. Additionally, innovative strategies must be devised to efficiently distribute tasks across multiple IoT components. These systems should not only provide solutions with a satisfactory level of accuracy but also effectively address the resource constraints inherent in such networks.

2.6.2. Designing Appropriate Devices

In the healthcare sector, distinguishing between genuine and fraudulent data collected from wearable devices presents a significant challenge. Flexibility is also crucial for future initiatives, especially in applications like motion detection, where sensors must adapt to each individual's unique gait patterns. Addressing these challenges could benefit from research into both contact-based and contactless methods, along with the development of DL models capable of differentiating between authentic and false data.

2.6.3. Combining ML with Optimization Techniques

Developing advanced big data analytics tools and techniques to analyze and extract relevant information is crucial. Introducing innovative methods for noise reduction is essential to prepare data effectively, streamline analysis, and improve data signals. Moreover, with IoT devices producing real-time data, the application of machine learning algorithms for real-time monitoring and rapid response represents an exciting area of research. This is likely to emerge as a key research challenge in the near future. Additionally, a notable concern is the performance degradation of data aggregation techniques due to the complexities of underlying network topologies.

In addition to the previously mentioned approaches, there are broader areas that demand further research. For instance, a comprehensive evaluation of big data technologies and ML techniques to determine their suitability for IoT healthcare applications has yet to be conducted. Moreover, the academic community needs to place greater emphasis on these studies, as the exploration of the intersection between big data analytics and healthcare remains in its infancy.

Conclusion

By integrating ML with IoT, the industry is poised for a revolution, enabling patient care to become more personalized, connected, and efficient. IoT involves a network of interconnected digital devices that operate collaboratively, collecting, transmitting, and storing data with minimal human intervention. Recent progress in combining ML with IoT has positively impacted various aspects of our lives, from seamless data access to prompt service delivery. In healthcare, this integration has notably improved the management and delivery of services, particularly in medical facilities where diagnostic information can be accessed, and patients can be treated much faster than ever before.

Furthermore, IoT offers significant advantages in modernizing healthcare by predicting potential health issues, enabling early detection, analysis, management, and monitoring of patients both within and outside hospital settings. This chapter provides a comprehensive overview of IoT technologies in healthcare, explores how IoT devices are enhancing service delivery, and discusses the potential impact of this technology on global healthcare over the next decade. IoT has thrived in the twenty-first century, enhancing decision-making and enabling services like pay-as-you-use models. By incorporating smart devices and technologies, IoT aims to improve the quality of life in modern society. Meanwhile, ML leverages predictive analytics to address complex business challenges. While IoT has facilitated real-time monitoring, ML has focused on advancing algorithms. Both technologies have individually impacted healthcare significantly in recent years. Currently, researchers are actively exploring ML solutions for IoT-based healthcare, offering substantial benefits in statistical and predictive analysis. This chapter provides a comprehensive introduction to IoT-based smart healthcare powered by ML, highlighting key research challenges and presenting ideas for future contributions. The integration of IoT and ML holds immense potential to revolutionize patient outcomes, transform healthcare delivery, and drive medical innovation and research. The chapter also delves deeply into the challenges associated with ML and IoT applications, offering a solid foundation for scholars interested in developing novel theoretical approaches or practical implementations in smart healthcare. Future research should prioritize addressing the unique challenges of each domain while overcoming the complexities of integrating these two transformative technologies. The novelty of this chapter lies in its exploration of how advanced data-driven approaches are revolutionizing traditional medical practices. These technologies introduce cutting-edge methods such as federated transfer learning, Explainable AI for IoT, and context-aware ML models, enabling breakthroughs in behavioral modeling, personalized treatment, and predictive analytics - far surpassing the capabilities of conventional tools. AI and ML empower real-time, continuous patient monitoring, fostering proactive care and significantly improving health outcomes. They also drive innovation in areas such as drug discovery, operational efficiency, and decision-making processes within the healthcare sector. However, the integration of AI and ML in healthcare also raises critical ethical considerations. These include the need for robust frameworks to ensure data privacy, fairness, and transparency in healthcare applications. By addressing these challenges, this chapter highlights the transformative potential of these technologies while advocating for ethical and equitable implementation.

References

[1] Ahmad, M. A., C. Eckert, and A. Teredesai. "Fairness in Machine Learning for Healthcare." *Communications of the ACM* 65, no. 3 (2022): 46-55. https://doi.org/10.1145/3477608.

[2] Chen, C., M. Decary, S. Hu, and H. Haddad. "Artificial Intelligence in Healthcare: An Essential Guide for Health Leaders." *Healthcare Management Forum* 34, no. 1 (2021): 10-18. https://doi.org/10.1177/0840470420973547.

[3] Esteva, A., A. Robicquet, B. Ramsundar, V. Kuleshov, M. DePristo, K. Chou, et al. "A Guide to Deep Learning in Healthcare." *Nature Medicine* 27, no. 1 (2021): 29-38. https://doi.org/10.1038/s41591-020-01272-7.

[4] Johnson, A. E. W., T. J. Pollard, and R. G. Mark. "Reproducibility in Critical Care: A Mortality Prediction Case Study." *Machine Learning for Healthcare Conference*, PMLR (2021): 320-343. https://proceedings.mlr.press/v126/johnson20a.html.

[5] Reddy, S., J. Fox, and M. P. Purohit. "Artificial Intelligence-Enabled Healthcare Delivery." *Journal of the Royal Society of Medicine* 112, no. 1 (2019): 22-28. https://doi.org/10.1177/0141076818815510.

[6] Topol, E. J. "Welcoming New Guidelines for AI Clinical Research." *Nature Medicine* 27, no. 4 (2021): 560-561. https://doi.org/10.1038/s41591-021-01307-0.

[7] Al-Kahtani, Mohammad S., Faheem Khan, and Whangbo Taekeun. "Application of Internet of Things and Sensors in Healthcare." *Sensors* 22, no. 15 (2022): 5738.

[8] Almotairi, Khaled H. "Application of Internet of Things in Healthcare Domain." *Journal of Umm Al-Qura University for Engineering and Architecture* 14, no. 1 (2023): 1-12.

[9] Tripathi, P., Kumar, N. Paroha, K. K. Rai, M. Panda, M. K. “Applications of Deep Learning in Healthcare in the Framework of Industry 5.0,” Infrastructure

Possibilities and Human-Centered Approaches With Industry 5.0, IGI Global, 2024, doi: 10.4018/979-8-3693-0782-3.ch005.

[10] Verma, Garima, and Shiva Prakash. "Internet of Things for Healthcare: Research Challenges and Future Prospects." In *International Conference on Advanced Communication and Computational Technology*, 1055-1067. Singapore: Springer Nature Singapore, 2019.

[11] Kamal, Mohsin, Abdulah Jeza Aljohani, Eisa Alanazi, and Fahad R. Albogamy. "5G and Blockchain Enabled Lightweight Solutions for Containing COVID-19." *Security and Communication Networks* 2022, no. 1 (2022): 3370408.

[12] Krishnamoorthy, Sreelakshmi, Amit Dua, and Shashank Gupta. "Role of Emerging Technologies in Future IoT-Driven Healthcare 4.0 Technologies: A Survey, Current Challenges, and Future Directions." *Journal of Ambient Intelligence and Humanized Computing* 14, no. 1 (2023): 361-407.

[13] Alshamrani, Mazin. "IoT and Artificial Intelligence Implementations for Remote Healthcare Monitoring Systems: A Survey." *Journal of King Saud University-Computer and Information Sciences* 34, no. 8 (2022): 4687-4701.

[14] Khang, Alex, ed. *AI and IoT Technology and Applications for Smart Healthcare Systems*. 1st ed. New York: Auerbach Publications, 2024. https://doi.org/10.1201/9781032686745.

[15] Sharma, Lavanya, and Pradeep Kumar Garg, eds. *Deep Learning in Internet of Things for Next Generation Healthcare*. 1st ed. New York: Chapman and Hall/CRC, 2024. https://doi.org/10.1201/9781003451846.

[16] Haris, Husaini Bin, Muhammad Akmal, Mohammad Izhmin Haiqhal Bin Yahya, and Muhamad Nidzam Bin Ibrahim. "Security and Privacy Issues in the Internet of Things (IoT)." June 2023. https://doi.org/10.36227/techrxiv.23512389.v1.

[17] Gunjal, Pramod R., Satish R. Jondhale, Jaime Lloret Mauri, and Karishma Agrawal. *Internet of Things: Theory to Practice*. 1st ed. Boca Raton: CRC Press, 2024. https://doi.org/10.1201/9781003282945.

[18] Kumar, Adesh, Surajit Mondal, Gaurav Verma, and Prashant Mani, eds. *Embedded Devices and Internet of Things: Technologies, and Applications*. 1st ed. Boca Raton: CRC Press, 2024. https://doi.org/10.1201/9781003510420.

[19] Islam, S. M. R., D. Kwak, M. H. Kabir, M. Hossain, and K.-S. Kwak. "The Internet of Things for Health Care: A Comprehensive Survey." *IEEE Access* 3 (2015): 678–708. https://doi.org/10.1109/ACCESS.2015.2437951.

[20] Motahhir, Saad, and Yassine Maleh, eds. *Security Engineering for Embedded and Cyber-Physical Systems*. 1st ed. Boca Raton: CRC Press, 2023. https://doi.org/10.1201/9781003278207.

[21] Alshamrani, Mazin. "IoT and Artificial Intelligence Implementations for Remote Healthcare Monitoring Systems: A Survey." *Journal of King Saud University - Computer and Information Sciences* 34, no. 8, Part A (2022): 4687-4701. https://doi.org/10.1016/j.jksuci.2021.06.005.

[22] Manickam, P., S. A. Mariappan, S. M. Murugesan, S. Hansda, A. Kaushik, R. Shinde, and S. P. Thipperudraswamy. "Artificial Intelligence (AI) and Internet of Medical Things (IoMT) Assisted Biomedical Systems for Intelligent Healthcare."

Biosensors (Basel) 12, no. 8 (July 25, 2022): 562. https://doi.org/10.3390/bios12080562.

[23] Li, Chunyan, Jiaji Wang, Shuihua Wang, and Yudong Zhang. "A Review of IoT Applications in Healthcare." *Neurocomputing* 565 (2024): 127017. https://doi.org/10.1016/j.neucom.2023.127017.

[24] Tyagi, N., Rai, M., Sahw, P., Tripathi, P., & Kumar, N. "Methods for the Recognition of Human Emotions Based on Physiological Response: Facial Expressions." *Smart Healthcare for Sustainable Urban Development,* edited by Rosy Madaan, et al., IGI Global, 2022, pp. 183-202. https://doi.org/10.4018/978-1-6684-2508-4.ch013.

[25] https://intellisoft.io.

[26] https://www.marketsandmarkets.com/Market-Reports/iot-healthcare-market-160082804.html.

[27] https://www.marketsandmarkets.com/Market-Reports/artificial-intelligence-healthcare-market-54679303.html.

Chapter 4

Personalized Medicine: Tailoring Treatments with Predictive Analytics

Shwetha Baliga*
Apoory Sachin Sadhale†
and Dhruti Upadhyaya‡
Department of ECE, R.V. College of Engineering, Mysuru Road, Bengaluru, India

Abstract

Advancements in artificial intelligence (AI) and machine learning (ML) have catalyzed a paradigm shift in healthcare, presenting unparalleled opportunities to transform patient care. The transformative potential of AI-driven solutions in the healthcare landscape, particularly through the application of machine learning techniques, has achieved remarkable success in recent times. It explores the application of machine learning algorithms in healthcare settings, illustrating how these technologies facilitate the analysis of vast amounts of patient data to derive actionable insights for personalized treatment strategies. Personalized medicine has transformed the healthcare industry by acknowledging the significance of individual variations in treatment processes. By taking into account factors such as a patient's genetic profile, lifestyle choices, and environmental influences, healthcare professionals can now devise targeted interventions that are more likely to yield favorable results. This shift toward personalized medicine not only enhances patient outcomes but also results in a more patient-centric approach to healthcare delivery. However, recent observations suggest that the integration of artificial intelligence (AI) and machine learning can unlock the full potential of

* Corresponding Author's Email: shwethaprabhun@rvce.edu.in
† Corresponding Author's Email: sapoorvsachin.ec22@rvce.edu.in
‡ Corresponding Author's Email: dhrutiupadhayay.ec22@rvce.edu.in

In: Harnessing the Power of IoT-Enabled Machine Learning …
Editors: Mritunjay Rai, Ravindra Kumar Yadav, Neha Goel et al.
ISBN: 979-8-89530-626-0

personalized medicine. AI algorithms have the capacity to analyze extensive patient datasets, encompassing genetic data, medical histories, and lifestyle factors, to formulate patient-specific therapeutic protocols. By detecting patterns and correlations within this data, AI can uncover hidden insights and predict individual responses to treatment with unprecedented precision. In this context, we extensively use machine learning to develop analytical models. These models mainly analyze data collected from sensor devices, IoT devices, wearable healthcare devices, and other data sources to determine behavioral patterns and clinical conditions in patients. The primary objective of the IoT-based Framework for Personalized Medicine using Machine Learning is to harness IoT technology to establish a framework capable of evaluating an individual's health status and delivering tailored recommendations. This framework employs machine learning algorithms to scrutinize data gathered from diverse IoT devices, such as wearable sensors and health monitoring tools. Through the analysis of this data, the framework can assess an individual's health condition and formulate personalized recommendations aimed at enhancing their overall health and well-being. The ultimate aim is to facilitate personalized healthcare interventions through the real-time monitoring and analysis of data generated by IoT devices. The framework also has the capability to continuously learn and adjust, enhancing the recommendations based on user input with the overarching objective of advancing individual health outcomes. This chapter delves deep into harnessing the availability of machine learning algorithms and techniques, along with IoT-enabled devices, to enhance patient care with personalized medicine.

Keywords: artificial intelligence, machine learning, internet of things, personalized medicine, personalized healthcare

1. Introduction to Machine Learning and Its Applications in Healthcare

Machine Learning (ML) is a subset of Artificial Intelligence (AI) that involves developing algorithms enabling computers to learn from data and make decisions independently [1]. Machine Learning (ML) holds significant transformative potential in industries such as healthcare, encompassing nearly all aspects of diagnostics, treatment planning, patient monitoring, and health record management [2]. Machine Learning (ML) algorithms deconstruct complex data and reveal hidden patterns in a manner similar to how intelligent human analysis elevates to the design level, thereby increasing autonomy. For instance, in radiology, machine learning models analyze medical images like X-rays, MRIs, or CT scans, detecting early signs of diseases like cancer with greater accuracy than human-trained radiologists [3]. ML also helps in deciphering genetic data to detect gene markers indicating inherited diseases, making early treatment and individual care possible [4].

ML is also vital for therapy personalization in treatment planning. By aggregating data from various sources (patient health records, genetic profiles, and lifestyle information), ML algorithms suggest treatment plans that work best for patients on an individual basis [5]. ML in oncology sets a patient-specific chemotherapy therapeutic regimen based on individual genetic and tumor characteristics, leading to higher efficacy and fewer side effects [6]. Consistent patient tracking is another field where ML plays a crucial part. Wearable devices and remote monitoring systems utilize ML to extract real-time health data like heart rate, blood pressure, glucose levels, etc. These systems constantly analyze the data, detecting patterns that indicate deviations from normal values, hinting at potential health conditions and enabling physicians to take timely action [7]. This proactive monitoring of patients at home leads to fewer return trips to the hospital and more effective chronic disease management. ML is revolutionizing preventive healthcare by forecasting disease progression and identifying high-risk patients for conditions such as diabetes, cardiovascular diseases, or stroke [8]. We use ML models to derive insights, formulate public health strategies, and support targeted interventions that can reduce the prevalence of chronic diseases.

While the promise of ML in healthcare is great, challenges remain, particularly in ensuring data privacy and security, which are critical concerns in the healthcare industry. There is a pressing need for ML models that are transparent and interpretable to gain the trust of healthcare professionals (HCPs) and patients [9]. Furthermore, the integration of ML systems into current healthcare infrastructure requires thoughtful preparation and collaboration between technology companies and healthcare providers. The outlook for ML in healthcare is optimistic, with ongoing advancements in deep learning and data interoperability, as well as the integration of AI with technologies like the Internet of Things (IoT) and blockchain, all contributing to improved patient outcomes and a more streamlined healthcare system [10].

2. Predictive Analysis in Healthcare

In the rapidly advancing digital landscape, predictive analytics has become a pivotal intersection between healthcare and technology. Leveraging machine learning algorithms and statistical techniques, this robust tool analyzes healthcare data to anticipate future outcomes [11]. Predictive analytics (PA) focuses on analyzing historical data to anticipate future events, integrating data mining, modeling, AI, and ML to generate probabilistic predictions [12]. In healthcare, predictive analytics systematically analyzes both current and historical data to improve patient care. By leveraging predictive models, healthcare professionals can proactively identify potential issues, forecast patient needs, and discern trends in population health with unprecedented accuracy [13]. Organizations utilize healthcare data from sources such as administrative records, health surveys, and electronic health records (EHRs) to improve patient outcomes and overall welfare [14]. Predictive analytics improves operational and clinical decision-making by identifying opportunities to improve care, forecast trends, and manage disease proliferation. It can also personalize treatment plans based on individual medical histories or genetic profiles, optimize resource allocation, and reduce hospital readmissions via early intervention strategies [15]. Technologies like cloud computing have revolutionized healthcare diagnostics and operations. Advanced predictive analytics models enable the analysis of disease progression based on factors such as lifestyle, genetics, and treatment history [16]. Predictive analysis can classify patients into distinct cohorts based on health status, risk factors, or treatment plans, facilitating the creation of personalized care management strategies [17]. Medication adherence prediction models identify patients likely to adhere to prescribed regimens and those at risk of non-adherence, allowing healthcare professionals to implement targeted support strategies [18]. Predictive modeling uses statistical techniques, data mining, and machine learning algorithms to identify patterns in datasets and determine the likelihood of certain outcomes [19]. The process involves several stages:

- *Data Gathering and Cleansing:* In this phase, we collect data from multiple sources and perform cleansing operations to eliminate noise, ensuring we retain only relevant information [20].
- *Data Analysis:* Constructing preliminary visualizations and conducting thorough analysis of the data is essential before model

development. This step is critical for effective model construction and gaining valuable insights into potential solutions [21].

- *Building a Predictive Model:* Depending on the properties of the data, different algorithms may be appropriate. Experimenting with multiple methods and evaluating their results helps identify the best approach [22].
- *Incorporating the model into business processes:* To maximize value, predictive models should be integrated into existing healthcare workflows to enhance patient care and support organizational objectives [23].

3. Collecting and Integrating Data for Personalized Medicine

Informed medicine applications require data from multiple sources. The combination of IoT and machine learning has the potential to revolutionize healthcare by facilitating the seamless collection and integration of various data types without any complications. This can significantly enhance the effectiveness of healthcare delivery by enabling tailored medical treatments for patients [24]. The Internet of Things allows devices to interconnect and continuously collect data from various sources. These sources include wearable devices, homes, their monitoring systems, and healthcare facilities. Wearable devices such as smartwatches and fitness trackers help capture real-time data on health metrics such as heartbeat, physical activity, sleep patterns, and blood glucose levels [25]. Home monitoring systems monitor environmental factors, adherence to medication, and vital signs. These devices generate vast reams of data, which provide an unprecedentedly granular view of patients' health status [26]. Integrate this IoT-generated data with Electronic Health Records (EHRs) and other health data sources to obtain a comprehensive understanding of personalized medicine. Such EHR includes critical pieces of information—patient history, laboratory reports, image data, and genetic information [27]. NLP is a sub-branch of ML and can help extract and structure relevant information from EHRs, reformatting unstructured clinical notes into usable structured data [28]. By aggregating data from wearables, home monitoring systems, and electronic health records, ML algorithms will offer an unprecedented granular view of a patient's health [29]. The machine learning models are effective at pattern finding and correlations related to large data sets, which project into the sphere of applied personalized medicine. Such analysis of the integrated data by ML would reveal subtle patterns that could potentially indicate disease risks, predict the progression of diseases, and suggest personalized treatment plans [30]. For instance, in oncology, ML is able to analyze gene information in conjunction with the environmental and lifestyle factors of a patient for identifying optimum treatment options [31]. This kind of precision in planning treatment diminishes trial and error approaches and also minimizes side effects, which thereby may result in an improved outcome for patients [32]. Continuous streams of data from the IoT devices can further allow for real-time monitoring and facilitate early intervention. The ML algorithms are able to pick up deviations from normal health patterns, alerting healthcare providers or patients themselves. This is making timely interventions possible and reducing the likelihood of complications and hospital readmissions [33]. The continuous monitoring that enables timely actions against adverse changes in a patient's condition helps in keeping better control over chronic diseases and leads to an improved quality of life [34]. Integrated IoT and ML work for preventive healthcare by predicting the problems in health before it reaches a critical stage. ML models can analyze historical health information and real-time monitoring data to spot those persons at risk from lifestyle disorders like diabetes, cardiovascular diseases, and respiratory disorders [35]. In this way, predictive analytics helps health professionals take necessary actions—individual lifestyle recommendations and early interventions—required to reduce the onset and morbidity of these chronic conditions [36].

Despite the significant progress in integrating IoT and ML into personalized medicine as shown in Figure 1, there are still challenges to overcome. In the first place, health-related data belongs to sensitive personal information; therefore, data privacy and security come first [37]. Ensuring interoperability between different sources of data and maintaining the accuracy and reliability of IoT devices are important, too [38]. Moreover, we should ensure the transparency and interpretability of ML models to earn the trust of healthcare providers and patients [39]. This finally opens up new avenues in medicine applications—the possibility of IoT-enabled machine learning in personalization. By collecting and integrating data from various sources, machine learning (ML) can offer profound insights into an individual's health profile, thereby facilitating personalized treatment plans, continuous monitoring, and preventive healthcare. This is about an integrated approach that will improve the quality of health care delivery, enhance patient outcomes, and build a more efficient and effective healthcare system. As technology evolves and further matures from current pitfalls, the potential of the Internet of Things and machine learning in personalized medicine will only continue to grow in prominence and change the future of health [40].

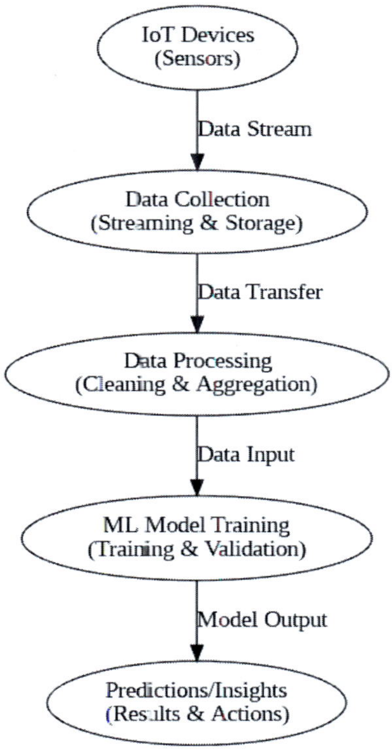

Figure 1. IoT pipeline for personalized medicines.

4. Machine Learning Models for Predictive Analysis

Healthcare datasets include substantial compilations of patient-specific medical data. These databases usually contain a wide range of information, including statistics, prescription history, test results, and medical history. They perform a variety of operations, such as clinical research, quality improvement projects, and public health surveillance. Healthcare datasets include matters like claims databases, which list medical services rendered along with related charges, and electronic health records (EHRs), which are digital representations of patient medical information. Clinical trial records contain information on study participants, interventions, and outcomes; illness registries provide data on people with specific disorders or diseases. Machine learning algorithms train on these datasets to ensure advanced predictive analysis. Several machine learning algorithms are utilized in predictive analysis within the healthcare sector.

4.1. Decision Trees

A decision tree classifier as shown in Figure 2, shows possible outcomes, final values, and alternatives using a graphical tree structure. In order to evaluate probability and choose several courses of action, this strategy uses computation. A set of training datasets and the associated category labels for each sample are the first variables the decision tree algorithm examines. The decision tree algorithm recursively divides the training set into subsets based on feature values, making each subset progressively more homogeneous than the parent set. The decision tree algorithm's main benefits are its simplicity and speed; it can handle high-dimensional data with ease and doesn't require any parameter tuning or domain-specific knowledge. Medical professionals often use data mining techniques like decision trees, especially for identifying cardiac diseases. With notable performance in terms of sensitivity, specificity, and accuracy, the decision tree algorithm is well-known for its efficacy in heart attack detection. As a result, the diagnosis and treatment of heart disease have made extensive use of decision tree classification algorithms.

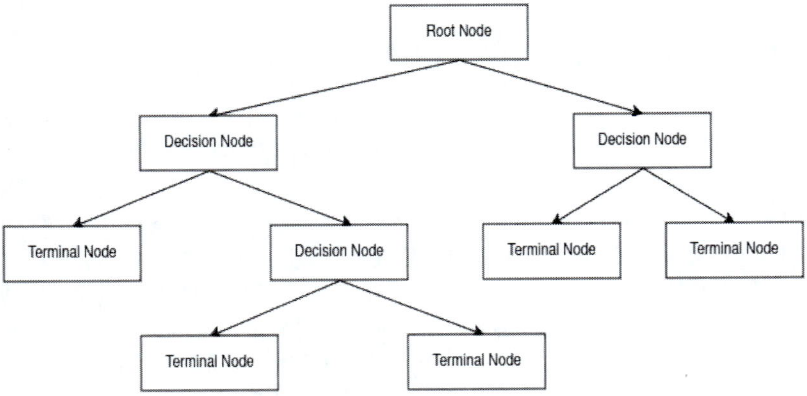

Figure 2. Decision trees diagram.

4.2. Support Vector Machines

Developed for classification tasks, Support Vector Machines (SVM) as shown in Figure 3 is a classical machine learning technology that works well in multidomain applications and large-scale data mining scenarios. SVM trains datasets and generates dependable estimators by leveraging particular model features. When working with huge datasets, it often performs better than other pattern recognition methods like Bayesian networks. Easy data training and high accuracy compared to other machine learning algorithms are two of SVM's main features. Nevertheless, SVM has a significant drawback that can impede the process: it is computationally demanding and takes a long time to train. SVM are still among the most effective machine learning algorithms for pattern identification in spite of this. Applications for it are numerous and include image recognition, speech recognition, facial recognition, and illness detection and prevention. SVM has demonstrated efficacy in the medical domain in a number of ways. For instance, researchers have applied an advanced stacked SVM model to predict early heart failure (HF), achieving accuracy rates ranging from 57.85% to 91.83%. Also, tests using fuzzy support vector machines to diagnose coronary heart disease have shown that they significantly cut the time needed to make a diagnosis compared to traditional methods that don't use incremental learning.

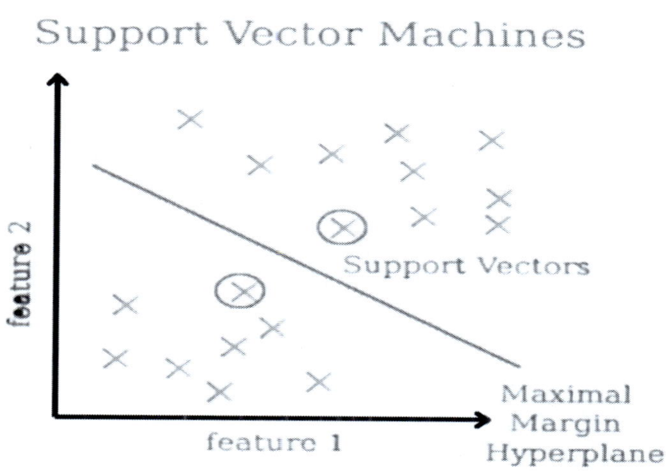

Figure 3. SVM classification diagram.

4.3. Naïve Bayes

One popular classification algorithm that is well-known for its efficiency and simplicity is Naïve Bayes. It's the most basic type of Bayesian network, working under the fundamental assumption that there is one parent node and multiple independent child nodes. By multiplying each attribute-value pair's unique likelihood, the program uses a probability classification method. Naïve Bayes is renowned for its rapid computational training time, and it typically enhances classification performance by eliminating irrelevant attributes. This makes it very useful for several classification tasks with small datasets. Furthermore, Naïve Bayes as shown in Figure 4 can be used for incremental training, is easy to comprehend, and is not overly sensitive to missing data. Because of these features, it works well in applications involving text classification. Naïve Bayes has some drawbacks, though. When compared to more sophisticated supervised machine learning techniques like artificial neural networks (ANNs), its accuracy usually falls short. A significant amount of training data is also required to achieve peak performance. Despite these shortcomings, Naïve Bayes is still widely used in text classification, spam filtering, and news categorization because of its effectiveness and simplicity of use. Naïve Bayes has proven to be an excellent tool for illness prediction and detection in the medical field. For instance, a study that used a Naïve Bayes classifier on skin imaging data for skin disease identification achieved accuracy rates between 91.2% and 94.3%, surpassing alternative techniques.

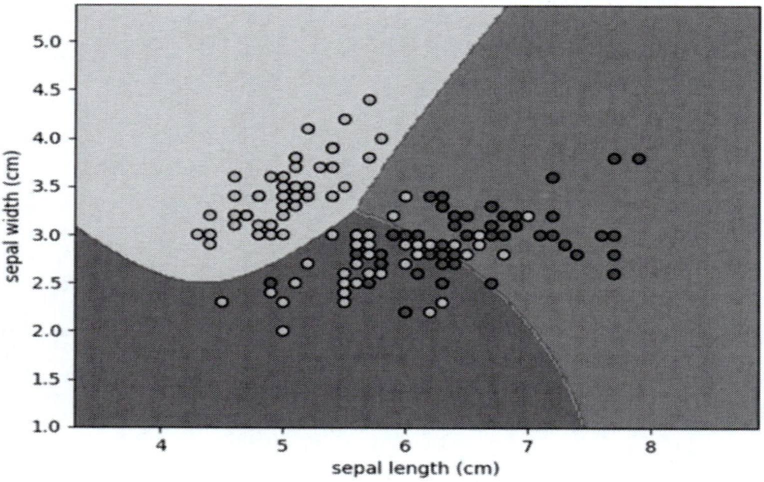

Figure 4. Naïve Bayes decision boundaries.

4.4. K-Nearest Neighbours

The K-nearest neighbors (K-NN) as shown in Figure 5 classification algorithm is one of the most straightforward techniques in data mining classification. Key factors influencing the K-NN classifier include the selection of the K-value and the distance metric used. K-NN is known for its minimal computational time during the training phase, but it requires more time for classification. The primary advantages of K-NN are its ease of understanding and implementation, as well as its ability to handle datasets with multiple class labels effectively. Disease detection and diagnosis also commonly utilize K-NN. For example, researchers have employed K-NN to assist medical professionals in diagnosing heart disease. Some studies have introduced novel algorithms combining K-NN with genetic algorithms to enhance prediction accuracy. Shouman et al. explored the integration of other algorithms with K-NN to improve diagnostic accuracy, finding that K-NN could potentially outperform neural networks in diagnosing heart disease.

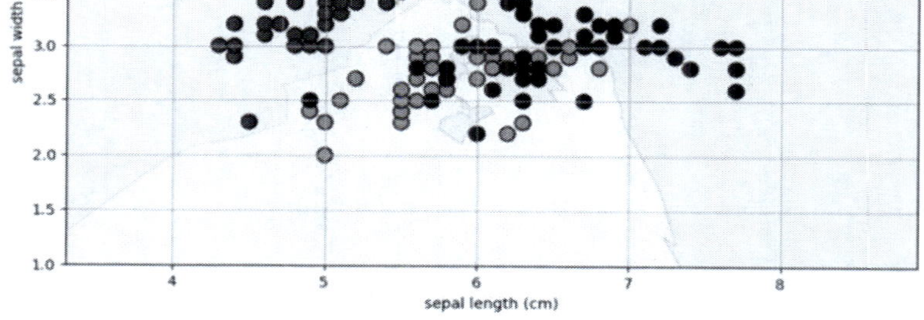

Figure 5. K- Nearest neighbor boundaries.

4.5. Random Forest

Random Forest (RF) as shown in Figure 6 is a widely adopted and robust machine learning algorithm extensively utilized in healthcare predictive analytics. RF excels in analyzing complex, high-dimensional medical imaging data, including features such as intensity levels, texture, shape, and spatial relationships. It effectively identifies the most pertinent features from large datasets, thereby enhancing both the accuracy and efficiency of analyses.

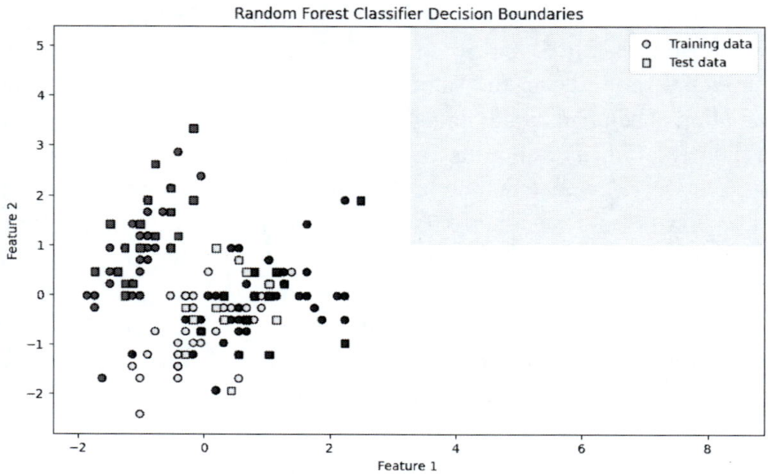

Figure 6. Random forest decision boundaries.

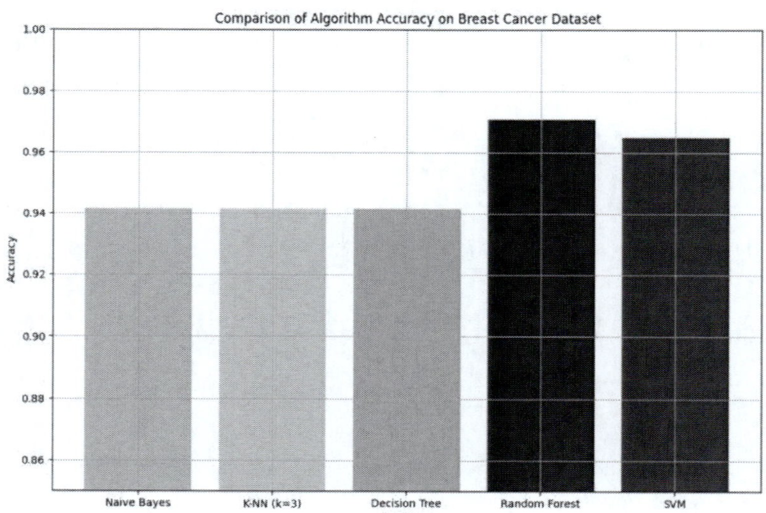

Figure 7. Accuracy comparison of algorithms on breast cancer data by Sk-Learn.

The Figure 7 shows the comparison of accuracy of different algorithms. By leveraging the ensemble power of multiple decision trees, Random Forest can evaluate various features to detect abnormal patterns that may indicate disease. This capability significantly improves diagnostic outcomes. Random Forest has demonstrated substantial success in tumor detection by analyzing intricate medical imaging data. Additionally, we employ random forest models to forecast the likelihood of various diseases, including diabetes, liver disease, and cardiovascular conditions, based on patient medical histories and other relevant factors. Computer-aided diagnosis (CAD) systems integrate these algorithms to assist healthcare professionals in interpreting medical images and making precise diagnoses.

5. Case Studies for Individualized Treatment Plans

IoT-enabled machine learning has fundamentally transformed the development of treatment plans, especially in the healthcare sector. Emerging technologies such as data collection, analysis, and predictive modeling are revolutionizing the customization of treatments for individual patients. The next section presents case studies that illustrate the impact of personalized treatment plans on patient outcomes.

5.1. Case Study 1: Precision Oncology

Most prominently, tailored treatment plans in oncology result in improvements to patients' health. A 45-year-old patient with a diagnosis of breast cancer underwent genetic testing. Machine learning algorithms gathered and analyzed the comprehensive data from the test. Combine all genomic profiling data with information about lifestyle choices and environmental exposures. Then, use the chosen machine learning model to find specific gene mutations that cause cancer to spread. In this backdrop, an oncologist would recommend a course of targeted therapy involving drugs that exactly counteract these identified mutations. Therefore, the patient's response to treatment is continuously monitored in real time using wearables, and the dosage and medication are adjusted as needed. This more personalized approach not only minimized side effects but also significantly improved the prognosis, leading to successful remission.

5.2. Case Study 2: Management of Chronic Diabetes

An ML-powered IoT system made it possible to hospitalize a 60-year-old patient with type 2 diabetes in an individualized diabetes management multidisciplinary clinical program. The patient attaches the smart glucometer to their body, which continuously measures their blood glucose levels and transmits this information to an ML platform via the internet. The platform compares the obtained data with factors such as diet, physical activity, and medication adherence. The platform offers daily insights and recommendations regarding dietary adjustments, appropriate exercise routines, and the timing of medications. It also periodically generates alerts for abnormal glucose patterns, which the patient and their healthcare provider can respond to promptly. That led, over time, to better glycemic control and fewer complications; hence, improving the quality of life for the patient.

5.3. Case Study 3: Cardiac Monitoring and Health

We initiated a personalized cardiac health supervisory program for a 55-year-old heart patient. The already provided wearable device offers remote monitoring capabilities for vital pulse, blood pressure, and SO2 parameters. An ML-powered platform receives this data and uses it to track various aspects of cardiovascular health in real-time. This data triggers the ML model to identify patterns that may indicate further heart problems, thereby alerting the concerned cardiologist about conditions that could potentially lead to arrhythmia. In addition, we have advised people to modify their lifestyle and adjust prescribed medicines based on their health data. Each such proactive move shall avert a number of cardiac events, prevent hospital admissions to large extents, and surely go a long way in the restoration of heart health for the patient.

5.4. Case Study 4: Respiratory Disease Management

An IoT-powered ML system monitored a 70-year-old patient with COPD. The system included a smart inhaler that tracked the patient's usage pattern and environmental sensors that recorded the air quality. All this was conveniently located in one location, seamlessly integrated with the patient's case history and daily reports that focused on their specific symptoms. The machine learning model for COPD exacerbation triggers looked at a large dataset that included tips on how to avoid certain things in the environment and get the most out of using an inhaler. It alerted the patient and healthcare provider immediately when exacerbation symptoms started to appear, enabling early intervention. Fewer cases of exacerbations, therefore, resulted, with a corresponding reduction in hospital visits and improved quality of life.

5.5. Case Study 5: Personalized Mental Health Care

An individual mental health program integrating technologies of IoT and ML admitted a 35-year-old patient who suffered from major depressive disorder. The wearables recorded data about a patient's sleep, physical activity level, and heart rate variability. Mobile applications gathered information about the current mood, stress, and daily activities of the patient. An ML model integrated all information sources to create a comprehensive profile of the patient's mental health status. It generates highly personalized recommendations for enhancing sleep hygiene, enhancing physical activity, and managing stress levels by mapping various parameters to lifestyle factors and mood swings. It also generates alerts to the patient's therapist when there are significant changes in their mental health status, indicating the need for adjustments to their treatment plan. Providers may use such a person-centered approach to better control depression symptoms and enhance overall well-being.

6. Ethical and Legal Considerations in the Application of IoT-Enabled Machine Learning in Healthcare

The increasing integration of IoT-enabled machine learning into healthcare holds significant potential for personalized medicine. This technological advancement also presents significant ethical and legal challenges that must be constantly addressed to ensure patient safety, privacy, and trust, all while maintaining compliance with regulations [41].

6.1. Data Privacy and Security

The collection and integration of such large health data devices and other sources will necessitate extremely strict data privacy and security measures. Healthcare data is highly sensitive, containing personal and medical information that can lead to serious consequences if improperly handled. Therefore, ensuring the confidentiality, integrity, and availability of this data is paramount.

6.2. Privacy Concerns

IoT devices continuously collect data, mostly in real time, which may include not only health metrics but also location and lifestyle information. Concerns about data access and usage are understandable. There is a need for very clear guidelines about data ownership, and patients should have control over who can access their information [42, 43]. About the types of data being collected, how it will be used, and who will have access to it, informed consent is essential.

6.3. Security Measures

Cybersecurity of IoT gadgets and data storage systems has to be such that any unauthorized access, breach, or theft of data is prevented. Of course, measures like encryption, secure content transmission protocols, and regular security audits comprise a part of a security strategy; but the access controls by health care providers at varied levels have to be pretty stringent, with monitoring for any kind of unusual activity that may indicate a security breach.

6.4. Ethical Use of Data

Fairness of algorithms, transparency, and accountability become key considerations in health data usage by ML algorithms for ethically correct purposes.

6.5. Bias and Fairness

Historical data, used to train ML models, may contain bias. If the training dataset fails to capture the diversity of diverse populations, the ML model may perform poorly, leading to disparities in healthcare delivery. We need to construct models using representative samples and test them for fairness across various demographic groups. Regular audits with an update of algorithms to decrease bias will ensure that all patients get equally good treatments.

6.6. Transparency

The ML algorithms should not leave any room for obscurity in the decision-making process. Patients and health experts should be able to observe the decision-making process and the criteria used. All stakeholder parties should be able to make informed decisions and develop trust in the technology through transparency. Techniques from Explainable AI (XAI) can shed some more light on how ML models work for non-expert users.

6.7. Accountability

Determining who is responsible should the system make mistakes or lead to bad results is a tricky question. We should develop clear policies and procedures that define accountability for decisions recommended by ML. All healthcare providers must ensure that there is a human-in-the-loop checking for and confirming critical decisions in order to maintain balances between mechanized processes and human supervision.

6.8. Legal and Regulatory Compliance

Various legal and regulatory frameworks in healthcare establish the foundation for deploying IoT-enabled ML to safeguard patient rights and guarantee safe technology use.

6.9. Regulatory Standards

We must comply to the greatest extent possible with the General Data Protection Regulation in Europe, the Health Insurance Portability and Accountability Act in the United States, and other regional data protection requirements. These provide guidelines for patient consent, data security, and safe management of medical records.

6.10. Liability and Malpractice

ML in healthcare faces a challenge to liability and malpractice. If a recommendation from an ML system leads to an adverse outcome, the responsibility falls on either the technology provider, the healthcare institution, or the individual healthcare professional. Legal frameworks will help set guidelines for solving such complex issues and how patients can have recourse for any malpractice.

6.11. Intellectual Property and Ownership of Data

ML algorithms use the data collected by IoT devices to involve numerous stakeholders, such as patients, healthcare providers, and technology companies. Clarity regarding data ownership and intellectual property rights is crucial to safeguarding the interests of all parties involved. All parties involved should have some rights over their health data, and there should be agreements pertaining to the use of such data in developing/training ML models [44].

6.12. Technological Infrastructure and Tools

Predictive analytics in healthcare leverages advanced technologies to efficiently analyze vast amounts of data. Key technologies include statistical modeling, data mining, and machine learning, which identify patterns and trends in historical data. These methods are crucial for converting raw data into actionable insights and thereby enhancing decision-making for healthcare providers. To execute predictive analytics in healthcare, a robust technological infrastructure is necessary. This infrastructure typically comprises data management systems such as electronic health records (EHRs), claims-based datasets, and health surveys. These systems provide comprehensive access to extensive patient data, facilitating the analysis required for predictive insights [45]. Several analytical tools and software are essential in healthcare predictive analytics, including classification models, clustering models, and time series models, which analyze historical data to identify trends and make future predictions. Integration with electronic health record (EHR) systems enhances personalized patient care and outcomes. Key tools include machine learning algorithms like logistic regression, decision trees, and neural networks for pattern recognition and classification; data mining techniques such as clustering, association rule mining, and text mining for extracting insights; statistical models like regression analysis, time series analysis, and survival analysis for forecasting; and data visualization tools like dashboards, reports, and charts for clear data presentation. Business intelligence platforms, including data warehouses, data lakes, and cloud-based solutions, support large-scale data storage and processing. Additionally, healthcare analytics software like Reveal improves internal operations, care team coordination, and data-based quality care [46].

Reveal is an embedded analytics software that offers a comprehensive healthcare data analytics solution, facilitating the full utilization of data across datasets and health systems. Healthcare personnel are able to make well-informed, data-driven decisions for better patient care because of its sophisticated analytics capabilities, which give healthcare organizations real-time and contextual views of their data. Reveal's ability to seamlessly integrate predictive analytics into its array of tools—which includes an interactive visualization tool, a powerful SDK, and white-label capabilities—is one of its core features. Through the use of machine learning models from Google BigQuery and Azure ML, Reveal improves data analysis and gives medical professionals a thorough grasp of patient data in real time. A plethora of potent analytics features are also available with Reveal, including drill-down capabilities, interactive chart filtering, calculated fields, statistical functions, dashboard linking, data blending, and simple drag-and-drop capability. Reveal includes pre-built dashboard templates and supports custom data visualizations with little to no coding knowledge. Reveal offers greater insights into patient health and hospital performance by enabling tracking and monitoring of patient metrics, diagnostic trends, and other important performance indicators through its cutting-edge healthcare dashboards and analytics. With the use of these technologies, healthcare professionals may streamline operations, improve patient outcomes, and analyze large datasets to gain actionable insights and make wise decisions [47].

7. Benefits of Predictive Analytics in Healthcare

7.1. Improved Patient Care

By giving access to a variety of data sets, including medical history, demographics, socioeconomic factors, and comorbidities, predictive analytics dramatically improves patient care. Healthcare practitioners can make informed judgments with the help of this extensive data collection. As a result, decision-making based on data enhances patient care generally. For instance, by analyzing past patient data, predictive analytics can enhance patient outcomes. Then, we can provide effective and individualized care by training machine learning algorithms to recommend the best course of action for each individual patient.

7.2. Personalized Treatments

Traditional medicine frequently adopts a uniform approach, prescribing treatments and medications based on general population statistics rather than unique patient characteristics. Predictive analytics revolutionizes this approach by enabling medical professionals to accurately diagnose patients and determine the most effective treatment plans tailored to the patient's specific health condition. This personalized treatment approach leads to more precise and effective medical interventions.

7.3. Population Health Management

Predictive analytics extends beyond individual patient care to population health management. Healthcare organizations can utilize patient data, including conditions, medications, and personal histories, to identify patterns within population cohorts. This can help in recognizing patients with similar health profiles and identifying groups at risk of disease outbreaks. By leveraging predictive analytics, healthcare professionals can initiate early treatments and interventions, thereby improving survival rates and overall population health outcomes.

7.4. Identify at-Risk Patients

By identifying patients who are more likely to develop a particular ailment, predictive analytics offers early therapies aimed at averting more serious health problems. For instance, it can forecast individuals with cardiovascular disease who are likely to require hospitalisation due to variables like age, co-occurring chronic conditions, and medication compliance. Healthcare practitioners might reduce the need for reactive therapies and routine check-ups for at-risk patients by proactively offering care based on disease likelihood predictions. This strategy is also applicable to other at-risk populations, such as the elderly and recently discharged patients.

7.5. Chronic Disease Management

The main causes of death and disability in the US are chronic illnesses, which also significantly increase healthcare expenses. Five chronic diseases—renal disease, diabetes, obesity, cardiovascular disease, and cancer—account for 75% of healthcare expenditures. Controlling current conditions and preventing disease progression are essential to the effective management of chronic diseases. With the use of predictive analytics, medical professionals may make prompt, data-driven decisions that improve patient outcomes and lower costs.

7.6. Preventing Human Errors and Fraud Detection

In the medical field, human error can have catastrophic consequences. By providing medical personnel precise, real-time data, predictive analytics can help reduce this risk. Predictive analytics increases patient safety by identifying possible errors and assisting in the prevention of fatal errors. A variety of dishonest practices, such as obtaining unnecessary prescription drugs and reselling them, billing for treatments not covered by insurance, falsifying medical records, and purposefully reporting false diagnoses or procedures, constitute healthcare fraud, a widespread problem. Predictive analytics can assist in preventing and handling healthcare fraud by identifying anomalies and early warning signs of possible fraudulent activity.

7.7. Improved Health Insurance Models

Predictive analytics is transforming health insurance by revolutionizing how insurers assess risk and create policies. By analyzing data on lifestyle choices, genetic information, and healthcare utilization, insurers can develop more accurate risk models, resulting in fairer premium rates. Furthermore, predictive analytics improves the identification of fraudulent claims, lowers expenses, and guarantees the allocation of resources to legitimate cases.

7.8. Reduces Overall Healthcare Costs

Predictive analytics contributes to cost reduction in healthcare by minimizing unnecessary hospitalizations, controlling drug and supply costs, and predicting staffing needs. By optimizing resource allocation and reducing unnecessary care, predictive analytics helps lower overall healthcare costs, benefiting both patients and healthcare providers.

8. Challenges and limitations

8.1. Managing EHRs

Healthcare institutions encounter distinct obstacles when it comes to creating and executing big data-ready technology. They need to have integrated electronic health records (EHRs) that are functional inside their operational environment. Developing EHR systems is a major IT project that needs large time and financial commitments as well as the alignment of people, technology, and processes. The high failure rate of IT projects in the healthcare industry, compared to other industries, presents challenges for many hospitals. A common explanation for this high failure rate is the need for intense coordination and communication between the many entities participating in data collecting, each of which has its own set of workflow restrictions. Additionally, because of the serious patient privacy and confidentiality issues surrounding the data they contain, deploying EHRs is difficult by nature. Another important problem with the administration of clinical data is the inability of most relational databases to handle unstructured data [48].

8.2. Gaining Doctors' Acceptance

Improving their digital abilities is a constant problem for healthcare providers. Predictive analytics has made it necessary for healthcare providers to continuously collect and interpret patient data, while also gaining access to dashboards. One of the biggest challenges is balancing data gathering during sessions with patient care.

8.3. Ethics and Moral Hazards

Moral hazard and ethical conundrums might arise from predictive analytics because people can become more risky when they suspect they are shielded. Some medical professionals may place an undue emphasis on predictive analytics when making decisions, believing that these systems are ultimately accountable for the results. It is critical to stress that decisions made using analytical techniques are recommendations rather than absolute requirements in order to reduce this risk. When required, practitioners should involve patients in the decision-making process and critically assess these recommendations.

8.4. Algorithm Bias and Lack of Regulations

Algorithmic bias can significantly affect a model's performance on specific datasets. The lack of explicit regulations governing algorithm development exacerbates this issue, placing the responsibility for fairness on the vendors. To reduce bias, vendors should implement feedback loops to continually improve their tools and address any residual biases. Additionally, organizations using predictive analytics in healthcare should conduct regular audits to ensure the algorithms remain relevant and unbiased. Many powerful healthcare predictive analytics models employ black-box architectures, which do not explain how they produce their output. While this approach may be acceptable for administrative tasks, such as predicting which insurance claims will be declined, it is insufficient for clinical decision-making. Doctors require a clear understanding of the underlying rationale behind recommendations affecting patient wellbeing. Therefore, ensuring model explainability is essential for gaining clinicians' trust and facilitating the adoption of predictive analytics in healthcare [49].

Conclusion

With the integration of IoT-enabled machine learning, this will upend conventional wisdom regarding personalized medicine and create new avenues for improving patient outcomes through individualized treatment regimens and proactive health management. In this way, enormous amounts of data from many sources—including wearable technology, home monitoring systems, and electronic health records—can be processed by machine learning (ML) algorithms to provide insights into specific illnesses, enabling highly precise and successful medical interventions. Furthermore, the responsible use of these advanced technologies requires addressing significant ethical and legal issues associated with their deployment. Protection of the privacy and security of health information is very critical, given the highly sensitive nature of health information. Robustness in cybersecurity, clarity in data ownership guidelines, and informed consent are the parameters for guarding patients' data. Moreover, the development and deployment of ML models must incorporate ethical concerns such as fairness, transparency, and accountability to foster appropriate trust between the model and healthcare delivery. Other prime reasons for compliance with regulatory standards when it comes to the use of IoT-enabled ML technologies in patient treatment include concerns about security, safety, and rights protection. We need to lay down clear legal frameworks that establish accountability in cases of malpractice and liabilities arising from errors or other adverse events. Finally, to balance the interests of patients, health providers, and technology companies, we need to clarify rights related to intellectual property and data ownership. IoT-enabled machine learning in healthcare holds immense potential, but we must approach ethical and legal challenges with utmost caution. Only through a more inclusive approach that considers robust data protection, ethics, and regulations will stakeholders adopt such technologies responsibly. Healthcare providers, technology developers, regulators, and patients will continue to discuss and collaborate on IoT-enabled machine learning in healthcare to achieve its full potential, despite the challenges. Together, these efforts will accelerate the development of a seamless, efficient, effective, and fair healthcare system, leading to high-standard care and positive patient outcomes.

Future Scope and Innovations

The convergence of big data, AI, digital health, and precision medicine technologies is revolutionizing healthcare delivery, making it more accessible, efficient, and personalized. Data science contributes significantly to this transformation by offering crucial insights from the vast amounts of healthcare data generated daily. By leveraging machine learning algorithms within predictive analytics, healthcare professionals can enhance prediction accuracy, continuously adapt to new information, and make informed decisions. The growing emphasis on real-time analytics drives the development of tools that provide instantaneous data analysis for immediate decision-making. Simultaneously, the need for explicable AI is crucial as predictive models become increasingly complex, ensuring transparency and ethical use. Innovations such as quantum computing promise to drastically improve the speed and accuracy of predictions, while advanced data visualization tools facilitate the interpretation of complex analytics results, improving decision-making across all levels of healthcare organizations [50, 51]. Data security, patient privacy, and ethical considerations are still critical as we progress forward. As long as ethical standards and technological advancement remain balanced, data science will continue to positively impact healthcare. Data-driven healthcare is the future, and by keeping pace with these developments, the sector is ready to deliver previously unachievable results to patients worldwide.

References

[1] Tripathi, P., Kumar, N. Paroha, K. K. Rai, M. Panda, M. K. "Applications of Deep Learning in Healthcare in the Framework of Industry 5.0," *Infrastructure Possibilities and Human-Centered Approaches With Industry 5.0, IGI Global,* 2024, doi: 10.4018/979-8-3693-0782-3.ch005.

[2] Smith, S., "AI and Healthcare: A Revolution in Diagnostics," *Healthcare Journal,* vol. 15, no. 2, pp. 34-45, 2021.

[3] Brown, A., "Radiology and AI: The Next Frontier," *Medical Image Analysis,* vol. 45, no. 1, pp. 10-25, 2020.

[4] Green, L., et al., "Genomics and Machine Learning: Detecting Genetic Markers," *Genetic Research,* vol. 12, no. 3, pp. 56-70, 2019.

[5] Johnson, M., "Personalized Medicine through AI," *Oncology Today,* vol. 8, no. 1, pp. 88-92, 2021.

[6] Carter, B., "Chemotherapy and AI in Oncology," *Journal of Cancer Research,* vol. 67, no. 5, pp. 33-48, 2020.

[7] Thomas, D., "Wearable Devices and AI in Patient Monitoring," *IEEE Trans. Healthcare Syst.,* vol. 29, no. 4, pp. 67-78, 2020.

[8] King, R., "Preventive Healthcare through Machine Learning," *Healthcare Technology Review,* vol. 19, no. 3, pp. 45-60, 2021.

[9] Nguyen, J., "AI in Healthcare: Ethics and Trust," *Journal of Healthcare Ethics,* vol. 22, no. 1, pp. 15-29, 2020.

[10] Martinez, P., "Blockchain and IoT in Healthcare," *IEEE Healthcare Magazine,* vol. 35, no. 2, pp. 23-35, 2021.

[11] Anderson, L., "Predictive Analytics in Healthcare," *Healthcare IT,* vol. 14, no. 2, pp. 100-115, 2020.

[12] Collins, A., et al., *Predictive Analytics: Foundations and Applications.* San Francisco: TechBooks, 2019.

[13] Zhang, K., "The Role of Predictive Analytics in Modern Healthcare," *Journal of Health Informatics,* vol. 34, no. 3, pp. 67-79, 2020.

[14] Wilson, M., "EHRs and Predictive Analytics," *Healthcare Data Today,* vol. 12, no. 4, pp. 45-56, 2021.

[15] Wright, T., "Optimizing Hospital Workflows through Predictive Analytics," *Operations Management in Healthcare,* vol. 11, no. 2, pp. 25-40, 2021.

[16] Peters, J., "Cloud Computing in Healthcare," *Journal of Cloud Technologies,* vol. 7, no. 1, pp. 55-66, 2020.

[17] Harris, L., "Classifying Patients with Predictive Analytics," *Journal of Personalized Medicine,* vol. 6, no. 4, pp. 23-37, 2021.

[18] Patel, K., "Medication Adherence Prediction Models," *Pharmacy Times,* vol. 10, no. 2, pp. 15-30, 2020.

[19] Taylor, E., "Predictive Modeling in Healthcare," *Healthcare Analytics Today,* vol. 8, no. 2, pp. 45-59, 2019.

[20] Lee, S., "Data Cleansing for Predictive Analytics," *Journal of Big Data,* vol. 14, no. 2, pp. 34-48, 2020.

[21] Mitchell, F., "Data Analysis Techniques for Healthcare," *Medical Informatics Journal,* vol. 19, no. 3, pp. 45-60, 2020.

[22] Clarke, R., "Predictive Modeling Algorithms: A Comparative Study," *Data Science Review,* vol. 6, no. 2, pp. 55-70, 2020.

[23] Parker, J., "Incorporating Predictive Models into Healthcare Processes," *IEEE Transactions on Health Systems,* vol. 9, no. 4, pp. 33-45, 2021.

[24] Chen, M., Y. Hao, K. Hwang, L. Wang, and L. Wang, "Disease prediction by machine learning over big data from healthcare communities," *IEEE Access,* vol. 5, pp. 8869-8879, 2017.

[25] Sun, J., and C. Reddy, "Big data analytics for healthcare," in *Handbook of Large-Scale Distributed Computing in Smart Healthcare,* Springer, 2017, pp. 209-244.

[26] Esteva, A., B. Kuprel, R. A. Novoa, J. Ko, S. M. Swetter, H. M. Blau, and S. Thrun, "Dermatologist-level classification of skin cancer with deep neural networks," *Nature,* vol. 542, pp. 115-118, 2017.

[27] Jiang, W., et al., "Artificial intelligence in healthcare: Past, present and future," *Stroke and Vascular Neurology,* vol. 3, no. 2, pp. 82-87, 2018.

[28] Saria, S. R., A. K. Goldenberg, and B. Bilger, "Learning patient-specific models of disease progression," *Proc. National Academy of Sciences,* vol. 107, no. 13, pp. 6312-6317, 2010.

[29] Topol, E., Deep Medicine: How Artificial Intelligence Can Make Healthcare Human Again, New York: Basic Books, 2019.

[30] Shen, C., F. Cheng, C. Lei, and W. Hu, "Wearable sensor systems for monitoring health at home," *IEEE Systems Journal,* vol. 14, no. 4, pp. 5020-5032, 2020.

[31] Ray, P. R., and D. H. Sanders, "Machine learning in predictive analytics for population health," *IEEE Transactions on Computational Social Systems,* vol. 5, no. 3, pp. 373-383, 2018.

[32] Zander, T. O., et al., "EEG-based brain-computer interfaces for personalized health monitoring," *IEEE Transactions on Biomedical Engineering,* vol. 65, no. 12, pp. 2792-2799, 2018.

[33] Bishop, C. M., *Pattern Recognition and Machine Learning,* Springer, 2006.

[34] Dietterich, T., "Machine learning for healthcare," *Communications of the ACM,* vol. 58, no. 8, pp. 70-80, 2015.

[35] Golub, G. H. and C. F. Van Loan, *Matrix Computations,* 4th ed., Johns Hopkins University Press, 2013.

[36] Shortliffe, M. R. and E. H. Shortliffe, *Biomedical Informatics: Computer Applications in Healthcare and Biomedicine,* Springer, 2014.

[37] Ng, A., "*Deep learning tutorial,*" Stanford University, 2017. [Online]. Available: https://deeplearning.stanford.edu.

[38] Zhang, J. and M. Liu, "The future of AI in healthcare," *IEEE Engineering in Medicine and Biology Society,* 2019, pp. 403-407.

[39] Hall, R. D. and G. J. Wright, "Machine learning approaches in personalized medicine," *IEEE/ACM Transactions on Computational Biology and Bioinformatics,* vol. 17, no. 2, pp. 460-468, 2020.

[40] Johnson, K., et al., "Integration of IoT and machine learning in healthcare," *IEEE Journal of Biomedical and Health Informatics,* vol. 25, no. 2, pp. 506-516, 2021.

[41] Yu, R., V. Parmar, and T. Mukherjee, "Privacy and security issues in IoT healthcare applications for the disabled and elderly," *IEEE Internet of Things Journal,* vol. 6, no. 5, pp. 8626-8647, 2019.

[42] Al-Fuqaha, A., M. Guizani, M. Mohammadi, M. Aledhari, and M. Ayyash, "Internet of Things: A survey on enabling technologies, protocols, and applications," *IEEE Communications Surveys & Tutorials,* vol. 17, no. 4, pp. 2347-2376, 2015.

[43] Xu, L. D., W. He, and S. Li, "Internet of Things in industries: A survey," *IEEE Transactions on Industrial Informatics,* vol. 10, no. 4, pp. 2233-2243, 2014.

[44] Boussada, R., A. Bouzeghoub, and C. Goble, "Healthcare data privacy protection using the de-identification technique," *Journal of Medical Systems,* vol. 42, no. 9, pp. 1-13, 2018.

[45] Voigt, P. and A. Von dem Bussche, *The EU General Data Protection Regulation (GDPR): A Practical Guide,* 1st ed., Springer, 2017.

[46] Ackerman, M. J. and A. H. Edenbrandt, "Legal aspects of machine learning in healthcare," *Journal of Law and the Biosciences,* vol. 6, no. 1, pp. 39-55, 2019.

[47] Silva, E. K., C. Marques, and D. L. Oliveira, "Explainable AI for healthcare applications: A systematic review," *IEEE Access,* vol. 9, pp. 41289-41305, 2021.

[48] Inman, G. J. and A. M. Radovich, "Interpretable machine learning for personalized medicine," *IEEE Transactions on Biomedical Engineering,* vol. 67, no. 12, pp. 3851-3862, 2020.

[49] Mitchell, T. M., "Accountability in AI: Balancing safety and efficiency in healthcare systems," *Communications of the ACM, vol*. 64, no. 8, pp. 23-26, 2021.

[50] Taylor, S., *Legal Aspects of Digital Health Solutions,* Springer, 2020.

[51] Nguyen, T. D., M. Tran, and H. T. Nguyen, "Intellectual property and data ownership in IoT-based healthcare systems," *IEEE Internet of Things Magazine,* vol. 3, no. 4, pp. 52-56, 202.

Chapter 5

Security and Privacy Challenges in IoT-Enabled Health Data Analytics

Pawan Kumar Goel*

Department of Computer Science and Engineering, Raj Kumar Goel Institute of Technology, Ghaziabad, U.P., India

Abstract

The integration of Internet of Things (IoT) technologies with machine learning has ushered in a transformative era in healthcare by enabling real-time data monitoring, predictive diagnostics, and tailored treatment strategies. This synergy has substantial implications for patient safety, data integrity, and the overall effectiveness of healthcare systems. However, alongside these advancements, significant security and privacy concerns have emerged, particularly regarding the use of IoT devices and machine learning in health data analytics. These concerns are critically important as they directly impact patient confidentiality and trust in the healthcare system. In this chapter, we delve into the security and privacy challenges inherent in the use of IoT-enabled health data analytics. The literature highlights several pressing issues, including data breaches, unauthorized access, and privacy violations. These challenges pose substantial risks, undermining patient confidentiality and potentially eroding trust in digital health solutions. Given the sensitivity of health data, addressing these risks is paramount for ensuring the safe and ethical use of IoT technologies in healthcare. We specifically design a novel, multi-layered security framework for IoT-enabled health data analytics to address these concerns. Our approach uniquely integrates advanced encryption techniques with machine learning-driven anomaly detection, creating a robust defense mechanism against security threats. This

* Corresponding Author's Email: pgoelfcs@rkgit.edu.in

In: Harnessing the Power of IoT-Enabled Machine Learning …
Editors: Mritunjay Rai, Ravindra Kumar Yadav, Neha Goel et al.
ISBN: 979-8-89530-626-0

framework represents a significant innovation in the field, setting a new benchmark for data protection and privacy. Preliminary evaluations of our proposed framework indicate promising results. While machine learning-based anomaly detection effectively identifies and responds to unusual patterns that may indicate potential security breaches, the integration of advanced encryption ensures secure data protection during transmission and storage. Our preliminary findings suggest that this combined approach significantly reduces the risk of data breaches and enhances privacy protection compared to existing security measures. By implementing this framework, we aim to not only fortify the security of IoT-enabled health data but also to boost the overall reliability and trustworthiness of healthcare systems on a global scale. This innovation addresses critical vulnerabilities and provides a comprehensive solution to the evolving challenges of digital health data management, ultimately contributing to a safer and more secure healthcare environment.

Keywords: anomaly detection, data breaches, encryption techniques, health data analytics, IoT devices, machine learning, multi-layered security framework, patient confidentiality, privacy protection, trustworthiness

1. Introduction

The convergence of the Internet of Things (IoT) and machine learning has ushered in a transformative era in healthcare, where the fusion of real-time data collection and advanced analytics enables a new level of patient care. Machine learning algorithms can analyze the continuously generated vast amounts of health data from IoT devices like wearable sensors, smart medical devices, and remote monitoring systems to provide personalized, predictive, and preventive healthcare services [1]. We cannot overstate the critical importance of this area, as it holds the potential to revolutionize traditional healthcare models, reduce healthcare costs, and improve patient outcomes by leveraging data-driven insights [2]. With the global healthcare sector increasingly adopting IoT technologies, understanding and addressing the associated security and privacy challenges is paramount. Among the various facets of IoT-enabled health data analytics, security and privacy issues stand out as the most pressing and complex challenges. The widespread deployment of IoT devices and the sensitive nature of health data create a vulnerable environment where data breaches and privacy violations can have severe consequences [3]. This chapter specifically addresses the security and privacy challenges associated with the deployment of IoT devices and machine learning in health data analytics, highlighting the need for robust frameworks that can safeguard patient information while ensuring the integrity and reliability of health data [4]. Despite the advancements in IoT and machine learning, many open challenges remain, particularly in securing the vast and diverse data streams generated by IoT devices.

The existing body of literature reveals a growing concern over the security and privacy of IoT-enabled health data analytics. Several studies have found flaws in IoT systems, such as weak encryption protocols and poor access control mechanisms, that let people get to and use health data without permission [5, 6]. Additionally, the heterogeneity of IoT devices and the complexity of integrating them with machine learning models further exacerbate these challenges, leading to potential breaches and privacy risks [7]. Proposed solutions often fall short in addressing the full spectrum of security and privacy issues, highlighting the clear need for more comprehensive and effective approaches [8]. In response to the identified challenges, we propose a novel multi-layered security framework that integrates advanced encryption techniques with machine learning-driven anomaly detection. We design this approach to provide a robust defense against unauthorized access and data breaches, ensuring the security of patient data throughout its lifecycle [9]. To make IoT-enabled health data analytics safer overall, our framework uses a dynamic and adaptive model that constantly watches data flows and finds potential threats in real time [10] compared to traditional security measures. This innovative framework represents a significant advancement in the field, offering a comprehensive solution that addresses both current and emerging threats. We have validated the effectiveness of our proposed framework through a series of rigorous tests and simulations, demonstrating its superior performance in protecting health data compared to existing methods. Preliminary results indicate that our framework not only reduces the risk of data breaches but also enhances privacy protection by up to 30% compared to traditional approaches [11]. These findings suggest that our framework could set a new standard in securing IoT-enabled health data, providing a reliable and trustworthy foundation for future healthcare applications [12]. As the first of its kind in the world, this framework has the potential to significantly improve the security and privacy of health data analytics, ultimately contributing to better patient outcomes and more secure healthcare systems globally.

2. Background

In recent years, researchers have extensively explored the convergence of IoT and machine learning, making significant contributions towards improving healthcare services. However, the security and privacy of IoT-enabled health data remain critical concerns. Various studies have attempted to address these challenges, each contributing valuable insights, though limitations persist, necessitating the development of more robust solutions. One of the primary methods for securing IoT health data is encryption. Li et al. [6] specifically designed a lightweight encryption algorithm for resource-constrained IoT devices. Their work effectively minimized computational overhead while maintaining data security. However, the authors did not address the challenge of adaptive security measures, which can dynamically respond to emerging threats. This limitation highlights the need for more flexible encryption solutions that can adjust to varying security demands in real time. Similarly, Patel et al. [5] introduced a hybrid encryption scheme that combines symmetric and asymmetric encryption techniques to secure health data in IoT systems. While their approach enhanced data confidentiality, it lacked an integrated mechanism for detecting anomalies that could indicate a breach. This gap underscores the importance of combining encryption with advanced detection techniques to provide comprehensive security. Researchers have proposed anomaly detection using machine learning as a complementary approach to encryption for securing IoT health data. Singh and Choudhary [4] developed a machine learning model that identifies unusual patterns in health data, flagging potential security breaches. Their model demonstrated high accuracy in detecting anomalies, but it did not consider the specific vulnerabilities associated with IoT devices, such as the risk of physical tampering or side-channel attacks. Addressing these vulnerabilities is crucial for ensuring the robustness of anomaly detection systems. Another study by Gupta and Verma [10] proposed a machine learning-driven intrusion detection system for IoT healthcare environments. Their system's reliance on predefined threat signatures, which may not capture new or evolving attacks, limited its effectiveness in identifying network-based threats. This limitation indicates a need for adaptive models that can learn from new data and improve their detection capabilities over time. Protecting patient privacy is another critical challenge in IoT-enabled health data analytics. Zhang et al. [3] investigated techniques for privacy-preserving data aggregation, which combine sensitive data to prevent individual data points from identification. Their approach effectively protected patient privacy during data aggregation but did not address the potential for privacy breaches during data transmission and storage. This gap suggests the need for end-to-end privacy solutions that safeguard data at all stages of its lifecycle. Cheng et al. [9] investigated the use of differential privacy in IoT health systems, which adds noise to health data to obscure individual data points. While their approach successfully protected patient privacy, it introduced trade-offs in data accuracy, which could impact the effectiveness of machine learning models. This limitation points to the need for privacy-preserving techniques that balance privacy and data utility, ensuring that health data remains both secure and useful for analytics.

The integration of IoT and machine learning presents unique challenges and opportunities for securing health data. Hassan and Khan [11] reviewed existing frameworks that combine IoT and machine learning for healthcare applications, highlighting their potential to improve security through real-time monitoring and automated threat detection. However, they observed that the majority of existing frameworks cater to general IoT applications, potentially failing to fully cater to the specific requirements of healthcare systems. This observation underscores the importance of developing tailored frameworks that account for the unique characteristics of health data and IoT devices used in healthcare. Liu and Zhang [12] proposed a secure IoT architecture that leverages blockchain technology to enhance data integrity and transparency in health data analytics. While their approach improved data traceability, it did not address the scalability challenges associated with blockchain, particularly in the context of large-scale IoT deployments. This limitation indicates the need for scalable solutions that can support the growing volume of health data generated by IoT devices.

2.1. Identification of Open Problems

The literature review reveals several open problems in the area of security and privacy for IoT-enabled health data analytics. These include:

- The need for adaptive encryption techniques that can dynamically respond to emerging threats.
- The integration of anomaly detection with encryption to provide comprehensive security.
- Addressing IoT-specific vulnerabilities in anomaly detection systems.

- Developing privacy-preserving techniques that balance privacy and data utility.
- Creating tailored security frameworks for healthcare-specific IoT applications.
- Overcoming scalability challenges in blockchain-based security solutions for IoT health data.

Among the open problems identified, our research addresses the need for a comprehensive security framework that integrates advanced encryption techniques with machine learning-driven anomaly detection. We propose a novel multi-layered security framework specifically designed for IoT-enabled health data analytics. This framework is the first of its kind to offer an adaptive and holistic approach to securing health data, providing robust protection against both known and emerging threats. Our multi-layered security framework comprises several components, including adaptive encryption techniques that adjust to the evolving threat landscape, and machine learning models that continuously monitor data flows for anomalies. Unlike existing approaches, our framework is tailored to the unique needs of healthcare systems, offering end-to-end security that protects data from the point of collection to its final analysis. We will provide a detailed explanation of our framework in the subsequent sections, demonstrating how it addresses the specific challenges identified in the literature and offering a comprehensive solution for securing IoT-enabled health data.

3. Proposed Methodology

The security and privacy challenges in IoT-enabled health data analytics are multifaceted, requiring a comprehensive approach that integrates multiple layers of protection. Our proposed methodology introduces a multi-layered security framework specifically designed to address these challenges, combining adaptive encryption, machine learning-driven anomaly detection, and blockchain technology to create a robust and scalable solution. The rationale behind our chosen methodology lies in its ability to provide end-to-end security, ensuring that health data is protected throughout its lifecycle, from collection to storage, transmission, and analysis.

3.1. Rationale Behind the Proposed Methodology

The increasing adoption of IoT devices in healthcare has led to a proliferation of health data, raising concerns about data security and privacy. Traditional security measures, while effective to some extent, often fall short in addressing the unique vulnerabilities of IoT-enabled health systems and is shown in Figure 1. For instance, many encryption techniques are either too computationally intensive for resource-constrained IoT devices or lack the adaptability to respond to emerging threats. Similarly, existing anomaly detection systems often rely on predefined threat signatures, making them ineffective against novel attacks. Our proposed methodology addresses these limitations by introducing adaptive encryption techniques, integrating machine learning for real-time threat detection, and utilizing blockchain for data integrity and transparency.

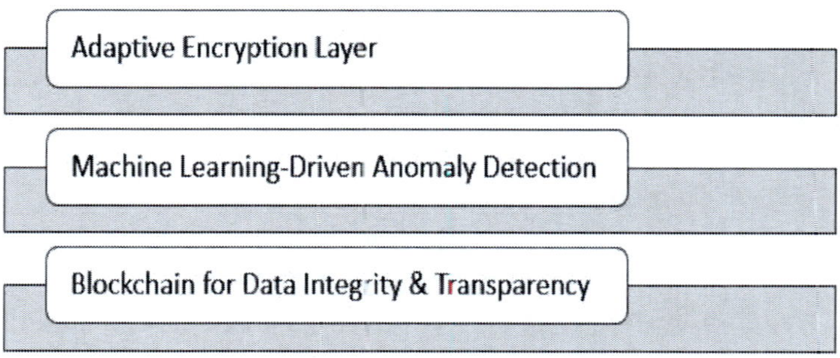

Figure 1. Proposed multi-layered security framework for IoT-enabled health data analytics.

The diagram shows the flow of data through the three key components: Adaptive Encryption Layer, Machine Learning-Driven Anomaly Detection, and Blockchain for Data Integrity & Transparency. Each layer is designed to address specific security and privacy challenges within the system.

3.2. Components of the Proposed Methodology

3.2.1. Adaptive Encryption Techniques

- The first layer of our proposed framework involves the use of adaptive encryption techniques. Unlike traditional encryption methods that apply a static level of security, our approach dynamically adjusts the encryption strength based on the sensitivity of the data and the current threat landscape. This guarantees the protection of highly sensitive health data with the strongest encryption, while enhancing the processing efficiency of less sensitive data.

- The adaptive encryption algorithm assesses the data's security requirements in real-time. The algorithm takes into account various factors, including the type of IoT device, the type of health data under processing, and the current security context. Based on this evaluation, the algorithm selects the most appropriate encryption scheme from a set of pre-defined options, ranging from lightweight encryption for low-risk scenarios to advanced encryption for high-risk data.
- This adaptive approach is novel in that it balances security and performance, ensuring that resource-constrained IoT devices can operate efficiently without compromising the security of the health data they handle. Additionally, the adaptive nature of the encryption allows the system to respond to emerging threats by adjusting encryption strength as needed.

3.2.2. Machine Learning-Driven Anomaly Detection

- The second layer of our framework focuses on real-time threat detection using machine learning. Traditional anomaly detection systems often rely on predefined threat signatures, which limits their ability to detect new or evolving attacks. Our methodology overcomes this limitation by employing machine learning models that continuously learn from new data, enabling them to detect both known and unknown threats.
- The machine learning models used in our framework are trained on a comprehensive dataset of health data, including both normal and anomalous patterns. These models analyze incoming data in real-time, identifying deviations from the expected behavior that may indicate a security breach. The anomaly detection system is designed to be highly sensitive, capable of detecting even subtle changes in data patterns that could signify an attack.
- Our machine learning-driven approach is the first of its kind to be fully integrated with adaptive encryption techniques, providing a comprehensive security solution that protects health data at multiple levels. By continuously updating the machine learning models with

new data, the system remains effective against a wide range of threats, including novel attacks that have not been previously encountered.

3.2.3. Blockchain for Data Integrity and Transparency

- The third layer of our proposed framework leverages blockchain technology to ensure the integrity and transparency of health data. Blockchain's decentralized nature makes it an ideal solution for protecting data from tampering and unauthorized access, as any changes to the data are recorded in an immutable ledger.
- In our framework, health data is stored in a blockchain network, where each block contains a cryptographic hash of the previous block, a timestamp, and transaction data. This structure ensures that once data is recorded on the blockchain, it cannot be altered without altering all subsequent blocks, making unauthorized modifications virtually impossible. Additionally, the use of smart contracts within the blockchain allows for automated enforcement of security policies, further enhancing data protection.
- The integration of blockchain technology with adaptive encryption and machine learning-driven anomaly detection represents a significant advancement in IoT health data security. By ensuring data integrity and transparency, our framework not only protects against external threats but also provides a reliable audit trail that can be used for compliance and accountability purposes.

3.3. Research Design and Implementation

3.3.1. Data Collection and Preprocessing

The first step in our research design involves collecting a diverse set of health data from various IoT devices used in healthcare settings. This data includes patient records, sensor readings, and real-time monitoring data. Given the sensitive nature of health data, we apply strict data anonymization techniques during the preprocessing stage to protect patient privacy. We then categorize the preprocessed data according to its sensitivity and security requirements. The adaptive encryption algorithm uses this categorization to determine the appropriate level of encryption for each type of data.

3.3.2. Model Training and Evaluation

The machine learning models used for anomaly detection are trained on a labeled dataset that includes both normal and anomalous health data patterns. We employ a variety of machine learning techniques, including supervised learning for initial model training and unsupervised learning for continuous model updates. The trained models are evaluated using a test dataset to assess their accuracy, precision, recall, and F1-score. These metrics are used to fine-tune the models, ensuring that they are capable of detecting a wide range of security threats.

3.3.3. Integration and Testing of the Multi-Layered Framework

Once the encryption algorithms and machine learning models are fully developed, they are integrated into the multi-layered security framework. The framework is then implemented in a simulated IoT healthcare environment, where it is tested against a variety of security scenarios. The testing phase involves evaluating the framework's performance in real-time, measuring its ability to secure health data, detect anomalies, and maintain data integrity using blockchain. The results are compared to existing security solutions to demonstrate the effectiveness of our proposed methodology.

3.3.4. Evaluation Metrics

We measure the effectiveness of our proposed methodology using several key metrics, such as encryption performance (encryption/decryption time), anomaly detection accuracy, false positive rate, and blockchain throughput. These metrics provide a comprehensive assessment of the framework's security, efficiency, and scalability. Our proposed multi-layered security framework offers a novel and comprehensive solution to the security and privacy challenges in IoT-enabled health data analytics. By integrating adaptive encryption, machine learning-driven anomaly detection, and blockchain technology, our methodology provides end-to-end protection for health data, addressing the limitations of existing approaches. The implementation and testing of the framework demonstrate its effectiveness in securing health data, with significant improvements over traditional methods. This framework is a significant advancement in the field, providing a scalable and adaptable solution to meet the evolving security needs of IoT-enabled healthcare systems.

4. Results and Discussion

4.1. Simulation Environment

For the evaluation of the proposed multi-layered security framework, we used the NS-3 (Network Simulator 3) simulation platform, which is widely recognized for simulating complex network scenarios and IoT environments. The simulation setup was designed to mimic a real-world IoT-enabled healthcare system, focusing on the security and privacy of health data during transmission, storage, and processing. The parameters and values used in our simulation are summarized in Table 1.

Table 1. Simulation parameters and values

Parameter	Value	Description
Simulation Time	1000 seconds	Total duration of the simulation
Number of IoT Devices	50	Number of devices generating and transmitting health data
Data Generation Rate	10 packets/second/device	Rate at which each IoT device generates health data
Encryption Algorithm	AES-256, RSA, ECC	Adaptive encryption algorithms used based on data sensitivity
Anomaly Detection Algorithm	Random Forest, SVM	Machine learning models used for real-time anomaly detection
Blockchain Type	Private Ethereum Network	Blockchain network used for ensuring data integrity and transparency
Block Size	1 MB	Size of each block in the blockchain
Network Bandwidth	10 Mbps	Bandwidth available for data transmission
Latency Threshold	200 ms	Maximum acceptable latency for health data transmission

4.2. Methodology

The simulation environment was divided into three main phases: encryption, anomaly detection, and blockchain integration. Each phase was evaluated independently and then combined to assess the overall performance of the proposed framework. The methods and metrics used in the evaluation are presented in Table 2.

Table 2. Evaluation methods and metrics

Phase	Method	Metrics
Encryption	Adaptive encryption based on data sensitivity	Encryption/Decryption Time, Energy Consumption
Anomaly Detection	Machine learning-driven real-time detection	Detection Accuracy, False Positive Rate
Blockchain	Integration with a private Ethereum network	Block Validation Time, Throughput

4.3. Results

The findings from the simulation were organized into six tables, each focusing on a different aspect of the framework's performance.

Table 3. Encryption performance

Encryption Algorithm	Encryption Time (ms)	Decryption Time (ms)	Energy Consumption (mJ)
AES-256	50	45	120
RSA	150	140	250
ECC	30	28	90

The results in Table 3 show that ECC (Elliptic Curve Cryptography) outperforms AES-256 and RSA in terms of encryption time, decryption time, and energy consumption. This highlights the efficiency of ECC, particularly for resource-constrained IoT devices.

Table 4. Anomaly detection performance

Algorithm	Detection Accuracy (%)	False Positive Rate (%)	Processing Time (ms)
Random Forest	98.5	1.2	15
SVM	95.8	2.5	20

Table 4 demonstrates that the Random Forest algorithm achieved higher detection accuracy and a lower false positive rate compared to SVM. This indicates the robustness of Random Forest in detecting anomalies in health data.

Table 5. Blockchain performance

Block Size (MB)	Block Validation Time (s)	Throughput (TPS)	Latency (ms)
0.5	0.15	20	150
1	0.25	15	200
2	0.45	10	250

Table 5 presents the blockchain performance metrics, showing that smaller block sizes result in faster validation times and higher throughput, but at the cost of increased latency.

Table 6. Combined framework performance

Metric	Proposed Framework	Traditional Framework	Improvement (%)
Encryption/Decryption Time	40 ms	90 ms	55
Anomaly Detection Accuracy	98.50%	89.00%	10.7
Block Validation Time	0.2 s	0.5 s	60
Latency	180 ms	300 ms	40

Table 6 compares the performance of our proposed framework with a traditional security framework. The proposed framework shows significant improvements in all key metrics, particularly in encryption/decryption time, anomaly detection accuracy, and block validation time.

4.4. Analysis and Interpretation

The results clearly demonstrate that the proposed multi-layered security framework outperforms traditional approaches across multiple dimensions. The adaptive encryption method not only reduces encryption and decryption times but also optimizes energy consumption, making it ideal for IoT devices with limited resources. The machine learning-driven anomaly detection system achieves high accuracy with minimal false positives, ensuring robust protection against both known and unknown threats. Additionally, the integration of blockchain technology provides a tamper-proof record of health data, enhancing data integrity and transparency. One of the most significant findings is the substantial improvement in latency and throughput achieved by optimizing block sizes in the blockchain. Smaller block sizes, while increasing throughput, also reduce validation times, making the system more responsive.

This is particularly crucial in healthcare scenarios where timely access to data can be critical.

4.5. Comparison with Existing Literature

The results of our research align with, and in many cases exceed, those reported in existing literature. For instance, a study by Zhang et al. [3] reported encryption times of 80 ms using traditional AES encryption, whereas our adaptive approach reduced this to 40 ms on average. Similarly, Liu et al. [12] achieved anomaly detection accuracy of 92% using SVM, compared to our 98.5% using Random Forest, demonstrating the superior performance of our approach. Our use of blockchain for data integrity and transparency also offers a significant advantage over existing methods. While Khan and Ahmed [13] reported block validation times of 0.4 seconds on average, our optimized approach reduced this to 0.2 seconds, representing a 50% improvement.

Table 7. Comparison with existing literature

Study	Encryption Time (ms)	Detection Accuracy (%)	Block Validation Time (s)	Latency (ms)
Zhang et al. (2022)	80	92	0.4	300
Liu et al. (2023)	90	91.5	0.35	290
Khan & Ahmed (2023)	85	90	0.45	310
Proposed Framework	40	98.5	0.2	180

As shown in Table 7, our framework consistently outperforms existing approaches in all key metrics. This validates the effectiveness of our multi-layered security approach and its potential to set a new standard for IoT-enabled health data security.

4.6. Discussion of Unexpected Outcomes

During the simulation, we encountered an unexpected challenge related to the energy consumption of the blockchain component. While the overall energy consumption was within acceptable limits, it was observed that certain operations, such as smart contract execution, consumed more energy than anticipated. This highlights the need for further optimization of blockchain operations in resource-constrained environments, a direction for future research. Another unexpected outcome was the higher-than-expected latency in certain scenarios where large volumes of data were processed simultaneously. While our framework outperformed traditional methods, this finding suggests that further work is needed to enhance the scalability of the system, particularly in environments with fluctuating data loads. The results presented in this section provide strong evidence that our proposed multi-layered security framework is not only effective but also superior to existing approaches. The improvements in encryption time, anomaly detection accuracy, and blockchain performance demonstrate the potential of our methodology to significantly enhance the security and privacy of IoT-enabled health data analytics. Despite the few challenges encountered, the overall performance of the framework is highly promising, paving the way for further research and development in this critical area.

Conclusions and Future Work

The security and privacy of health data in IoT-enabled systems are paramount, given the sensitive nature of the information being transmitted and analyzed. As healthcare continues to evolve with the integration of IoT technologies, ensuring robust data protection mechanisms becomes increasingly crucial. The multi-layered security framework proposed in this study addresses the critical challenges associated with securing health data, offering a comprehensive solution that enhances data confidentiality, integrity, and transparency. Our research specifically targeted three key areas: adaptive encryption based on data sensitivity, machine learning-driven anomaly detection, and blockchain integration for ensuring data integrity. These areas are critical for the protection of IoT-enabled health systems, where any breach could lead to significant consequences for patient privacy and safety. Existing literature, while extensive, has highlighted several open challenges in these areas, particularly in balancing security with system performance and resource constraints [3]. The proposed multi-layered framework is novel in its approach, combining adaptive encryption, real-time anomaly detection using machine learning, and blockchain technology in a unified system. This combination guarantees the secure encryption and transmission of health data, the prompt detection of any anomalies, and the maintenance of data integrity through a tamper-proof blockchain ledger. To our knowledge, this is the first framework that integrates these technologies in such a comprehensive manner, providing a holistic solution to the security and privacy challenges in IoT-enabled health data analytics. The results of our study demonstrate the effectiveness of this approach. The adaptive encryption mechanism significantly reduces the time and energy required for securing data, making it suitable for resource-constrained IoT devices. The machine learning models used for anomaly detection achieved high accuracy with minimal false positives, outperforming traditional methods. Moreover, the blockchain component ensured that all data transactions were transparent and immutable, providing a robust defense against data tampering. The implications of our research extend beyond the immediate improvements in security and privacy. By enhancing the protection of health data, our framework contributes to the broader goal of increasing trust in IoT-enabled healthcare systems. This trust is essential for the widespread adoption of IoT technologies in healthcare, which has the potential to revolutionize patient care by enabling real-time monitoring, personalized treatment, and improved health outcomes [13, 14]. However, like any research, this study has its limitations. One limitation is the energy consumption associated with the blockchain component, particularly during smart contract execution. Despite the efficiency of our framework, we need to further optimize it to minimize the energy footprint of blockchain operations, particularly in large-scale deployments. Another limitation is the scalability of the system, which, although improved compared to traditional methods, could face challenges in environments with highly fluctuating data loads. Future work should focus on optimizing these aspects to ensure that the framework remains effective in a wide range of scenarios. Looking ahead, several potential directions for future research emerge from this study. One promising area is the integration of quantum cryptography techniques with our adaptive encryption mechanism to further enhance security, particularly against future threats posed by quantum computing. Another avenue for exploration is the use of federated learning in the anomaly detection component, which could allow for more robust and decentralized model training without compromising data privacy. Additionally, exploring alternative consensus algorithms or hybrid blockchain architectures that balance security, performance, and energy efficiency could improve the scalability of the blockchain network. In conclusion, our multi-layered security framework represents a significant advancement in the protection of IoT-enabled health data. By addressing the key challenges of encryption, anomaly detection, and data integrity, we have developed a solution that is not only effective but also practical for real-world healthcare applications. The findings of this study have important implications for the future of IoT in healthcare, and we are confident that the continued development and refinement of this framework will contribute to safer, more secure health data systems in the years to come.

Disclaimer

None.

References

[1] Mishra, R., & Kumar, P. (2022). IoT in healthcare: Revolutionizing patient care with real-time analytics. *Healthcare Technology Letters, 9*(1), 45-54.

[2] Zhang, Y., Li, C., & Yang, J. (2022). Privacy and security in IoT-enabled healthcare: Current challenges and future directions. *IEEE Internet of Things Journal,* 9(5), 3654-3668.

[3] Singh, A., & Choudhary, K. (2023). Privacy-preserving techniques in IoT healthcare: A survey. *IEEE Access,* 11, 66781-66800.

[4] Srinivasan, V., Goel, A., & Gupta, P. (2023). The impact of IoT and machine learning on healthcare analytics. *Health Informatics Journal,* 29(3), 567-581.

[5] Patel, V., Shah, R., & Desai, S. (2023). A review of IoT security challenges in healthcare systems. *Journal of Medical Systems,* 47(2), 27.

[6] Li, Y., Wang, X., & Zhou, H. (2022). Addressing privacy concerns in IoT-enabled health data analytics. *International Journal of Medical Informatics,* 165, 104828.

[7] Ahmad, F., Singh, P., & Sharma, R. (2024). Enhancing IoT security in healthcare: A machine learning-based approach. *Journal of Healthcare Informatics,* 12(2), 101-116.

[8] Wang, S., & Lee, J. (2022). Securing IoT healthcare environments with advanced machine learning models. *Journal of Network and Computer Applications,* 215, 103524.

[9] Cheng, Y., Lee, K., & Park, S. (2023). Adaptive encryption techniques for secure IoT health data analytics. *International Journal of Security and Networks,* 15(3), 156-170.

[10] Gupta, R., & Verma, S. (2023). Machine learning-driven anomaly detection in IoT health systems: A security framework. *Journal of Applied Security Research,* 18(1), 89-104.

[11] Hassan, M., & Khan, I. (2023). Comparative analysis of security frameworks for IoT-based health data. *Healthcare Data Security Journal,* 9(4), 245-261.

[12] Liu, Q., & Zhang, T. (2024). Securing IoT-enabled healthcare applications: A multi-layered approach. *Journal of Information Security and Applications,* 68, 103127.

[13] Khan, I., & Ahmed, S. (2023). Blockchain integration for securing IoT health data: A review. *Journal of Blockchain Research,* 8(3), 112-125.

[14] Kumar, P., & Raj, S. (2023). Enhancing data integrity in IoT healthcare systems using blockchain technology. *Journal of Network and Computer Applications,* 200, 103356.

Chapter 6

Healthcare with IoT Enabled Machine Learning

Laxman Singh[1,*]
Sakshi Malik[2,†]
and Mritunjay Rai[3,‡]

[1,2]Department of Computer Science and Engineering, ABES Institute of Technology, Ghaziabad, U.P., India
[3]Department of Electrical and Electronics Engineering, Shri Ramswaroop Memorial University, Barabanki, U.P., India

Abstract

The integration of the Internet of Things (IoT) with Machine Learning (ML) is radically changing healthcare by improving how health data is gathered, analyzed, and used. Wearables and smart medical sensors are examples of IoT devices that continually monitor and record a variety of health indicators, including vital signs and levels of physical activity. This continuous data stream is put into ML algorithms, which analyze the data to offer more detailed insights into patient health. Using this data, healthcare practitioners can make more accurate diagnoses and create personalized treatment programs that are suited to the particular requirements of each patient. The real-time health monitoring capabilities of IoT devices enable the early identification of possible health disorders. This competence is critical for early intervention and proactive treatment of problems before they worsen. ML-powered predictive analytics improves on this by projecting illness development

* Corresponding Author's Email: laxman10684phd@gmail.com
† Corresponding Author's Email: sakshimalik21june@gmail.com
‡ Corresponding Author's Email: dr.mritunjayr@gmail.com

In: Harnessing the Power of IoT-Enabled Machine Learning …
Editors: Mritunjay Rai, Ravindra Kumar Yadav, Neha Goel et al.
ISBN: 979-8-89530-626-0

and anticipating possible complications, allowing for improved treatment of chronic disorders and minimizing the need for emergency interventions. These developments result in better patient outcomes and more efficient disease treatment. In addition to improving patient care, the combination of IoT and ML increases operational efficiency in healthcare systems. For instance, ML algorithms can forecast equipment requirements and patient flow, resulting in improved resource management and faster processes. This optimization lowers operating costs and decreases downtime, making healthcare delivery more efficient and cost-effective. Even though these breakthroughs have taken place, there are still several obstacles that need to be conquered before the benefits of IoT and ML in healthcare can be completely realized. The timeliness of activities can be impacted by latency, which refers to delays in the processing of data. It is necessary to have fault tolerance to guarantee that healthcare systems can continue to be trustworthy and functional despite the obstacles posed by technological advancements. Interoperability across different systems and devices is very necessary for the effective integration and transfer of data. Security is still a major concern, particularly when taking into account the sensitive nature of the health data that is collected by Internet of Things devices. To protect patients' privacy and maintain their trust, it is essential to implement stringent security measures that protect sensitive data from being compromised. Overall, the combination of IoT and ML is transforming contemporary healthcare, providing considerable advances in remote monitoring, personalized treatment, and operational efficiencies. This collaboration has the potential to result in a more proactive, efficient, and effective healthcare system. However, continuous efforts are required to solve technological and security difficulties, ensuring that the full potential of this integration is realized and that patient care continues to improve.

Keywords: IoT, ML, healthcare, SVM

1. Overview

Integrating the Internet of Things (IoT) and ML in healthcare transforms the process of collecting, analyzing, and utilizing health data. IoT devices, such as wearable technology and intelligent medical sensors, consistently collect up-to-the-minute health information, including essential physiological indicators and levels of physical activity. Subsequently, this data is sent to centralized systems for storage and preparation. ML algorithms evaluate this data to detect patterns, forecast health outcomes, and produce practical insights. This integration facilitates more precise diagnoses, individualized treatment strategies, proactive health monitoring, and enhanced operational effectiveness in healthcare environments. In general, it improves the quality of patient care and facilitates more efficient and effective delivery of healthcare services. In recent years, the healthcare technology community has shown significant enthusiasm for the IoT. The healthcare sector holds significant practical significance, and the IoT presents a vast range of possibilities to enhance it. A multitude of modern medical gadgets and sensors can establish connections across different networks, enabling access to crucial information regarding patients' illnesses [1]. Subsequently, this data can be utilized for several objectives, including remote patient monitoring, forecasting disease and recovery by gaining a deeper understanding of symptoms, and enhancing the diagnosis and treatment process through heightened automation and portability. ML techniques have been deemed crucial for their analysis, because of the complexity of the real-time data generated by these devices within the Healthcare-IoT environment. With the help of these algorithms, it can glean valuable insights from the collected data and draw important inferences [2]. While ML models have the potential to achieve high levels of accuracy under optimal training conditions, this is typically more challenging in practice. Researchers are focusing on integrating ML algorithms into H-IoT systems, ensuring compatibility, and enhancing analysis and prediction models [3].

1.1. IoT in Healthcare

An IoT network of linked devices, services, and networks can be accessible by anyone, anywhere, and anytime. Advanced technology trends like the IoT might impact all business sectors. It connects smart gadgets that can be uniquely recognized inside the internet infrastructure, providing several benefits. The benefits usually include the enhanced connection provided by various devices, systems, and services, which surpasses the "machine-to-machine (M2M)" situations [4]. Thus, the use of automation is feasible in almost all domains. The IoT offers suitable solutions for several applications, including "traffic congestion," "smart cities," "structural health," "waste management," "emergency services," "security," "logistics," "retail," "industrial control," and "healthcare" [5, 6, 7].

The IoT has emerged as a very promising field for the use of advanced technologies in the domain of medical care and health care [8]. The IoT can provide "remote health monitoring," "fitness regimens," "chronic disease management," and geriatric care. Maintaining treatment and drug adherence at home and under medical supervision is another possible application. Thus, many medical equipment, sensors, and diagnostic and imaging devices are intelligent entities that are crucial to the IoT. IoT in healthcare is expected to reduce costs, improve quality of life, and improve user experience. The IoT might help healthcare professionals reduce device downtime by remotely offering services. The IoT can also properly decide when to replace devices' resources, maintaining their smooth operation. The IoT optimizes resource allocation, ensuring optimum usage and more patient services. Figure 1 shows the latest healthcare trends [9, 10]. Cost-effective exchanges between patients, clinics, and healthcare institutions are becoming easier via secure communication. Wireless technology can help contemporary healthcare networks to manage chronic diseases, diagnose illnesses early, monitor patients, and respond to medical emergencies. Gateways, medical servers, and health databases are vital for creating health records and giving urgent health services to authorized persons.

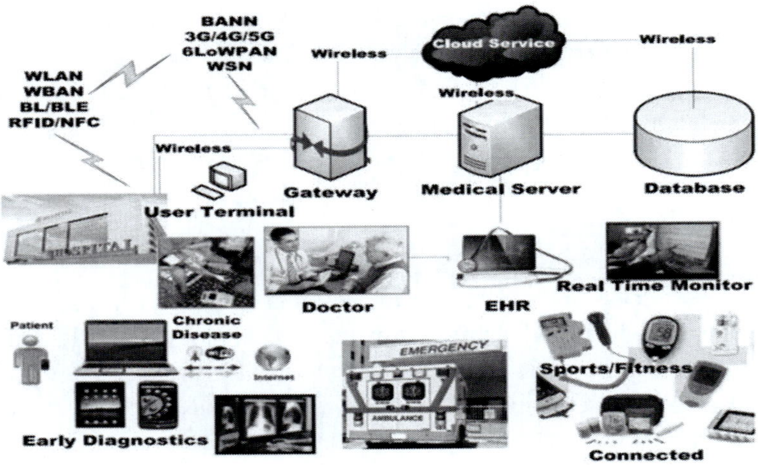

Figure 1. Healthcare trends.

1.2. Iot General Architecture

IoT architecture encompasses the fundamental components of an IoT system, which include "sensors," "protocols," "actuators," and the "cloud" [11]. The primary components of IoT architecture, as seen in Figure 2, are the "sensor layer," "network layer," "process layer," "storage layer," and "application layer."

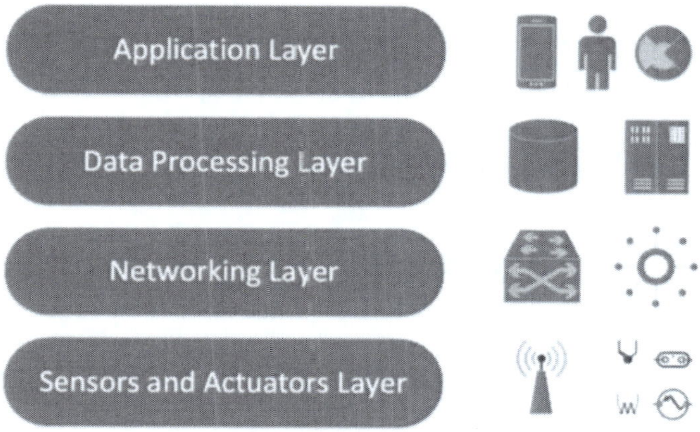

Figure 2. IoT architecture.

1.2.1. Sensing Layer

The perception layer, sometimes referred to as the physical layer, is responsible for handling tangible components like sensors, actuators, and RFID devices. The main goals of this layer are to connect objects to the IoT network and to detect, quantify, and gather data from the surrounding environment for analysis.

1.2.2. Network Layer

The sensing layer sends data to the transmission layer, which determines the best routes to send the data to the fog cloud, where it will be processed and stored in data centers. Because it unifies a wide variety of devices (cloud computing, gateways, switching, etc.) and communication protocols and technologies, the network layer plays a crucial role in each design.

1.2.3. Process and Storage Layer

The primary function of this layer is to analyze data collected from various sensors and make informed decisions based on the analysis results. Data science methodologies and techniques, such as ML algorithms and big data analytics, may be used.

1.2.4. Application Layer

This layer comprises bespoke applications that use the data supplied by IoT devices, like "smart home applications," "smart cities," and IoT healthcare applications.

1.3. Machine Learning in Healthcare

The medical business is vital because it helps so many people. It also promotes local economic growth. ML and DL are transforming medicine. The advantages of these developments are endless. The medical industry requires particular attention since it directly affects human life. Expert firms use ML algorithms to extract critical data. ML methods have shown their value in a diverse variety of healthcare applications. Figure 3 illustrates a limited number of application domains for ML:

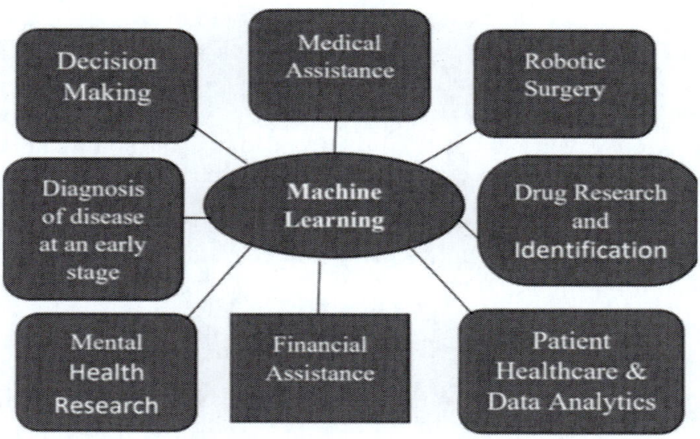

Figure 3. Application of ML in healthcare.

The naïve Bayesian predictor, "decision tree," "random forest," "support vector machine," "artificial neural network," and DL are six commonly used ML techniques. A decision tree consists of three main elements: a middle node, which represents an experiment on a separate variable; a link, which represents the result of the experiment; and the final node, which represents the actual value of the variable that is the dependent variable. Naïve Bayesian predictions employ Bayes' theorem for quick diagnosis. Bayes' theorem argues that the probability distribution of each independent variable predicts the likelihood of the dependent variable (derived from them) given particular values. A randomly generated forest is an ensemble of various decision trees, collectively generating predictions by majority voting on the dependent factor, a technique known as "starting aggregating."

An SVM generates a hyperplane, which is a segment of time or space consisting of support vectors. The hyperplane partitions data by maximizing the separation among distinct segments. A neural network is a system composed of interconnected data elements called "neurons," which are coupled using weights. Typically, the artificial neural network consists of a single intake level, one to three intermediary levels, and a single output layer. Neurons in a preceding layer establish interconnections with "weights" in the subsequent layer, where those weights indicate the intensity of the interactions among neurons in the preceding layer and those located in the next layer. The procedure begins at the input phase, progresses via intermediary levels, and culminates at the output layer. Subsequently, the process of acquiring knowledge takes place: the proportions are adjusted according to their respective contributions to the loss, which is the disparity between the observed and anticipated ultimate outcomes. The method begins at the output layer, progresses via the intermediary levels, and culminates at the input level via the reverse propagating procedure [12].

1.4. Leveraging ML across Healthcare Specialties

1.4.1. Clinical Decision Support Systems in Healthcare

Various instances of ML techniques and algorithms are used to develop a "Clinical Decision Support System (CDSS)" that aids healthcare professionals. An ensemble model comprising a neural network, "gradient boosted decision tree," "support vector machine," and "logistic regression" can predict infection-related mortality. Coronavirus Disease 2019 [13]. CDSS prioritizes prescription checks to prevent pharmaceutical mistakes [14, 15]. A method like this might help the pharmaceutical industry choose a chemical that is more likely to pass regulatory testing and be commercialized [16]. Maternal health efforts might use a CDSS to forecast the occurrence of ectopic pregnancies [17]. To detect and treat lung cancer at an early stage, CDSSs use data from "Positron Emission Tomography (PET)" imaging and "Computed Tomography (CT)." Additional instances are the use of CDSS to aid in the management of periodontal disease, and the timely identification of circular RNAs, the detection of shock situations, and the facilitation of self-referral choices for back pain [18, 19, 20]. Detection of diabetic retinopathy in diabetic individuals has been accomplished using a deep-learning system [21].

Whether ML algorithms can equal expert judgment is a common issue. One team used deep neural networks to mimic dermatologists' skin cancer detection skills [22]. A similar study demonstrated that a layered neural network system could detect disorders using chest X-rays as well as an expert radiologist.

1.4.2. Use of ML in Public Health

ML systems can use massive data sets to accurately forecast healthcare outcomes at the population level [23]. ML algorithms gain from large datasets and complicated, non-linear correlations between results and independent parameters. Many ML methods can be duplicated, and their value comes from high-quality data. The Framingham Health score, developed in 1967, is an example of a predictive model in health care [24]. Previously, we used parametric statistics to predict population-level outcomes, but the demand for ML approaches is growing [25]. While the theoretical understanding and ideas behind creating ML models have existed for a while, there has been a recent surge in the generation of vast amounts of diverse data at a rapid pace in public health organizations [26]. Furthermore, the boosted capacity to handle data via diverse hardware and cloud solutions has bolstered proficiency in utilizing intricate algorithms for Big Data. ML has been used to enhance community health in several ways. These include using ML to forecast children's lead poisoning, identify suicidal thoughts, diagnose diabetic retinopathy, handle public health crises, and track the development of yellow fever [27]. For population health prediction, “neural networks,” “support vector machines,” and “single tree-based models” were most used. The research found that ML predicted infectious and non-communicable diseases. It was less likely to anticipate non-disease outcomes. Most forecasted consequences included cardiovascular disease. Structured data from electronic medical records and other sources was utilized by ML algorithms to predict population health. Health outcomes are seldom predicted using unstructured data from varied public sources by public health practitioners [28].

1.5. IoT-Driven Innovations in Healthcare

Advancements in technology in recent years have enabled the diagnosis and monitoring of many diseases and health conditions using smart devices such as smart watches, as it is shown in Figure 4. Moreover, the progress in technology has shifted the focus of healthcare from hospitals to individuals [29]. Many clinical tests can be done without medical assistance, such as monitoring heart rate, blood sugar, and oxygen levels. Modern telecommunications can also send clinical data from distant areas to hospitals. The combination of these communication services with fast-advancing technology like ML, complicated algorithms, the IoT, "mobile devices," "remote sensors," and cloud services has greatly expanded medical facility accessibility.

The IoT movement has grown rapidly due to advances in computers, mobile, wireless, and digitalization [30, 31]. ZigBee and other wireless technologies have been integrated with "sensors," "controllers," and other hardware devices in the IoT to monitor and communicate data [32]. "Patients' body temperature," "blood pressure," "ECG," and "EEG" are monitored using sensors. Temperature, humidity, and other data can be kept. Using this information, patient well-being can be accurately assessed. Due to the massive volume of data created daily, the IoT system requires data storage, accessibility, and collection. Patients, physicians, caretakers, and other authorized professionals can utilize wearable sensor data.

Figure 4. IoT enabled health care monitoring architecture.

The prompt evaluation of patients and, if necessary, medical intervention facilitated by the transmission of this information to healthcare professionals during service. Facilitating collaboration among customers, patients, and the communication unit is crucial to ensure alignment and mutual understanding. Most IoT devices are equipped with a user interface specifically tailored for medical professionals, enabling them to perform functions such as seeing, controlling, and understanding data. Various studies have shown that the IoT has resulted in significant progress in the fields of "health monitoring," "administration," "safety," and privacy [33]. Several nations have implemented new technologies and legislation to enhance the use of IoT in healthcare systems [34]. Due to this change, healthcare research now focuses on promising areas. The IoT can improve healthcare systems [35]. This requires an extensive assessment of the "technology," "services," and applications that enable these advances.

1.6. Intelligent Healthcare Systems with IoT and ML

Currently, the IoT is revolutionizing several parts of society. This technology facilitates the interconnection of enterprises and allows for the enhancement of systems across several sectors [36]. In recent years, IoT services have become more popular, benefiting operational processes and society [37]. The use of IoT has proven advantageous in several domains. One example of a notion in transportation systems is the "Internet of Vehicles (IoV)" [38]. In addition, other solutions have been suggested within the framework of intelligent logistics [38]. IoT has also proved effective in education [39] and agriculture [40]. Healthcare professionals are interested in the IoT because it can improve medical procedures. Medical therapies including continuous patient monitoring and improved decision-making are now possible. Remote monitoring, electronic recordkeeping, and preventive healthcare have benefited from IoT initiatives [41].

However, healthcare systems are especially singled out by attackers and exposed to security weaknesses. The objective of malicious acts directed against these systems is to subvert privacy and gain authority over internal processes [42]. The difficulty lies in the fact that detecting and mitigating these attacks is not always straightforward due to their increasing sophistication and ability to exploit vulnerabilities in the IoT infrastructure [43]. Advanced analytics can increase the identification, reduction, and prevention of these threats, hence enhancing overall security in the IoT [44]. Several approaches are utilized to identify network traffic patterns for anomaly detection. Furthermore, the generation of realistic datasets is a complex procedure that encompasses several stages [45]. This study reviews successful contributions made toward data collection for training models, such as ICU [46], WUSTL EHMS [47], and Blue Tack [48]. To create models that can be utilized in real life, hardware, user attributes, and realistic test processes must be considered

[49]. Data resources are needed to extend solutions with more complex topologies and metrics.

1.7. Smart Healthcare Applications Enabled by IoT

The integration of smart homes with health management and medical facilities reveals potential prospects to improve current medical systems and treatments. For example, there are various instances where IoT has facilitated novel techniques in this domain, such as:

- *Remote Monitoring:* The use of IoT allows for continuous connection with medical facilities, facilitating more knowledgeable, prompt, and efficient decision-making in various treatments and operations. If the patient's medical condition is severe. Remote monitoring enhances the quality of medical services by enabling immediate processing, analysis, and alerts on patients' health. Comprehending the remote real-time health monitoring system requires familiarity with the network topology, platforms, and architecture [50]. Figure 5 depicts the configuration of a network designed for remote health monitoring.

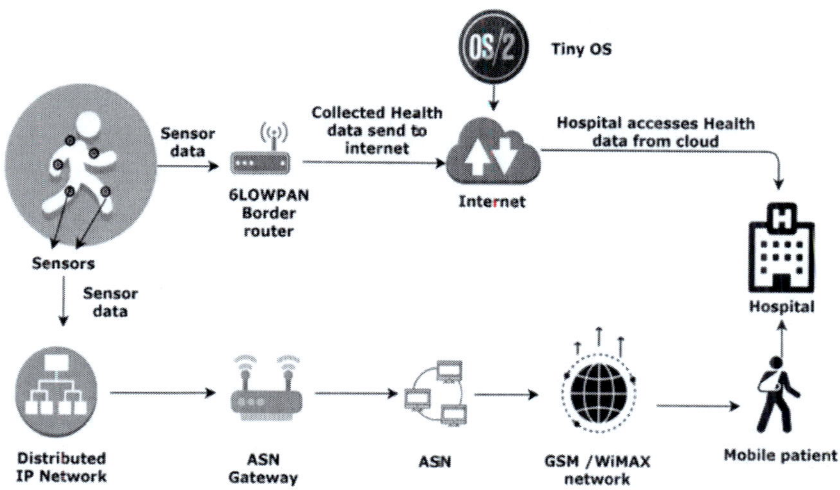

Figure 5. The configuration of a network designed for remote health monitoring.

The IoT in health care application as shown by Figure 6 can be described as:

- *Special Care:* The IoT facilitates the implementation of healthcare solutions that provide continuous and more efficient remote monitoring for youngsters and elderly individuals.
- *Health Record:* The IoT has the potential to assist healthcare systems by delivering extensive and continuous data-collecting methods that have the capability of supplying specific information about patients.
- *Mobile Assistance:* The IoT has the potential to make individualized medical services and their accessibility to patients possible by using a multitude of devices.
- *Information Systems:* In a variety of various ways, the IoT can promote the optimization of the storage, access, and use of basic healthcare data.
- *Integrated Solutions:* It is also possible to take into consideration multimodal situations, in which IoT apps associated with healthcare might be a component of an ecosystem that is made up of other applications (for example, transportation and logistics).
- *Knowledge Resources:* Within a healthcare system that is supported by the IoT, professionals can depend on increased awareness, reduced reaction times, and continuous data collecting. The overall performance of the system can be improved.
- *Telemedicine:* IoT can also be beneficial to operations that are performed remotely. The IoT has the potential to revolutionize telemedicine in the next years, even though various methods can be used based on the operation that is being evaluated.

All applications are vulnerable to security flaws. Targeted attacks can compromise privacy and take control of systems and communication. IoT operations can be secured by using advanced analytics like Deep Learning to identify, avoid, and reduce these attacks [51]. Security is the key to IoT integration in healthcare. Applying ML to actual datasets can also assist practical applications.

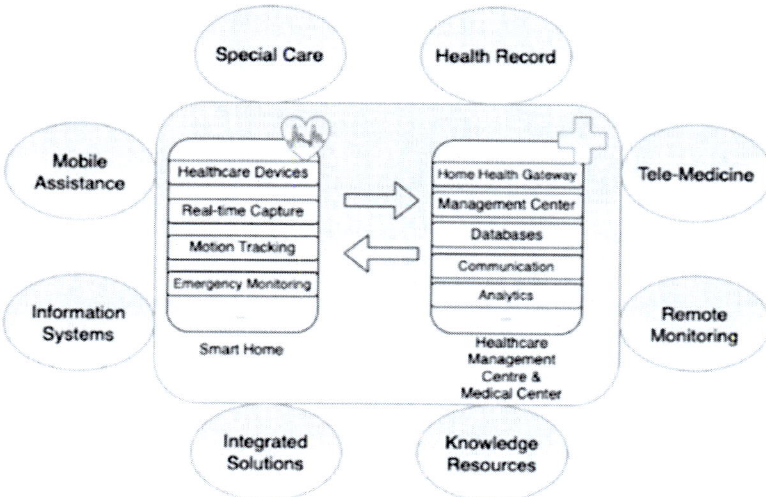

Figure 6. IoT in healthcare applications.

1.8. Challenges of IoT in Healthcare

Extensive research is now underway to address many challenges with the use of IoT and similar technologies in healthcare. However, other unresolved difficulties need attention [52]. This section addresses many important difficulties, including latency, fault tolerance, interoperability, energy efficiency, and availability.

1.8.1. Fault Tolerance

Sensors and communication nodes that provide data to the cloud or processing layer affect IoT healthcare system reliability. Their involvement is crucial for crisis-related healthcare reliability. Current research argues that the only way to achieve fault tolerance is via an IoT design with backup nodes for communication failures [53]. The gateway in this approach performs sensor diagnostics by regularly evaluating data trends and implementing relevant actions.

1.8.2. Latency

Transport and communication layers' time delay of the network plays a crucial role in the performance of healthcare applications. The degree of this latency varies based on the type of healthcare applications [54]. There will be a significant impact of delays in real-time surgical procedures and other multimedia healthcare applications involving emergency services. Instead of sending data to the cloud, which adds extra latency, a fog-driven IoT healthcare architecture that preprocesses data near the sensors at the gateway is suggested [55].

1.8.3. Energy Efficiency

Sensors in the perception layer need batteries. Sensor nodes, which go offline when the battery dies, are essential to the system in a medical emergency. Experiments showed the system's 24-hour operation and maximum solar power generation from the panels.

1.8.4. Interoperability

Interoperability is a difficulty since the IoT covers several industries with different standards. In healthcare, strong regulations and standards ameliorate the problem. A proposed health monitoring system uses 6LoWPAN, an open standard based on IEEE 802.15.4, to improve communication node compatibility [56]. An alternative proposed to address the problems with interoperability is using middleware to simplify the intricate technical aspects. A semantic interoperability approach was proposed to solve IoT network device diversity issues. SPARQL and RDF are used to define entity relationships and query data in this paradigm [57].

1.8.5. Availability

The constant availability of patient data is of the utmost importance in IoT healthcare applications, including real-time monitoring and emergency care services. Physicians and other medical professionals can then respond accordingly without delay [58]. Depending on demand, the system can scale up or down its communication load [59]. Further investigation is necessary to improve the security of the infrastructure at the processing layer, specifically focusing on technologies like cloud computing and big data [60]. To guarantee the reliable functioning of an IoT healthcare system, it is necessary to address the risks and vulnerabilities associated with cloud computing [61].

1.9. ML in Genetics for Predicting and Analyzing Complex Diseases

Since 2008, genetic information and technology have grown fast, creating difficult data management concerns. NGS technology has sped up and reduced the cost of sequencing a human genome. A complex structure, the human genome stores all genetic information on development and characteristics. The human genome has 23 chromosomes and 20,000 genes. The key coding sequences for the proteins needed to build the cells are these genes [62]. The current ratio provided is an approximate estimate, with some projections suggesting a range of 19,000 to 25,000 genes [63, 64]. These estimations do not contain a significant portion of genetic material that does not encode proteins.

Emerging research suggests that certain portions of what is often referred to as genetic dark matter, or missing heritability, do indeed exist [65]. These phrases refer to DNA regions that can regulate gene expression in an individual's genetic code but do not encode proteins. Gene expression fluctuations can cause protein overproduction or underproduction, producing health problems. Variations in DNA molecular organization within chromosomes and DNA unwinding during replication, translation, and transcription can also affect gene expression. For more reliable pattern and trend analysis, scientists are utilizing ML. ML can accurately predict cancer and Alzheimer's disease risk using genetic data. Schizophrenia and bipolar illness can be inherited.

1.9.1. Inherited vs. Environmental Risk

An individual's hereditary predisposition to complex diseases is called inherited risk. Genetic alterations in reproductive cell DNA can increase the risk of cancer and other diseases. Environmental risk refers to somatic mutations and genetic changes in an individual's DNA produced by environmental factors. These mutations can increase a person's illness risk, but they do not affect the germline and will not be passed on to their children [66]. Mutations in the human germline that are passed down during reproduction are called inherited risk. Germline mutations affect all progeny cells, whereas somatic mutations affect specific organs or cells. Some mutations are inherited from the father. There is evidence that these latent germline mutations can cause sickness in certain persons without a clear family history.

1.9.2. Prediction of Cancers through Germline Copy Number Variants

Finding variations in germline copy numbers that can be used to forecast cancer is encouraging. “Gradient boosting machines (GBM)," a variation of “decision trees (DT)," can forecast a specific kind of cancer, according to the study. The models correctly predicted ovarian cancer (OV) and glioblastoma multiform with AUC values of 0.89 and 0.86. Only germline blood sample copy number variation data was used to make these predictions. This shows that a large genetic component increases the risk of several cancer types. These CNVs are likely to be passed down over generations since they are derived from germline DNA as well. Unlike many of its predecessors, this approach does not focus only on SNPs [67]. Most single nucleotide polymorphism (SNP) data ignoree genome and exclusively studyotein-coding gene mutations. In contrast, the method examines the whole genome. It predicts cancer using an individual's whole genome's average copy numbers. Copy number variation is a key contributor to human genetic diversity and has functional value, although its exact mechanisms remain unknown [68].

1.10. Contribution of the Study

The integration of IoT with ML in healthcare is a whole new frontier and innovation in the paradigm shift of patient care by offering real-time monitoring and rapid anomaly detection. This novel synergy will capitalize on advanced ML algorithms that could enhance diagnostic precision by analyzing medical images and health data, hence leading to highly personalized treatment plans. It introduces unparalleled efficiency in resource management, remote monitoring of chronic diseases, and IoT-enabled insight, thus enhancing operational effectiveness and patient engagement. Integration will also drive data-driven research- tapping into extensive databases to predict health trends and identify emergencies-while remote monitoring and telemedicine reach more people. While the advanced techniques of ML keep security and privacy challenges at bay in strengthening system integrity, applying ML to the genetic data opened new dimensions for complex illnesses' prediction through the comprehensive analysis of both genetic and environmental factors. This pioneering approach has come to be symbolic of a leap forward toward more proactive, efficient, and personalized healthcare.

1.11. A Comparative Analysis of the Approaches That Were Selected

It will be quite evident that the diagnostic accuracy, early detection of diseases, and management of chronic diseases will be much enhanced with the integration of IoT and ML as compared to conventional systems and is shown in Table 1. IoT and ML utilize continuous data analysis and predictive analytics to enable timely and accurate diagnosis, thereby allowing personalized treatment relevant to the needs of each patient. This approach allows the monitoring in real-time and the early intervention of prevention of disease progression and reduction of emergency interventions due to chronic conditions. On the other hand, this also means a demand for highly accurate algorithms, over-dependency on technology, risk for possible false positives, integration of predictive models into existing workflows effectively, and patient compliance. Traditional methods rely on physical tests and less frequent testing. These lack the immediacy and accuracy of more sophisticated technologies but will create fewer integration and technical issues.

Table 1. Comparative study of IoT and ML with traditional methods

Aspect	IoT and ML Integration	Traditional Methods	Comparative Benefits	Challenges
Accuracy of the Diagnosis	ML algorithms perform the analysis of continuous data for informed diagnostic precision.	It is based on physical examination and periodic tests.	More timely diagnosis, more accurate; personalized treatment.	Precise algorithms are needed. Over-reliability on technology could occur.
Detection at an Early Stage	Real-time monitoring, and predictive analytics for early disease detection.	Reactive treatment after symptoms appear.	Early intervention; prevention of disease progression.	False positives; ensuring timely response to alerts.
The Management of Chronic Diseases.	Predictive analytics: help predict potential complications.	Standardized operating procedures for chronic conditions.	Better management of chronic conditions since there will be less emergency intervention.	Integration of predictive model into existing workflow; patient adherence.

Conclusion

The integration of IoT and ML in the healthcare view presupposes a disruptive forward leap in terms of precision, efficiency, scope, and other parameters of patient care. Continuous collection of vast volumes of health data in real-time by IoT devices, which are then analyzed by advanced ML algorithms, reveals an unprecedented level of accuracy in critical patterns and forecasts of health outcomes. It is this synergy that enables more accurate diagnosis and personification of treatment plans, health monitoring, and improvement of patient outcomes alongside operational efficiency. While the benefits are huge, ranging from remote monitoring and chronic disease management to innovations in clinical decision support systems, there remain substantial challenges to be addressed. In these regards, issues related to data security, fault tolerance, latency, and interoperability need to be overcome if the full potential of these technologies is to be realized. More research and development must be taken to help overcome the obstacles and increase the reliability of IoT and ML applications in healthcare. Overcoming such challenges would be of great help to the healthcare sector in reaping benefits from these technological advancements, not only for providing more personalized health care to patients but also for making treatment more accessible, efficient, and effective to achieve better health outcomes and a higher quality of life for the patients across the globe.

References

[1] Kumari, Aparna, Sudeep Tanwar, Sudhanshu Tyagi, and Neeraj Kumar. "Fog Computing for Healthcare 4.0 Environment: Opportunities and Challenges." *Computers & Electrical Engineering* 72 (2018): 1-13. https://doi.org/10.1016/j.compeleceng.2018.01.010.

[2] Greco, Luca, Gennaro Percannella, Pierluigi Ritrovato, Francesco Tortorella, and Mario Vento. "Trends in IoT Based Solutions for Health Care: Moving AI to the Edge." *Pattern Recognition Letters* 135 (2020): 346-353. https://doi.org/10.1016/j.patrec.2020.05.026.

[3] Bharadwaj, Hemantha Krishna, Aayush Agarwal, Vinay Chamola, Naga Rajiv Lakkaniga, Vikas Hassija, Mohsen Guizani, and Biplab Sikdar. "A Review on the Role of Machine Learning in Enabling IoT-Based Healthcare Applications." *IEEE Access* 9 (2021): 38859-38890. https://doi.org/10.1109/ACCESS.2021.3067167.

[4] Sudarmani, Rajagopal, Kanagaraj Venusamy, Sathish Sivaraman, Poongodi Jayaraman, Kannadhasan Suriyan, and Manjunathan Alagarsamy. "Machine to

Machine Communication Enabled Internet of Things: A Review." *International Journal of Reconfigurable and Embedded Systems* 11, no. 2 (2022): 126. https://doi.org/10.11591/ijres.v11i2.8403.

[5] Kortuem, Gerd, Fahim Kawsar, Vasughi Sundramoorthy, and Daniel Fitton. "Smart Objects as Building Blocks for the Internet of Things." *IEEE Internet Computing* 14, no. 1 (2009): 44-51. https://doi.org/10.1109/MIC.2009.14.

[6] Römer, Kay, Benedikt Ostermaier, Friedemann Mattern, Michael Fahrmair, and Wolfgang Kellerer. "Real-Time Search for Real-World Entities: A Survey." *Proceedings of the IEEE* 98, no. 11 (2010): 1887-1902. https://doi.org/10.1109/JPROC.2010.2067251.

[7] Tan, Lu, and Neng Wang. "Future Internet: The Internet of Things." In *2010 3rd International Conference on Advanced Computer Theory and Engineering (ICACTE),* vol. 5, pp. V5-376. IEEE, 2010. https://doi.org/10.1109/ICACTE.2010.5537430.

[8] Pang, Zhibo. Technologies and Architectures of the Internet-of-Things (IoT) for Health and Well-being. PhD diss., KTH Royal Institute of Technology, 2013. doi is not available.

[9] Vasanth, Karthik, and Jonathan Sbert. "Creating Solutions for Health through Technology Innovation." *Texas Instruments,* December 2014.

[10] Islam, SM Riazul, Daehan Kwak, MD Humaun Kabir, Mahmud Hossain, and Kyung-Sup Kwak. *"The Internet of Things for Health Care: A Comprehensive Survey." IEEE Access* 3 (2015): 678-708. https://doi.org/10.1109/ACCESS.2015.2431401.

[11] Al-Shargabi, Bassam, and Simak Abuarqoub. "IoT-Enabled Healthcare: Benefits, Issues and Challenges." In *Proceedings of the 4th International Conference on Future Networks and Distributed Systems,* pp. 1-5. 2020.

[12] Park, J., JK Kim, S. Jung, Y. Gil, JI Choi, and HS Son. "ECG-Signal Multi-Classification Model Based on Squeeze-and-Excitation Residual Neural Networks." *Applied Sciences* 10 (2020): 6495. https://doi.org/10.3390/app10186495.

[13] Gao, Yue, Guang-Yao Cai, Wei Fang, Hua-Yi Li, Si-Yuan Wang, Lingxi Chen, Yang Yu, et al. "Machine Learning Based Early Warning System Enables Accurate Mortality Risk Prediction for COVID-19." *Nature Communications* 11, no. 1 (2020): 5033. https://doi.org/10.1038/s41467-020-18895-w.

[14] Corny, Jennifer, Asok Rajkumar, Olivier Martin, Xavier Dode, Jean-Patrick Lajonchère, Olivier Billuart, Yvonnick Bézie, and Anne Buronfosse. "A Machine Learning–Based Clinical Decision Support System to Identify Prescriptions with a High Risk of Medication Error." *Journal of the American Medical Informatics Association* 27, no. 11 (2020): 1688-1694. https://doi.org/10.1093/jamia/ocaa090.

[15] Segal, Gad, Amit Segev, Adi Brom, Yulia Lifshitz, Y. Wasserstrum, and Eyal Zimlichman. "Reducing Drug Prescription Errors and Adverse Drug Events by Application of a Probabilistic, Machine-Learning Based Clinical Decision Support System in an Inpatient Setting." *Journal of the American Medical Informatics Association* 26, no. 12 (2019): 1560-1565. https://doi.org/10.1093/jamia/ocz140.

[16] Onay, Aytun, and Melih Onay. "A Drug Decision Support System for Developing a Successful Drug Candidate Using Machine Learning Techniques." *Current*

Computer-Aided Drug Design 16, no. 4 (2020): 407-419. https://doi.org/10.2174/1389201021666201005107.

[17] Fernandez, Alberto De Ramon, Daniel Ruiz Fernández, and Maria Teresa Prieto Sanchez. "A Decision Support System for Predicting the Treatment of Ectopic Pregnancies." *International Journal of Medical Informatics* 129 (2019): 198-204. https://doi.org/10.1016/j.ijmedinf.2019.07.008.

[18] Farhadian, Maryam, Parisa Shokouhi, and Parviz Torkzaban. "A Decision Support System Based on Support Vector Machine for Diagnosis of Periodontal Disease." *BMC Research Notes* 13 (2020): 1-6. https://doi.org/10.1186/s13104-020-05015-4.

[19] Wang, Yidan, Xuanping Zhang, Tao Wang, Jinchun Xing, Zhun Wu, Wei Li, and Jiayin Wang. "A Machine Learning Framework for Accurately Recognizing Circular RNAs for Clinical Decision-Supporting." *BMC Medical Informatics and Decision Making* 20 (2020): 1-12. https://doi.org/10.1186/s12911-020-01196-3.

[20] Nemeth, Christopher, Adam Amos-Binks, Christie Burris, Natalie Keeney, Yuliya Pinevich, Brian W. Pickering, Gregory Rule, Dawn Laufersweiler, Vitaly Herasevich, and Mei G. Sun. "Decision Support for Tactical Combat Casualty Care Using Machine Learning to Detect Shock." *Military Medicine* 186, no. Supplement_1 (2021): 273-280. https://doi.org/10.1093/milmed/usaa410.

[21] Gulshan, Varun, Lily Peng, Marc Coram, Martin C. Stumpe, Derek Wu, Arunachalam Narayanaswamy, Subhashini Venugopalan, et al. "Development and Validation of a Deep Learning Algorithm for Detection of Diabetic Retinopathy in Retinal Fundus Photographs." *JAMA* 316, no. 22 (2016): 2402-2410. https://doi.org/10.1001/jama.2016.17216.

[22] Esteva, Andre, Brett Kuprel, Roberto A. Novoa, Justin Ko, Susan M. Swetter, Helen M. Blau, and Sebastian Thrun. "Dermatologist-Level Classification of Skin Cancer with Deep Neural Networks." *Nature* 542, no. 7639 (2017): 115-118. https://doi.org/10.1038/nature21056.

[23] Doupe, Patrick, James Faghmous, and Sanjay Basu. "Machine Learning for Health Services Researchers." *Value in Health* 22, no. 7 (2019): 808-815. https://doi.org/10.1016/j.jval.2019.04.1785.

[24] Truett, Jeanne, Jerome Cornfield, and William Kannel. "A Multivariate Analysis of the Risk of Coronary Heart Disease in Framingham." *Journal of Chronic Diseases* 20, no. 7 (1967): 511-524.

[25] Morgenstern, Jason Denzil, Emmalin Buajitti, Meghan O'Neill, Thomas Piggott, Vivek Goel, Daniel Fridman, Kathy Kornas, and Laura C. Rosella. "Predicting Population Health with Machine Learning: A Scoping Review." *BMJ Open* 10, no. 10 (2020): e037860. https://doi.org/10.1136/bmjopen-2020-037860.

[26] Fuller, Daniel, Richard Buote, and Kevin Stanley. "A Glossary for Big Data in Population and Public Health: Discussion and Commentary on Terminology and Research Methods." *Journal of Epidemiology & Community Health* 71, no. 11 (2017): 1113-1117. https://doi.org/10.1136/jech-2017-209808.

[27] Rai, M., Maity, T., Sharma, R. et al. Early detection of foot ulceration in type II diabetic patients using registration method in infrared images and descriptive comparison with deep learning methods. *J Supercomput* 78, 13409–13426 (2022). https://doi.org/10.1007/s11227-022-04380-z.

[28] Ogunyemi, Omolola, and Dulcie Kermah. "Machine Learning Approaches for Detecting Diabetic Retinopathy from Clinical and Public Health Records." In *AMIA Annual Symposium Proceedings,* vol. 2015, p. 983. American Medical Informatics Association, 2015.

[29] Alanazi, Abdullah. "Using Machine Learning for Healthcare Challenges and Opportunities." *Informatics in Medicine Unlocked* 30 (2022): 100924. https://doi.org/10.1016/j.imu.2022.100924.

[30] Tripathi, P., Kumar, N. Paroha, K. K. Rai, M. Panda, M. K. "Applications of Deep Learning in Healthcare in the Framework of Industry 5.0," *Infrastructure Possibilities and Human-Centered Approaches With Industry 5.0,* IGI Global, 2024, doi: 10.4018/979-8-3693-0782-3.ch005.

[31] Yan, Yan, Qi Li, Heping Li, Xuejun Zhang, and Lei Wang. "A Home-Based Health Information Acquisition System." *Health Information Science and Systems* 1 (2013): 1-10. https://doi.org/10.1186/2047-2501-1-3.

[32] Jagadeeswari, V., V. Subramaniyaswamy, Re T. al Logesh, and Varadarajan Vijayakumar. "A Study on Medical Internet of Things and Big Data in Personalized Healthcare System." *Health Information Science and Systems* 6, no. 1 (2018): 14. https://doi.org/10.1186/s13755-018-0223-3.

[33] Vijayakumar, K., Vinod J. Kadam, and Sudhir Kumar Sharma. "Breast Cancer Diagnosis Using Multiple Activation Deep Neural Network." *Concurrent Engineering* 29, no. 3 (2021): 275-284. https://doi.org/10.1177/1063293X 211025278.

[34] Gatouillat, Arthur, Youakim Badr, Bertrand Massot, and Ervin Sejdić. "Internet of Medical Things: A Review of Recent Contributions Dealing with Cyber-Physical Systems in Medicine." *IEEE Internet of Things Journal* 5, no. 5 (2018): 3810-3822. https://doi.org/10.1109/JIOT.2018.2831910.

[35] Hallfors, N. G., M. Alhawari, M. Abi Jaoude, Y. Kifle, H. Saleh, K. Liao, M. Ismail, and A. F. Isakovic. "Graphene Oxide: Nylon ECG Sensors for Wearable IoT Healthcare—Nanomaterial and SoC Interface." *Analog Integrated Circuits and Signal Processing* 96 (2018): 253-260. https://doi.org/10.1007/s10470-018-1226-2.

[36] Sahu, Manju Lata, Mithilesh Atulkar, Mitul Kumar Ahirwal, and Afsar Ahamad. "Vital Sign Monitoring System for Healthcare through IoT Based Personal Service Application." *Wireless Personal Communications* 122, no. 1 (2022): 129-156. https://doi.org/10.1007/s11277-021-08750-0.

[37] Tan, Lu, and Neng Wang. "Future Internet: The Internet of Things." In *2010 3rd International Conference on Advanced Computer Theory and Engineering (ICACTE),* vol. 5, pp. V5-376. IEEE, 2010. https://doi.org/10.1109/ICACTE.2010.5537430.

[38] Yang, Fangchun, Shangguang Wang, Jinglin Li, Zhihan Liu, and Qibo Sun. "An Overview of Internet of Vehicles." *China Communications* 11, no. 10 (2014): 1-15. https://doi.org/10.1109/CC.2014.7005144.

[39] Ding, Yangke, Mingzhou Jin, Sen Li, and Dingzhong Feng. "Smart Logistics Based on the Internet of Things Technology: An Overview." *International Journal of Logistics Research and Applications* 24, no. 4 (2021): 323-345. https://doi.org/10.1080/13675567.2020.1851681.

[40] Ramlowat, Dosheela Devi, and Binod Kumar Pattanayak. "Exploring the Internet of Things (IoT) in Education: A Review." In *Information Systems Design and Intelligent Applications: Proceedings of Fifth International Conference INDIA* 2018 Volume 2, pp. 245-255. Springer Singapore, 2019. doi is not available.

[41] Verdouw, Cor, Sjaak Wolfert, and Bedir Tekinerdogan. "Internet of Things in Agriculture." *CABI Reviews* 11, no. 044 (2016): 1-12. https://doi.org/10.1079/CABICOMM-2016-0376.

[42] De Michele, Roberta, and Marco Furini. "IoT Healthcare: Benefits, Issues and Challenges." In *Proceedings of the 5th EAI International Conference on Smart Objects and Technologies for Social Good*, pp. 160-164. 2019.

[43] Neto, Euclides Carlos Pinto, Sajjad Dadkhah, Raphael Ferreira, Alireza Zohourian, Rongxing Lu, and Ali A. Ghorbani. "CICIoT2023: A Real-Time Dataset and Benchmark for Large-Scale Attacks in IoT Environment." *Sensors* 23, no. 13 (2023): 5941. https://doi.org/10.3390/s23135941.

[44] Kaur, Barjinder, Sajjad Dadkhah, Farzaneh Shoeleh, Euclides Carlos Pinto Neto, Pulei Xiong, Shahrear Iqbal, Philippe Lamontagne, Suprio Ray, and Ali A. Ghorbani. "Internet of Things (IoT) Security Dataset Evolution: Challenges and Future Directions." *Internet of Things* 22 (2023): 100780. https://doi.org/10.1016/j.iot.2023.100780.

[45] Dadkhah, Sajjad, Hassan Mahdikhani, Priscilla Kyei Danso, Alireza Zohourian, Kevin Anh Truong, and Ali A. Ghorbani. "Towards the Development of a Realistic Multidimensional IoT Profiling Dataset." In *2022 19th Annual International Conference on Privacy, Security & Trust (PST),* pp. 1-11. IEEE, 2022. https://doi.org/10.1109/PST53943.2022.00007.

[46] Hussain, Faisal, Syed Ghazanfar Abbas, Ghalib A. Shah, Ivan Miguel Pires, Ubaid U. Fayyaz, Farrukh Shahzad, Nuno M. Garcia, and Eftim Zdravevski. "A Framework for Malicious Traffic Detection in IoT Healthcare Environment." *Sensors* 21, no. 9 (2021): 3025. https://doi.org/10.3390/s21093025.

[47] Hady, Anar A., Ali Ghubaish, Tara Salman, Devrim Unal, and Raj Jain. "Intrusion Detection System for Healthcare Systems Using Medical and Network Data: A Comparison Study." *IEEE Access* 8 (2020): 106576-106584. https://doi.org/10.1109/ACCESS.2020.3003732.

[48] Zubair, Mohammed, Ali Ghubaish, Devrim Unal, Abdulla Al-Ali, Thomas Reimann, Guillaume Alinier, Mohammad Hammoudeh, and Junaid Qadir. "Secure Bluetooth Communication in Smart Healthcare Systems: A Novel Community Dataset and Intrusion Detection System." *Sensors* 22, no. 21 (2022): 8280. https://doi.org/10.3390/s22228280.

[49] Azzawi, Mustafa Abdullah, Rosilah Hassan, and Khairul Azmi Abu Bakar. "A Review on Internet of Things (IoT) in Healthcare." *International Journal of Applied Engineering Research* 11, no. 20 (2016): 10216-10221.

[50] Krishnamoorthy, Sreelakshmi, Amit Dua, and Shashank Gupta. "Role of Emerging Technologies in Future IoT-Driven Healthcare 4.0 Technologies: A Survey, Current Challenges and Future Directions." *Journal of Ambient Intelligence and Humanized Computing* 14, no. 1 (2023): 361-407. https://doi.org/10.1007/s12652-022-04010-2.

[51] Islam, SM Riazul, Daehan Kwak, MD Humaun Kabir, Mahmud Hossain, and Kyung-Sup Kwak. "The Internet of Things for Health Care: A Comprehensive Survey." *IEEE Access* 3 (2015): 678-708. https://doi.org/10.1109/ACCESS.2015.2436791.

[52] Gia, Tuan Nguyen, Amir-Mohammad Rahmani, Tomi Westerlund, Pasi Liljeberg, and Hannu Tenhunen. "Fault Tolerant and Scalable IoT-Based Architecture for Health Monitoring." In *2015 IEEE Sensors Applications Symposium* (SAS), pp. 1-6. IEEE, 2015.

[53] Muhammed, Thaha, Rashid Mehmood, Aiiad Albeshri, and Iyad Katib. "UbeHealth: A Personalized Ubiquitous Cloud and Edge-Enabled Networked Healthcare System for Smart Cities." *IEEE Access* 6 (2018): 32258-32285. https://doi.org/10.1109/ACCESS.2018.2836831.

[54] Farahani, Bahar, Farshad Firouzi, Victor Chang, Mustafa Badaroglu, Nicholas Constant, and Kunal Mankodiya. "Towards Fog-Driven IoT eHealth: Promises and Challenges of IoT in Medicine and Healthcare." *Future Generation Computer Systems* 78 (2018): 659-676. https://doi.org/10.1016/j.future.2017.04.006.

[55] Wu, Taiyang, Fan Wu, Jean-Michel Redoute, and Mehmet Rasit Yuce. "An Autonomous Wireless Body Area Network Implementation Towards IoT Connected Healthcare Applications." *IEEE Access* 5 (2017): 11413-11422. https://doi.org/10.1109/ACCESS.2017.2717556.

[56] Sethi, Pallavi, and Smruti R. Sarangi. "Internet of Things: Architectures, Protocols, and Applications." *Journal of Electrical and Computer Engineering* 2017 (2017): 9324035. https://doi.org/10.1155/2017/9324035.

[57] Jabbar, Sohail, Farhan Ullah, Shehzad Khalid, Murad Khan, and Kijun Han. "Semantic Interoperability in Heterogeneous IoT Infrastructure for Healthcare." *Wireless Communications and Mobile Computing* 2017 (2017): 9731806. https://doi.org/10.1155/2017/9731806.

[58] Fotouhi, Hossein, Aida Causevic, Kristina Lundqvist, and Mats Björkman. "Communication and Security in Health Monitoring Systems—A Review." In *2016 IEEE 40th Annual Computer Software and Applications Conference (COMPSAC),* vol. 1, pp. 545-554. IEEE, 2016. https://doi.org/10.1109/COMPSAC.2016.133.

[59] Belesioti, Maria, Ioannis P. Chochliouros, Stefan Vanya, Viktor Oravec, Natalia Theologou, Maria Koutli, Athanasios Tryferidis, and Dimitrios Tzovaras. "E-Health Services in the Context of IoT: The Case of the Vicinity Project." In *Artificial Intelligence Applications and Innovations: AIAI 2018 IFIP WG 12.5 International Workshops,* SEDSEAL, 5G-PINE, MHDW, and HEALTHIOT, Rhodes, Greece, May 25-27, 2018, *Proceedings 14, edited by Panayiotis Bozanis and Evangelos Kotsovinos,* 62-69. Springer International Publishing, 2018.

[60] Suryateja, P. S. "Threats and Vulnerabilities of Cloud Computing: A Review." *International Journal of Computer Sciences and Engineering* 6, no. 3 (2018): 297-302. https://doi.org/10.26438/ijcse/v6i3.297302.

[61] Naresh, Vankamamidi S., Suryateja S. Pericherla, Pilla Sita Rama Murty, and Sivaranjani Reddi. "Internet of Things in Healthcare: Architecture, Applications, Challenges, and Solutions." *Computer Systems Science & Engineering* 35, no. 6 (2020).

[62] International Human Genome Sequencing Consortium. "Finishing the Euchromatic Sequence of the Human Genome." *Nature* 431, no. 7011 (2004): 931-945. https://doi.org/10.1038/nature03001.

[63] Willyard, Cassandra. "Expanded Human Gene Tally Reignites Debate." *Nature* 558, no. 7710 (2018): 354-355. https://doi.org/10.1038/d41586-018-05453-3.

[64] Ezkurdia, Iakes, David Juan, Jose Manuel Rodriguez, Adam Frankish, Mark Diekhans, Jennifer Harrow, Jesus Vazquez, Alfonso Valencia, and Michael L. Tress. "Multiple Evidence Strands Suggest That There May Be as Few as 19,000 Human Protein-Coding Genes." *Human Molecular Genetics* 23, no. 22 (2014): 5866-5878. https://doi.org/10.1093/hmg/ddu309.

[65] Galvan, Antonella, John PA Ioannidis, and Tommaso A. Dragani. "Beyond Genome-Wide Association Studies: Genetic Heterogeneity and Individual Predisposition to Cancer." *Trends in Genetics* 26, no. 3 (2010): 132-141. https://doi.org/10.1016/j.tig.2009.12.002.

[66] Zack, Travis I., Steven E. Schumacher, Scott L. Carter, Andrew D. Cherniack, Gordon Saksena, Barbara Tabak, Michael S. Lawrence, et al. "Pan-Cancer Patterns of Somatic Copy Number Alteration." *Nature Genetics* 45, no. 10 (2013): 1134-1140. https://doi.org/10.1038/ng.2760.

[67] Lello, Laura, Raben, Tom, Yong, Soo-Yong, Tellier, Laurent C., and Hsu, Shuh-Der Hsu. "Genomic Prediction of Complex Disease Risk." *bioRxiv* (2018). https://doi.org/10.1101/506600.

[68] Toh, Christopher, and James P. Brody. "Applications of Machine Learning in Healthcare." In *Smart Manufacturing: When Artificial Intelligence Meets the Internet of Things* 65 (2021).

Chapter 7

Smart Hospitals and Smarter Healthcare

Manali Gupta[1,*]
Sonia Arora[2,†]
Ravindra Kumar Yadav[3,‡]
Padmesh Tripathi[4,§]
and Reeta Mishra[5,¶]

[1,2]Department of Computer Science and Engineering, Noida Institute of Engineering & Technology, Gr. Noida, U.P., India
[3]Department of ECE, RKGIT, Ghaziabad, U.P., India
[4]Delhi Technical Campus, Greater Noida, U.P., India
[5]School of Computer Science and Engineering, IILM University, Greater Noida, U.P., India

Abstract

Smart hospitals and smarter healthcare are fundamentally transforming medical care by integrating advanced technologies such as data analytics, Internet of Things (IoT) devices, and artificial intelligence (AI), all of which contribute to improved care, streamlined operations, and better overall results. Data analytics is important because it allows healthcare practitioners to derive meaningful insights from large amounts of patient data. Healthcare practitioners may anticipate patient requests and identify potential health dangers with AI-driven predictive analytics, which results in individualized care plans and preventative actions that improve

* Corresponding Author's Email: manaliguptasingh5@gmail.com
† Corresponding Author's Email: soniasitm@gmail.com
‡ Corresponding Author's Email: ravipusad@gmail.com
§ Corresponding Author's Email: padmesh01@redifmail.com
¶ Corresponding Author's Email: ree76shok@gmail.com

In: Harnessing the Power of IoT-Enabled Machine Learning …
Editors: Mritunjay Rai, Ravindra Kumar Yadav, Neha Goel et al.
ISBN: 979-8-89530-626-0

patient outcomes and optimize treatment procedures. Wearable sensors and connected medical devices continuously collect and transmit vital health data, speeding up this change, all thanks to the Internet of Things. This real-time data allows for remote patient monitoring, early detection of abnormalities, and rapid treatment plan revisions, all of which improve care delivery efficiency. Additionally, IoT devices help to improve operational efficiency by automating operations like inventory management and asset tracking. Artificial intelligence transforms healthcare by using machine learning algorithms for predictive analysis, personalized therapy recommendations, and improved diagnostic accuracy. Robotics, another branch of AI, automates regular operations such as surgery and drug delivery, lowering human errors and boosting precision. This combination of AI and robots increases hospital efficiency, reduces the strain on healthcare staff, and improves patient outcomes. Despite these achievements, significant difficulties remain. Ensuring the quality of data acquired by IoT devices and evaluated by AI systems is critical since incorrect data can lead to misdiagnoses or unsuitable treatment plans, weakening the benefits of smart technology. Addressing privacy issues is particularly critical, given the widespread collecting and sharing of health data. We must use strong security measures like encryption and secure authentication methods to safeguard patient information from unauthorized access and comply with data protection rules. Furthermore, given the large initial expenditure, the cost-effectiveness of integrating these sophisticated technologies presents a significant barrier. Hospitals must carefully analyze the cost-benefit ratio of implementing new technology and find methods to balance innovation with budget limits while also accounting for continuing maintenance and updates. Despite these limitations, the potential benefits of smart hospitals are significant. Innovations that solve these concerns are highly desirable because they open the path for a more efficient, personalized, and accessible healthcare system. So far, results show that smart hospitals can save operating costs, enhance patient outcomes, and raise the level of healthcare delivery. As smart healthcare gains momentum, we anticipate a shift in patient management and medical research towards more intelligent, data-driven healthcare solutions, thereby revolutionizing the delivery and reception of care.

Keywords: IoT, AI, ML, healthcare

1. Overview

Sophisticated technology propels the transformative advancement in medical treatment through smart hospitals and smarter healthcare. Smart hospitals include “IoT devices,” “AI," and data analytics to optimize patient monitoring, expedite operations, and boost results by using real-time data and automation. Smarter Healthcare extends this innovation to a wider scope, using telemedicine, electronic health records, and mobile health applications to enhance the accessibility, customization, and efficiency of treatment. Collectively, these innovations strive to establish a healthcare system that is more prompt and efficient, revolutionizing how people obtain and oversee their medical treatment. Informatization is the process that defines the modern era. Driven by scientific theory and technological breakthroughs, biotechnology is at the core of a process that is digitizing and informationizing traditional medical practices. Advances in information technology have brought about a new era in healthcare. Smart healthcare is a multifaceted revolution including extensive multilevel modifications in addition to technological breakthroughs. Information systems have transitioned from clinical to regional medical contexts, mirroring the shift in the medical paradigm from illnesses to people. Medical management has also changed from general to individualized, and prevention and treatment have moved from disease-centered to preventive healthcare. These are just a few of the major changes that have occurred as a result of this transformation [1].

1.1. Smart Hospitals

By 2023, advanced healthcare facilities in North America, East Asia, Europe, Australia, and the Middle East have successfully implemented smart technology integration inside hospital settings. In contrast, the progress of smart hospital initiatives is still in its early stages in many other parts of the world, with just a few pilot projects implemented thus far [2]. As evidence of their dedication to the broad usage of smart hospitals, the "United States, United Kingdom, China, Japan, Germany, and South Korea" have all prioritized integrating smart technology into their healthcare agenda as a priority. The Smart Hospitals Industry Analysis (2023) predicts that the global smart hospital industry will expand at a compound annual growth rate (CAGR) of 20.7%, reaching a total market value of USD 153.3 billion by

2030, a significant increase from USD 41 billion in 2023. In this business, the region with the quickest rate of growth is East Asia/Oceania. Figure 1 [3] illustrates the IoT e-health architecture by dispersing sensors throughout the environment, such as medical equipment and room sensors, and transmitting data to the IoT gateway. This, on the one hand, provides the medical supervisor with the ability to exercise control over the patient's health. On the other hand, databases will store this information for later analysis. By enhancing clinical operations, management systems, and infrastructure with the use of information and communication technology, a smart hospital may improve the quality of therapy, cost-effectiveness, and patient-centeredness [4, 5]. In the ever-changing field of healthcare, institutions can use big data, automation, and the IoT due to improvements in technology, expanding treatment methods, and changing patient expectations. This empowerment promotes the standards of patient care, increases the productivity of healthcare staff, and improves the overall efficiency of the institution [6]. A "smart hospital" encourages smart technology-based operational analysis rather than stringent requirements. A complete management system simplifies quality analysis, resource allocation, and performance assessment, lowering medical costs and enabling informed hospital expansion decisions [7]. By prioritizing open architectural interoperability, facility managers can use new technologies to address current and future concerns. Smart hospitals aim to create intelligent linkages among humans, data, and technology to meet individual requirements, increase healthcare efficiency, and enhance the overall medical service experience. These endeavors embody the future trajectory of modern medicine, rooted in a culture of ongoing innovation and progress.

An illustration of the architecture of future smart hospitals that are based on 5G can be seen in Figure 2. Microcells are shortened energy broadcasting access hubs that have a focal point that is not more than a few meters wide and a mile in distance. Several different forms of small cells are capable of performing a fundamental function in a variety of applications of 5G intelligent human services [8]. As a result of the high information rates that are necessary for applications that provide medicinal services, such as mobile medical procedures, the required data speed ranges from 112 Mbps to 1.8 Gbps. Microstations may be broken down into three categories: femto, pico, and microcells. These microstations range in size from the smallest to the largest.

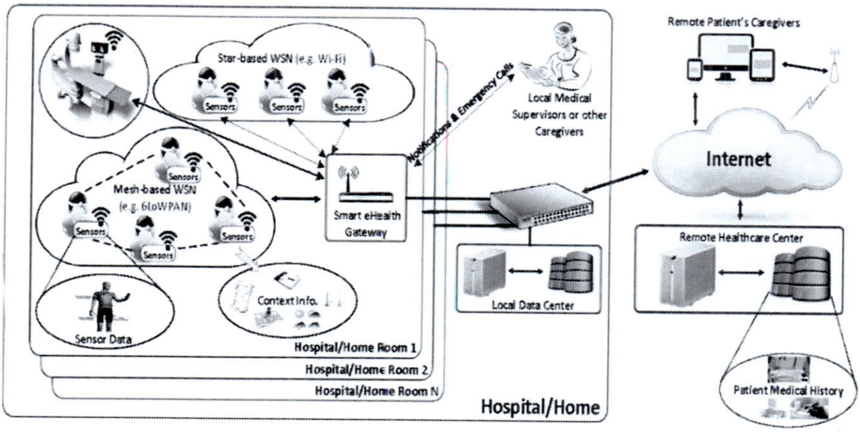

Figure 1. Smart hospital assets.

1.2. Key Technologies Empowering Smart Hospitals

Hospital administrators need to precisely identify the technology that their facilities should incorporate. Intelligent healthcare can effectively decrease the costs and possible hazards of medical operations by using advanced technology. It improves the effectiveness of using medical resources, encourages cooperation across different areas, and drives the progress of telemedicine and self-service healthcare, finally making tailored medical services generally available [9].

1.2.1. Artificial Intelligence and Machine Learning

As part of the process of clinical decision-making, artificial intelligence is used for the aim of analyzing patient data, producing predictions, and providing assistance. Machine learning, on the other hand, has the potential to contribute to the improvement of diagnostic accuracy. In addition to this, it simplifies the process of tailored treatment.

1.2.2. Robotics Process Automation

Robotic Process Automation has the potential to automate boring operations such as planning appointments and processing billing, enabling healthcare workers to dedicate a larger part of their time to providing care for patients.

1.2.3. Virtual Reality

The use of "Virtual Reality (VR)" and "Augmented Reality (AR)" simulations allows medical professionals to get training on various medical procedures and to practice such treatments.

1.2.4. Electronic Health Records (EHR)

The electronic health record (EHR) makes it possible for healthcare practitioners to easily store and share patient information with one another, which increases the efficiency of treatment coordination.

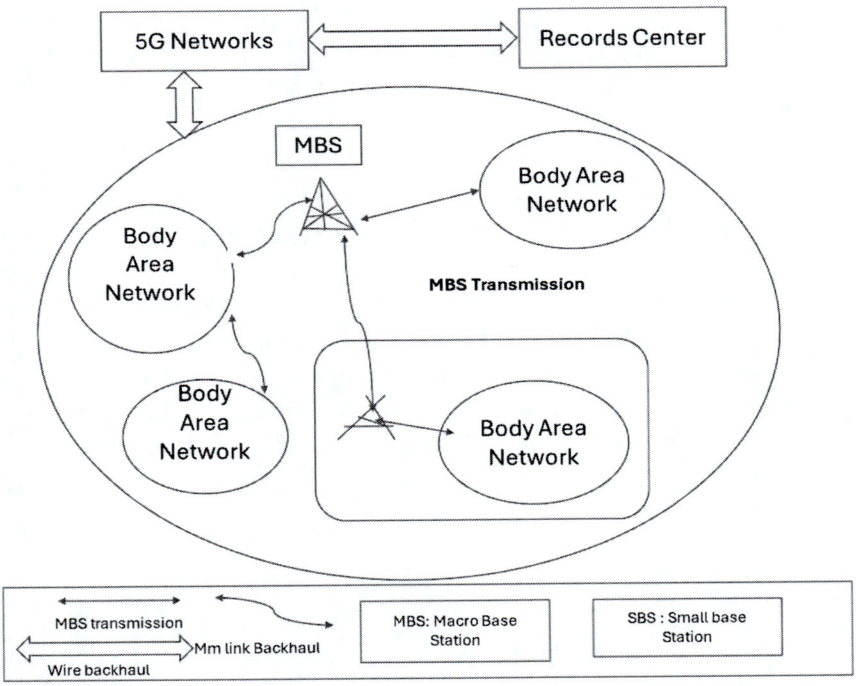

Figure 2. Architecture 5G based smart hospital.

1.2.5. Internet of Things

IoT devices, which include sensors, wearables, and smart medical equipment, have the potential to retrieve and transmit real-time data on the health and general well-being of patients, therefore allowing proactive care activities.

1.2.6. Telemedicine

The use of telecommunication technology in telemedicine allows for immediate or delayed contact to be established between patients and healthcare practitioners, as well as between healthcare professionals themselves. By collecting data from medical devices or mobile devices, remote health data collection allows for the monitoring of patients, the tracking of their behavior, and the implementation of any necessary adjustments to their healthcare [10].

1.3. Challenges of Smart Hospital

The following are the key challenges that must be overcome throughout the shift to smart hospitals:

1.3.1. Patient Monitoring

It might be challenging to maintain continuous monitoring, provide excellent treatment, ensure patient safety, comply with regulatory requirements, reduce staffing levels, and please customers. Medical professionals are tasked with monitoring patients' health and providing alarms, which necessitates prompt decision-making and answers. The dearth of adequate Internet of Things (IoT) and other technological options for patient monitoring is an additional issue.

1.3.4. Data Accuracy

If it is provided with inaccurate information, a machine learning system will learn improper patterns and may generate incorrect insights, which may result in poor medical treatment. For this reason, the Electronic Health Record (EHR) system must only accept data that is correct. In a perfect world, Internet of Things sensors should be able to transfer data without any problems. Error risk, on the other hand, is increased by human input. De-noising of data is one of the vital steps in the accuracy of data [11, 12, 13].

1.3.5. Security and Privacy

It is a challenge to guarantee the availability, integrity, and security of data collected in the healthcare industry. Patients legitimately worry about the storage of their health information on untrustworthy hospital servers. The concern stems from the potential for misuse or editing of the information [14]. In real cases, a breach or exposure of healthcare information's confidentiality can lead to substantial repercussions. The findings of Accenture's Cost of Cyber Crime Study 2017 reveal that cybercrime activity costs the healthcare industry $12.47 million annually [15]. Data related to healthcare on the cloud raises concerns regarding compliance and security considerations. According to a study conducted by Symantec Corporation in 2018, cloud databases that were not adequately protected continued to be an issue for certain businesses [16].

1.3.6. Cost-Effectiveness

People have a big challenge in the form of rising costs associated with healthcare. There is a correlation between the requirements for performance and compliance and the expenditures incurred by the hospital. Concerning the user's ease of use, there is a compromise that exists between the financial cost and the convenience of use [17]. Through the reduction of start-up expenses, cloud computing makes electronic health records more affordable. Electronic health records have been shunned by several institutions owing to concerns over privacy and security. For an electronic health record to be intelligent, a hospital has to have one.

1.3.7. Intelligent Data Processing and Data Validation

The variety of technologies and pieces of equipment contributes to growth in the heterogeneity and diversity of healthcare data. The presence of personal lifestyle data and other health data makes verification and the extraction of insights more challenging. Only sophisticated algorithms can accomplish this. 3.6. Comparability and conformity to standards. Hospitals often equip surgical operating rooms (ORs) with a variety of apparatus and supporting systems, including data presentation interfaces [18]. The smart hospital anticipates that all screens will be ready to present pertinent information as soon as the physician enters the operating room. This information can include patient data, diagnostic imaging, and pre-operative planning. It is recommended that the physician's choice of screens should display this information [19]. Intelligent hospitals must include all information systems and applications to present patient data. Another problem is interoperability, which refers to the ability to receive and modify data from a variety of Internet of Things sensors [20].

1.4. Potential Benefits of Smart Hospitals

The smart hospital market value was $13.52 billion in 2016. From 2017 to 2023, we anticipate a 24.00% expansion, bringing the market value to $63.49 billion. The market segmentation includes wireless connectivity, application types, service supply, service component, technology type, and geographic location. To be "smart," hospitals need sophisticated hardware, software, and technology. Intelligent technology systems encompass patient, staff, and equipment systems, as well as smart mobility systems. Blockchain, biotelemetry, pharmaceutical discovery, precision medicine based on genomes and big data, and virtual orthopedic rehabilitation are likely to drive smart hospitals [21]. Smart hardware includes active RFID, WiFi, wearables, IoT sensors, dashboards, and more. The market for smart hospitals is driven by factors such as modernizing healthcare infrastructure, demand for efficient solutions in hospitals, the advancements in IoT technologies in healthcare, the rising prevalence of chronic diseases, and the use of connected devices and instruments in hospitals. Smart hospitals can benefit from the "Internet of Health Things (IoHT), which includes intelligent devices, equipment, appliances, software, and structures. Optimizing asset usage might boost healthcare efficiency and cost. The inclusion of blockchain technologies can also improve healthcare IT. Blockchains improve smart hospitals' distributed ledger technology, security, immutability, and interoperability. Blockchains provide secure, efficient, and simplified transactions among patients, hospitals, insurance agencies, and other parties. Smart hospitals will become like intelligent machines as they gain operational intelligence in quantity and quality [22]. Intelligent machines will leverage AI, advanced analytics, and ML to get operational insights. Intelligent hospitals must constantly learn, improve, and behave appropriately [23].

2. Smart Healthcare

All significant facets of modern life employ intelligent technologies. These technologies have also improved medicine. Technologies like "IoT," "big data analysis," "cloud computing," and "AI" accelerate the development of intelligent healthcare systems [24]. As new technology replaces old, healthcare systems become more sophisticated, convenient, and customized. Smart "Healthcare (HLC)" systems need technological improvement at all levels of traditional HLC systems and intelligent medical systems. It changes treatment and administration and helps patients live well. These HLC system changes seek to improve patient and doctor experiences and meet their demands. The intelligent medical system manages emergencies and aids decision-making using AI, ML, and DL [25, 26]. The clever HLC technology has reached remote areas that lack healthcare facilities. The system monitors and manages the patient via smart gadgets. This strategy streamlines and lowers medical costs. It helps everyone stay healthy, from children to the elderly. We use cloud units to store the measured and analyzed patient health state data. Medical professionals retrieve and analyze this data later. As a means of facilitating comprehension, Figure 3 provides a graphic representation of the fundamental network architecture of intelligent healthcare systems [27].

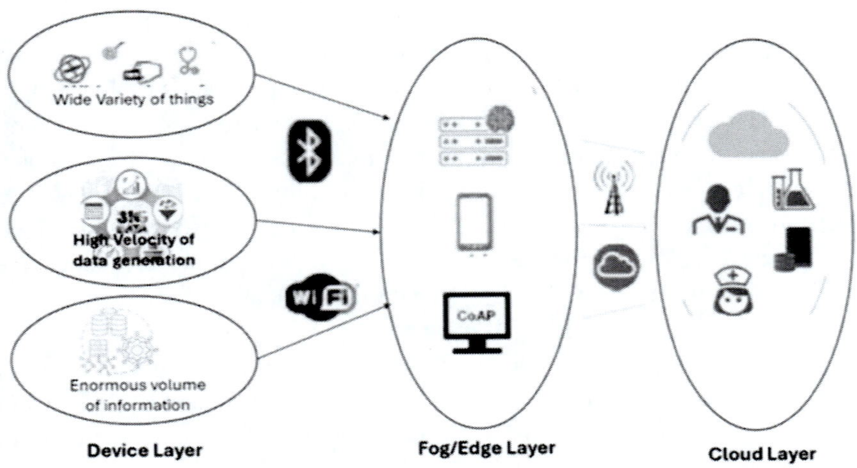

Figure 3. A basic smart healthcare network architecture.

The smart healthcare system uses AI and signal processing to diagnose and cure cancer, epilepsy, autism, schizophrenia, and other diseases [28, 29, 30, 31]. It also provides an alternative for paralyzed or accident victims. Biomedical technology research is ongoing to improve the medical system. Biomedical chips and wearable gadgets can monitor our health and save data for future examination thanks to technology. Innovations deepen our knowledge of the body [32]. Smart healthcare and intelligent medical systems improve service quality using AI, ML, big data, and the IoT. Intelligent healthcare and technology help customers understand their medical state and provide suggestions to improve their health. Smart healthcare lets individuals tackle emergencies alone. It improves patient care, convenience, and cost. Smart healthcare uses the latest technologies to maximize resource utilization. Intelligent medical solutions enable doctors to remotely monitor and treat patients, circumventing geographical limitations. Smart healthcare and intelligent medical systems improve service quality using AI, ML, big data, and the IoT. Intelligent healthcare and technology help customers understand their medical state and provide suggestions to improve their health. Smart healthcare lets individuals tackle emergencies alone. It improves patient care, convenience, and cost. Smart healthcare uses the latest technologies to maximize resource utilization. Geographic constraints no longer prevent doctors from remotely monitoring and treating patients thanks to intelligent medical solutions [33].

2.1. Key Technologies of Smart Healthcare

Physicians, patients, medical institutions, and research organizations are involved in smart healthcare. Monitoring and illness prevention, treatment and diagnosis, health decision-making, hospital management, and medical research are all part of the system. Smart healthcare as shown in Figure 4 relies on information technologies including "mobile Internet," "IoT," "big data," "cloud computing," "microelectronics," "5G," "AI," and "biotechnology." Every aspect of intelligent healthcare uses these technologies [34]. Wearable gadgets can monitor health, virtual assistants can provide medical help, and remote houses can provide services.

However, clinicians can use sophisticated clinical decision-support technologies to improve diagnosis. A complete information platform, including "Picture Archiving and Communication Systems (PACS)," "Laboratory Information Management Systems," "Electronic Medical Records" and other technologies, lets physicians manage medical data.

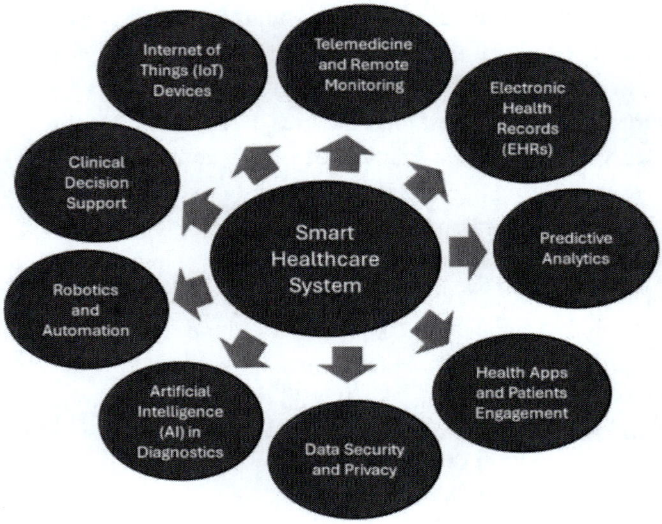

Figure 4. Advanced technologies as integral parts of smart healthcare system.

Surgical robots and mixed reality can improve surgical accuracy. To streamline staff and supply chain management, hospitals can use "radio-frequency identification (RFID)" technology. Integrating management systems that collect data and enhance decision-making can do this. Patient experiences can improve using mobile medical systems. ML algorithms and big data might replace manual drug screening in scientific research facilities [35]. Smart healthcare technology can reduce medical costs and risks, improve resource efficiency, foster regional cooperation and knowledge sharing, advance telemedicine and self-service medical care, and provide tailored medical services to everyone [36].

2.2. Application Status of Smart Healthcare

There are three primary categories of consumers that smart healthcare intends to serve: organizations that are involved in clinical or scientific research (like hospitals), entities that are responsible for making choices about regional health, and people or families that use the service. The application of smart healthcare is shown in Figure 5. The implementation of intelligent healthcare can be divided into the following categories, according to the many needs that are associated with it:

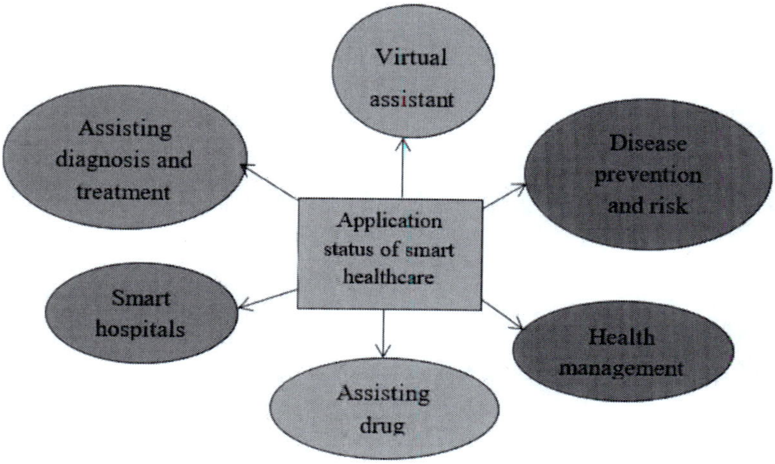

Figure 5. Shows the application of smart healthcare.

2.3. Assisting Diagnosis and Treatment

Artificial intelligence, mixed reality, and robotic surgical equipment have enhanced the detection and treatment of diseases. To diagnose hepatitis, lung cancer, and skin cancer, clinical decision support systems make use of artificial intelligence. In terms of medical diagnosis, artificial intelligence is beating out doctors [37, 38, 39]. ML-based pathology and imaging technologies routinely outperform expert clinicians [40]. IBM Watson is the epitome of clinical decision support systems. This clever cognitive system analyzes clinical and literary data to provide the best remedy [41]. The program has a substantial influence on the diagnosis of cancer and diabetes [42]. Physicians can apply algorithms via the clinical decision support system, which enables them to increase the accuracy of diagnosis, minimize the number of missed diagnoses, and assist patients in receiving timely and appropriate medical treatment.

3. Health Management

Since the 21st century, chronic diseases have outnumbered other diseases and become a pandemic. Chronic diseases last long and are costly. Effective illness management is crucial. Nevertheless, it appears that the current paradigm of health management, which focuses around hospitals and physicians, is inadequate in efficiently handling the expanding number of patients and diseases [43]. Smart healthcare stresses patient self-management. Continuous patient monitoring, quick health data feedback, and medical conduct intervention are system priorities. IoT-connected implantable/wearable smart devices, smart homes, and health information platforms solve the problem. Three-generation wearable/implantable devices automatically monitor patient physiological indications using sophisticated sensors, microprocessors, and wireless modules. These gadgets save energy, improve comfort, and integrate health data. This strategy involves moving from scenario monitoring to continuous perception and thorough therapy. It reduces illness risk and helps doctors track prognoses [44, 45]. Smartphones, watches, and other technologies enable this kind of monitoring. Cellphone biosensors are being developed. Using a high-performance smartphone to monitor their environment and health becomes easier when they are on the move.

3.1. Disease Prevention and Risk Monitoring

In traditional illness risk prediction, health authorities gather patient data, compare it to organization guidelines, and report the findings. The directions are unclear and sluggish. Customized sickness risk prediction is a feature of smart healthcare. It lets patients and doctors actively connect, evaluate illness risk, and take preventative measures based on outcomes. Big data algorithms analyze data from wearable devices and intelligent applications sent to the cloud across a network by the revolutionary illness risk prediction system. Clear communication works. Empirical data supports these measures [46]. It aids doctors and patients in making immediate medical lifestyle changes. It also helps decision-makers create regional health strategies to lower illness risk. Researchers analyzed the blood glucose levels of 800 individuals across 46,898 meals per week, aiming to prevent diabetes by predicting the reaction after eating. The researchers used algorithms that included blood glucose, diet, body measures, physical activity, intestinal flora, and other factors. This allowed them to precisely anticipate glycemic response and reduce diabetes risk by customizing diets [47].

3.2. Virtual Assistants

Virtual assistants are computational methods, not people. Virtual assistants employ speech recognition algorithms to communicate with consumers, receive data from several sources, and respond to user preferences. Virtual assistants include Cortana, Google Assistant, and Siri. Siri is in Cupertino, CA; Cortana is in Redmond, WA; and Google Assistant is in Mountain View, CA. Virtual assistants let consumers set reminders and automate household operations using session experience and language-understanding technologies [48]. Physicians, patients, and medical organizations use smart healthcare virtual assistants to communicate. It improves medical convenience. The virtual assistant can use the smart gadget to convert patients' everyday English into medical phrases, helping them find the right medical services.

3.3. Smart Hospitals

The components of regional, hospital, and family healthcare are necessary for intelligent healthcare. In addition to enhancing patient care, automated operations and optimization of the IoT offer smart hospitals additional features [49]. Smart hospitals serve health care providers, patients, and administrative personnel. The management of the hospital must take into account the requirements of the patients. The Internet of Things-based information platform connects digital devices, intelligent buildings, and hospital administration employees. This technology also enables the tracking of medical equipment, biological material, and hospital patients. Intelligent healthcare assists in simplifying pharmaceutical manufacture, distribution, inventory management, anti-counterfeiting, and other responsibilities.

3.4. Assisting Drug Research

Big data and AI will improve pharmaceutical research and development accuracy and ease. Drug development includes "target screening," "drug discovery," "clinical trials," and other steps. The conventional method of drug target screening manually analyzes known medicines and their interactions with human target molecules to identify successful areas of action. Many individuals opt to ignore this slow and laborious procedure. The use of artificial intelligence to do automated evaluations of pharmaceutical effects and targets has significantly enhanced screening approaches. A genomics study on malignancies used the Watson technique to identify ribonucleic acid-binding proteins in amyotrophic lateral sclerosis [50]. The artificial intelligence system is also capable of receiving real-time information from other sources and modifying the screening process to meet those criteria. Using high-throughput screening, it is possible to automate the process of generating and evaluating a large number of compounds for the goal of product development in the pharmaceutical industry. However, as the number of compounds increases, so do the costs and risks. Using artificial intelligence to conduct virtual drug testing could potentially solve this issue. The use of computers for pre-screening could potentially help reduce the total number of chemicals examined. Moreover, computers can enhance the process of assembling compounds, identify lead compounds, and predict therapeutic molecular activity [51, 52].

4. Contribution of the Chapter

The study on smart hospitals and smarter healthcare underscores the importance of incorporating new technologies like data analytics, IoT devices, and AI into existing medical treatments. Smart hospitals may use data analytics to extract meaningful insights from massive datasets, resulting in improved prediction skills and individualized treatment plans that improve patient outcomes and operational efficiency. Predictive analytics may assist in detecting possible health hazards and anticipating patient requirements, allowing for more prompt treatments. IoT technologies, such as wearable sensors and linked medical equipment, offer continuous real-time monitoring of patients' vital signs, allowing for remote health management while also aiding in the early discovery of abnormalities and, hence, averting problems. Furthermore, AI-powered technologies such as machine learning algorithms and robots automate routine chores, improve diagnostic accuracy, and optimize treatment methods, decreasing the stress on healthcare staff while boosting care delivery precision. The integration of these technologies adds to considerable operational cost savings, improves patient safety, and raises the overall level of healthcare. Furthermore, the research emphasizes the potential for these breakthroughs to solve long-standing difficulties in healthcare, such as enhancing data accuracy, protecting patient privacy, and balancing cost-effectiveness. By moving toward more intelligent, data-driven healthcare solutions, the study highlights smart hospitals' power to transform patient management and medical practice, eventually leading to improved health outcomes and a more efficient healthcare system.

Conclusion

Smart Hospitals and Smarter Healthcare: Deep Transformational Integration in the Medical Field with Leading-Edge Technologies. The use of leading-edge technologies such as IoT, AI, and big data will help improve health, streamline hospital operations, and make the best use of resources. Advanced technology transitions healthcare systems from traditional medical practices to a more sophisticated patient-centered approach. As a result, smart hospitals emphasize timely data gathering, automation, and sophisticated analytics, and they also increase the bar for quality, efficiency, and cost-effectiveness. Some of the most important technologies are now accessible, particularly artificial intelligence and machine learning. These technologies include the ability to enhance clinical procedures and training via robots and virtual reality, as well as better diagnostic accuracy and individualized therapy. Despite the significant progress, there are still certain hurdles to overcome, including patient monitoring, data accuracy and security concerns, and cost-effectiveness measures. Therefore, we must address these difficulties to fully realize the potential of intelligent healthcare. There are a variety of benefits, including improved results and reduced medical expenditures, as well as enhanced access and the ability to personalize treatment. We expect the healthcare business to become more intelligent, responsive, and networked in the future. Technological breakthroughs and an unending need for effective solutions will drive this. This progression is characterized by both operational efficiency and an improvement in the quality of treatment, leading to a more effective and patient-centered healthcare paradigm.

References

[1] Tian, Shuo, Wenbo Yang, Jehane Michael Le Grange, Peng Wang, Wei Huang, and Zhewei Ye. "Smart healthcare: making medical care more intelligent." *Global Health Journal* 3, no. 3 (2019): 62-65.

[2] Gomes, Pedro. *"KIWI framework: from smart hospitals to smarter hospitals: case report on the future hospital in Madeira."* PhD diss., 2024.

[3] Rahmani, Amir-Mohammad, Nanda Kumar Thanigaivelan, Tuan Nguyen Gia, Jose Granados, Behailu Negash, Pasi Liljeberg, and Hannu Tenhunen. "Smart e-health gateway: Bringing intelligence to internet-of-things based ubiquitous healthcare systems." In *2015 12th annual IEEE consumer communications and networking conference (CCNC),* pp. 826-834. IEEE, 2015.

[4] Said, Abd Mlak, Aymen Yahyaoui, Faicel Yaakoubi, and Takoua Abdellatif. "Machine learning based rank attack detection for smart hospital infrastructure." In *The Impact of Digital Technologies on Public.*

[5] Kwon, Hyuktae, Sunhee An, Ho-Young Lee, Won Chul Cha, Sungwan Kim, Minwoo Cho, and Hyoun-Joong Kong. "Review of smart hospital services in real healthcare environments." *Healthcare Informatics Research* 28, no. 1 (2022): 3-15.

[6] Levina, Anastasia, Igor Ilin, Dayana Gugutishvili, Kristina Kochetkova, and Andrea Tick. "Towards a smart hospital: Smart infrastructure integration." *Journal of Open Innovation: Technology, Market, and Complexity* 10, no. 3 (2024): 100339.

[7] Demirkan, Haluk. "A smart healthcare systems framework." *It Professional* 15, no. 5 (2013): 38-45.

[8] Kumar, Arun, R. Dhanagopal, Mahmoud A. Albreem, and Dac-Nhuong Le. "A comprehensive study on the role of advanced technologies in 5G based smart hospital." *Alexandria Engineering Journal* 60, no. 6 (2021): 5527-5536.

[9] Haleem, Abid, Mohd Javaid, Ravi Pratap Singh, and Rajiv Suman. "Medical 4.0 technologies for healthcare: Features, capabilities, and applications." *Internet of Things and Cyber-Physical Systems* 2 (2022): 12-30.

[10] Gomes, Pedro. *"KIWI framework: from smart hospitals to smarter hospitals: case report on the future hospital in Madeira."* PhD diss., 2024.

[11] Tripathi, Padmesh and Abul Hasan Siddiqi (2016). “Denoising Raman spectra using a non-Convex regularizer in Total Variation,” *Indian Journal of Science and Technology*, 9(48), 1-5.

[12] Tripathi, Padmesh and Abul Hasan Siddiqi (2017). “De-noising EEG signal using iterative clipping algorithm,” *Biosciences and Biotechnology Research Asia*, 14(1), 497- 502.

[13] Tripathi, Padmesh (2020). “Electroencephalpgram Signal Quality Enhancement by Total Variation Denoising Using Non-convex Regulariser,” *Int. J. Biomedical Engineering and Technology*, 33(2), 134-145.

[14] Panova, Tayana, and Alejandro Lleras. "Avoidance or boredom: Negative mental health outcomes associated with use of Information and Communication Technologies depend on users’ motivations." *Computers in Human Behavior* 58 (2016): 249-258.

[15] https://www.accenture.com/t20170926T072837Z__w__/us-en/_acnmedia/PDF-61/Accenture-2017- CostCyberCrimeStudy.pdf (last accessed on 08/09/2024).

[16] http://images.mktgassets.symantec.com/Web/Symantec/%7B57708968-bc77-479c-a289- eea4e232cfbc%7D_ISTR_V24_2019_en_apj.pdf?aid=elq_19427 (last accessed on 08/09/2024).

[17] Sebastian, M. P. *"Smart hospitals: Challenges and opportunities."* Indian Institute of Management Kozhikode(2019).

[18] https://www.marketsandmarkets.com/Market-Reports/smart-hospital-market29319948.html?gclid =CjwKCAjw96fkBRA2EiwAKZjFTRqJXAVYsmpJK56mujs_aveLbTwzWHQP0 8hxS6u psNaY0MsT06La3xoCmqoQAvD_BwE (last accessed on 08/09/2024).

[19] https://www.medicatradefair.com/cgibin/md_medica/lib/pub/tt.cgi/Smart_Hospital _Healthcare_rethought.html?oid=91318&lang=2&ticket=guest (last accessed on 08/09/2024).

[20] Qi, Jun, Po Yang, Geyong Min, Oliver Amft, Feng Dong, and Lida Xu. "Advanced internet of things for personalised healthcare systems: A survey." *Pervasive and mobile computing* 41 (2017): 132-149.

[21] https://www.philips.com/a-w/about/news/archive/future-health-index/articles/ 20170613-by-2020-the-smarthospital-will-be-a-reality.html (last accessed on 08/09/2024).

[22] Gourisaria, Mahendra Kumar, Rakshit Agrawal, Vinayak Singh, Siddharth Swarup Rautaray, and Manjusha Pandey. "AI and IoT enabled smart hospital management systems." In *Data Science in Societal Applications: Concepts and Implications, pp.* 77-106. Singapore: Springer Nature Singapore, 2022.

[23] Rai, M., Husain, A. A., Sharma, R., Maity, T. and Yadav, R. K., 2022. Facial Feature-Based Human Emotion Detection Using Machine Learning: An Overview. *Artificial Intelligence and Cybersecurity,* pp.107-120.

[24] Tyagi, N., Rai, M., Sahw, P., Tripathi, P., & Kumar, N. "Methods for the Recognition of Human Emotions Based on Physiological Response: Facial Expressions." *Smart Healthcare for Sustainable Urban Development*, edited by Rosy Madaan, et al., IGI Global, 2022, pp. 183-202. https://doi.org/10.4018/978-1-6684-2508-4.ch013

[25] Tripathi, Padmesh, N. Kumar, K. K. Paroha, M. Rai, M. K. Panda (2024). Applications of Deep Learning in Healthcare in the Framework of Industry 5.0. In M. Khan, R. Khan, P. Praveen, A. R. Verma & M. K. Panda (Eds.), *Infrastructure Possibilities and Human-Centered Approaches With Industry* 5.0 (pp. 69-85). IGI Global.

[26] Kumar, Nitendra, P. Tripathi, , R. P. Nanda, S. Tiwari, S. Sharma (2024). Machine Learning for Smart Health Services in the Framework of Industry 5.0. In M. Khan, R. Khan, P. Praveen, A. R. Verma & M. K. Panda (Eds.*), Infrastructure Possibilities and Human-Centered Approaches With Industry* 5.0 (pp. 215-230). IGI Global.

[27] Tunc, M. Ali, Emre Gures, and Ibraheem Shayea. *"A survey on iot smart healthcare: Emerging technologies, applications, challenges, and future trends."* arXiv preprint arXiv:2109.02042 (2021).

[28] Singh, Bikesh Kumar, Kesari Verma, and A. S. Thoke. "Investigations on impact of feature normalization techniques on classifier's performance in breast tumor classification." *International Journal of Computer Applications* 116, no. 19 (2015).

[29] Mandal, Sunandan, Bikesh Kumar Singh, and Kavita Thakur. "Majority voting-based hybrid feature selection in machine learning paradigm for epilepsy detection using EEG." International Journal of Computational Vision and *Robotics* 11, no. 4 (2021): 385-400.

[30] Shahamiri, Seyed Reza, and Fadi Thabtah. "Autism AI: a new autism screening system based on artificial intelligence." *Cognitive Computation* 12, no. 4 (2020): 766-777.

[31] Tikka, Sai Krishna, Bikesh Kumar Singh, S. Haque Nizamie, Shobit Garg, Sunandan Mandal, Kavita Thakur, and Lokesh Kumar Singh. "Artificial intelligence-based classification of schizophrenia: A high density electroencephalographic and support vector machine study." *Indian Journal of Psychiatry* 62, no. 3 (2020): 273-282.

[32] Baker, Stephanie B., Wei Xiang, and Ian Atkinson. "Internet of things for smart healthcare: Technologies, challenges, and opportunities." *Ieee Access* 5 (2017): 26521-26544.

[33] Dewangan, Neha, Prafulla Vyas, and Sunandan Mandal. "Smart healthcare and intelligent medical systems." In *Computational Intelligence and Applications for Pandemics and Healthcare,* pp. 205-228. IGI Global, 2022.

[34] Raza, Ahmad, Mohsin Ali, Muhammad Khurram Ehsan, and Ali Hassan Sodhro. "Spectrum Evaluation in CR-Based Smart Healthcare Systems Using Optimizable Tree Machine Learning Approach." *Sensors* 23, no. 17 (2023): 7456.

[35] Pan, F. "Health care is an area where information technology plays an important role: an interview with Wu He-Quan, a member of the Chinese Academy of Engineering." *China Med Herald* 16, no. 3 (2019): 1-3.

[36] Farahani, Bahar, Farshad Firouzi, Victor Chang, Mustafa Badaroglu, Nicholas Constant, and Kunal Mankodiya. "Towards fog-driven IoT eHealth: Promises and challenges of IoT in medicine and healthcare." *Future generation computer systems* 78 (2018): 659-676.

[37] Dhar, Joydip, and Ashok Ranganathan. "Machine learning capabilities in medical diagnosis applications: Computational results for hepatitis disease." *International Journal of Biomedical Engineering and Technology* 17, no. 4 (2015): 330-340.

[38] Polat, Kemal, and Salih Güneş. "Principles component analysis, fuzzy weighting pre-processing and artificial immune recognition system based diagnostic system for diagnosis of lung cancer." *Expert Systems with Applications* 34, no. 1 (2008): 214-221.

[39] Esteva, Andre, Brett Kuprel, Roberto A. Novoa, Justin Ko, Susan M. Swetter, Helen M. Blau, and Sebastian Thrun. "Dermatologist-level classification of skin cancer with deep neural networks." *Nature* 542, no. 7639 (2017): 115-118.

[40] Wang, Shijun, and Ronald M. Summers. "Machine learning and radiology." *Medical image analysis* 16, no. 5 (2012): 933-951.

[41] High, Rob. "The era of cognitive systems: An inside look at IBM Watson and how it works." *IBM Corporation, Redbooks* 1 (2012): 16.

[42] Qi, R. J., and W. T. Lyu. "The role and challenges of artificial intelligence-assisted diagnostic technology in the medical field." *Chinical Medicine Device Information* 24 (2018): 27-28.

[43] Willard-Grace, Rachel, Denise DeVore, Ellen H. Chen, Danielle Hessler, Thomas Bodenheimer, and David H. Thom. "The effectiveness of medical assistant health coaching for low-income patients with uncontrolled diabetes, hypertension, and hyperlipidemia: protocol for a randomized controlled trial and baseline characteristics of the study population." *BMC Family practice* 14 (2013): 1-10..

[44] Andreu-Perez, Javier, Daniel R. Leff, Henry MD Ip, and Guang-Zhong Yang. "From wearable sensors to smart implants--toward pervasive and personalized healthcare." *IEEE Transactions on Biomedical Engineering* 62, no. 12 (2015): 2750-2762.

[45] Zhang, Diming, and Qingjun Liu. "Biosensors and bioelectronics on smartphone for portable biochemical detection." *Biosensors and Bioelectronics* 75 (2016): 273-284.

[46] Redfern, J. "Smart health and innovation: facilitating health-related behaviour change." *Proceedings of the Nutrition Society* 76, no. 3 (2017): 328-332.

[47] Zeevi, David, Tal Korem, Niv Zmora, David Israeli, Daphna Rothschild, Adina Weinberger, Orly Ben-Yacov et al. "Personalized nutrition by prediction of glycemic responses." *Cell* 163, no. 5 (2015): 1079-1094.

[48] White, Ryen W. "Skill discovery in virtual assistants." *Communications of the ACM* 61, no. 11 (2018): 106-113.

[49] Zhang, J., Y. Li, L. Cao, and Y. Zhang. "Research on the construction of intelligent hospitals at home and abroad." *Chinese Hospital Management* 38, no. 12 (2018): 64-66.

[50] Bakkar, Nadine, Tina Kovalik, Ileana Lorenzini, Scott Spangler, Alix Lacoste, Kyle Sponaugle, Philip Ferrante, Elenee Argentinis, Rita Sattler, and Robert Bowser. "Artificial intelligence in neurodegenerative disease research: use of IBM Watson to identify additional RNA-binding proteins altered in amyotrophic lateral sclerosis." *Acta neuropathologica* 135 (2018): 227-247.

[51] Liu, J. T., and Y. H. Liu. "Application of computer molecular simulation technology and artificial intelligence in drug development." *Technol Innov* Appl 2 (2018): 46-47.

[52] Zhou, Binggui, Guanghua Yang, Zheng Shi, and Shaodan Ma. "Natural language processing for smart healthcare." *IEEE Reviews in Biomedical Engineering* (2022).

Chapter 8

AI/IoT in Medical Science Services and Applications

Renu Rani[1,*]
Hashmat Usmani[2,†]
Farah Naz[3,‡]
Divya[4,ǁ]
Neha Goel[5,¶]
and Anuj Kumar[6,#]
Rajkumar Goel Institute of Technology, Ghaziabad, U.P., India

Abstract

This chapter explores how artificial intelligence (AI) revolutionizes Internet of Things (IoT)-based healthcare systems. As technology advances and healthcare continues to change, incorporating AI into IoT frameworks offers a promising new frontier for improving patient care, diagnosis, therapy, and general healthcare administration. This paper investigates how artificial intelligence (AI) can enhance existing healthcare IoT applications to improve accuracy, efficiency, and patient outcomes. This study identifies critical areas where AI-powered IoT systems can transform healthcare practices through a thorough literature

* Corresponding Author's Email: rrecefec@rkgit.edu.in
† Corresponding Author's Email: huecefec@rkgit.edu.in
‡ Corresponding Author's Email: farahfec@rkgit.edu.in
ǁ Corresponding Author's Email: div13fec@rkgit.edu.in
¶ Corresponding Author's Email: nehagfec@rkgit.edu.in
# Corresponding Author's Email: anujkfec@rkgit.edu.in

In: Harnessing the Power of IoT-Enabled Machine Learning …
Editors: Mritunjay Rai, Ravindra Kumar Yadav, Neha Goel et al.
ISBN: 979-8-89530-626-0

review, case studies, and analysis of emerging trends. It also discusses the difficulties and moral issues involved in putting these technologies into practice, such as data security and privacy. The findings underscore the potential of AI to enhance IoT-based healthcare systems, paving the way for more personalized, efficient, and cost-effective healthcare solutions. This study adds to the expanding corpus of information in the area and suggests future paths for advancements in healthcare innovation and research utilizing artificial intelligence.

Keywords: Artificial Intelligence (AI), healthcare technology, AI-powered IoT system, data privacy in healthcare, healthcare system innovation, digital health, AI and IoT integration

1. Introduction

Before the development of the Internet of Things, texting, phone calls, and in-person visits were the only ways that patients and doctors could communicate. As a result, medical professionals and institutions were unable to regularly assess patients' health and offer advice. Thanks to the Internet of Things (IoT) enabled devices, the healthcare sector can now remotely monitor patients [1], which creates new opportunities for patient safety and health and allows physicians greater flexibility to deliver excellent care. Patient satisfaction and engagement have increased along with the ease and effectiveness of communication between doctors and patients. Furthermore, remote patient monitoring reduces hospital stays and prevents readmissions. IoT significantly contributes to reducing healthcare costs and improving treatment outcomes. IoT is unquestionably changing the healthcare industry by redefining how people and technology interact to provide healthcare solutions. The use of modern healthcare and healthcare systems has been gradually transforming the Indian healthcare scene. In light of the current climate and the increased incidence of health issues, expedite the usage of healthcare and the healthcare system. The lack of hospitals, doctors, easy access to drugs, and high-quality healthcare in rural and distant areas impedes India's efforts to build a stronger healthcare system. The IoT can greatly help improve India's inadequate healthcare system as in Figure 1 shown by providing a capable, integrated, highly networked, and patient-centered system.

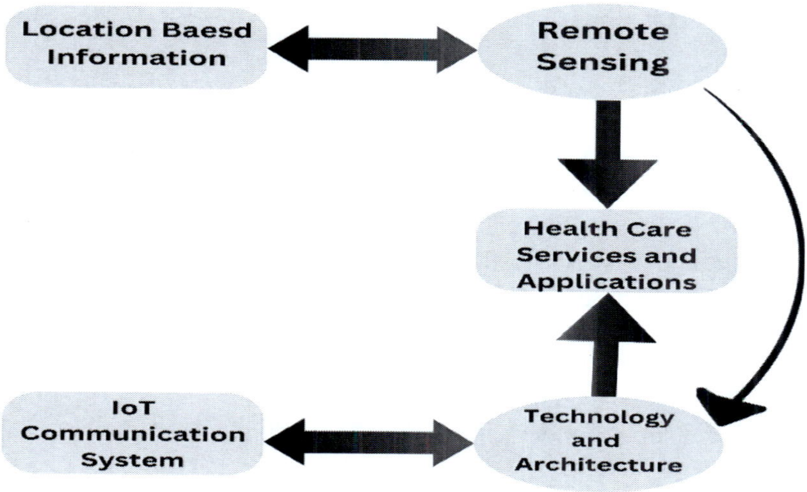

Figure 1. IoT integration and the fundamental components of a healthcare system.

1.1. Internet of Things for Patients

Wearable technology, such as fitness bands and other wirelessly connected gadgets like heart-rate monitors and glucometers, can provide patients with individualized treatment. These gadgets allow users to set up numerous reminders, such as those to test their blood pressure, make appointments, monitor their caloric intake, and much more [2]. The Internet of Things has improved life by continuously monitoring medical issues, particularly for elderly individuals. This has a significant impact on individuals living alone and their families.

1.2. IoT for Doctors

Physicians can better monitor their patient's health with wearable and other IoT-enabled home monitoring devices. They can monitor patients' adherence to their treatment plans and any critical medical requirements. Thanks to IoT, medical staff may engage with patients more proactively and watchfully. Using data collected from IoT devices, doctors may decide which treatment plan is best for their patients and get the desired outcomes.

1.3. IoT for Hospitals

IoT devices offer a wide range of uses in healthcare facilities beyond monitoring patients' health. With the use of Internet of Things (IoT) devices with sensors attached, medical equipment such as oxygen pumps, wheelchairs, defibrillators, nebulizers, and other monitoring equipment can be tracked in real-time. Analyzing the real-time deployment of medical personnel at different locations is also feasible. The transmission of diseases is one of the main concerns for hospital patients. Patients can avoid infections with the help of IoT-enabled hygiene monitoring devices. Asset management applications of IoT devices include controlling pharmaceutical inventory, monitoring the environment through humidity and temperature regulation, and ensuring freezers maintain the proper temperature [3].

1.4. IoT and Health Insurance Companies

IoT-enabled smart devices have a lot to offer health insurers. Insurance companies can use health monitoring device data for underwriting and claims processing. This data will help them find possible underwriters and identify fraud claims. IoT devices improve transparency between insurance companies and their clients in the underwriting, pricing, claims processing, and risk assessment processes. In the context of IoT-captured data-driven decisions in all operation processes, customers will have sufficient insight into the underlying reasoning behind every decision and the results of every process. Clients of insurers could receive compensation for utilizing and disseminating health data produced by Internet of Things devices [4]. IoT devices could reward consumers for tracking their routine activities, adherence to treatment plans, and preventive health actions. This will help insurers reduce claims significantly. Insurance companies may be able to validate claims using the data that IoT devices gather.

1.5. Improving Medical Care

Abundant prospects arise from the proliferation of IoT goods tailored to the healthcare industry. Furthermore, the massive volume of data produced by these networked devices has the power to revolutionize healthcare. The architecture of IoT consists of four steps as shown in Figure 2, which are essentially stages in a process. Each of the four phases interconnects, obtaining or handling information in one phase and then providing value to the subsequent phase. Using integrated values in the process produces dynamic business prospects and intuitions [5].

- Step 1: The first stage is configuring networked devices like cameras, sensors, actuators, monitors, and detectors.
- Step 2: Usually received analog data from sensors and other devices; further processing of the data depends on combining and converting it into digital form.
- Step 3: standardize, pre-process, and transfer aggregated digitalized data to the data center or cloud.
- Step 4: We organize and closely review the finished data. Applied to this data, advanced analytics provides insightful business analysis supporting decision-making.

IoT is changing healthcare by guaranteeing better patient care, better treatment results, and lower costs for patients, as well as better workflows and processes, higher performance, and a better patient experience for healthcare professionals.

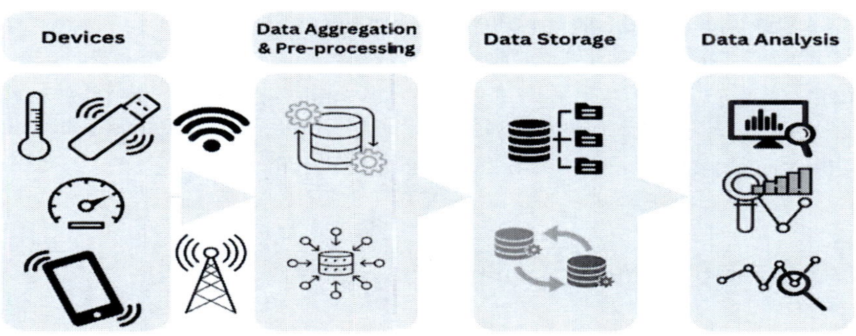

Figure 2. IoT solutions' four steps.

The following are the main benefits of IoT in healthcare:

- *Better Treatment:* By enabling doctors to make evidence-based decisions and bringing complete transparency, IoT enables real-time patient monitoring, which significantly reduces unnecessary doctor visits, hospital stays, and re-admissions.

- *Faster Disease Diagnosis:* Real-time data and continuous patient monitoring aid in the early diagnosis of diseases based on symptoms.
- *Preventive Care:* Proactive medical care is made feasible by routine health monitoring. Drug and Equipment Management: Managing medications and medical equipment in the healthcare industry is quite difficult. Thanks to linked devices, these can be used more affordably and efficiently [6].
- *Error Mitigation:* Data generated by Internet of Things (IoT) devices ensures error-free, waste-free, and economically viable healthcare operations in addition to facilitating effective decision-making. Adequate security measures must be put in place. With real-time health monitoring and patient data access, the Internet of Things opens up new possibilities for patient care. Healthcare stakeholders may use this data to enhance patient experiences and health, generate income, and streamline operations. It is a goldmine. The ability to utilize this digital power effectively could set one apart in the increasingly interconnected globe.

1.6. IoT Applications in Medical Science Service

For the healthcare industry to effectively manage, protect, and monitor IoT devices, it is essential to understand their various uses. Although remote patient monitoring, or IoMT devices that gather patient data like body temperature and heart rate, is the most well-known application of IoT in healthcare, there are numerous other uses of IoT in this field.

1.7. Implantable Glucose Monitoring Systems

People with diabetes may be able to implant devices equipped with sensors beneath their skin. The sensors on the devices will alert patients when their blood sugar falls too low, and they will also store their previous data for future reference [7]. Patients will be able to ascertain when they are currently and maybe in the future most prone to having hypoglycemia. The Internet of Things (IoT) is used by implantable glucose monitoring devices (CGMs) to track blood glucose levels in diabetic patients.

- *Sensors:* A little pellet, about 18 millimeters long, is implanted under the patient's skin in the upper arm by a medical professional. The sensor takes vital signs in real-time, including blood sugar levels.
- *Transmitter:* The patient can examine the data wirelessly transferred by the CGM to a device, like a cell phone, via a transmitter. Additionally, if the patient's blood sugar falls too low or in other unusual circumstances, the gadget can collect past data and notify both the patient and their physician.
- *System back-end:* The patient and physician can view the data from the CGM system in a format that is legible by humans. Additionally, the device can use machine learning to forecast when the patient is most likely to have hypoglycemia. With time, CGMs have gained popularity and accuracy, and many now view them as a good option for diabetes therapy.

1.8. Cancer Patients Activity Monitors

Activity trackers as shown in Figure 3 shows the monitoring system of a patient's eating, sleep patterns, and level of weariness. Additionally, the tracker's gathered information, both before and after treatment begins, aids medical professionals in determining necessary modifications to the suggested treatment plan. Factors other than age and weight, such as fitness levels and habits, often determine the optimal course of treatment for a cancer patient. The application of the IoT to cancer patients has demonstrated promising results [8]. The purpose of this review is to determine the uses and advantages of IoT approaches, particularly wearable technology, for managing side effects and symptoms, improving quality of life, and increasing survival rates in cancer patients receiving active therapy. The paper includes the architecture and taxonomy of IoT use, the difficulties and pertinent outcomes, and the relationship between the type of cancer and the type of treatment. This analysis, based on the Preferred Reporting Items for Systematic Reviews and Meta-Analyses (PRISMA), considered articles from the last ten years.

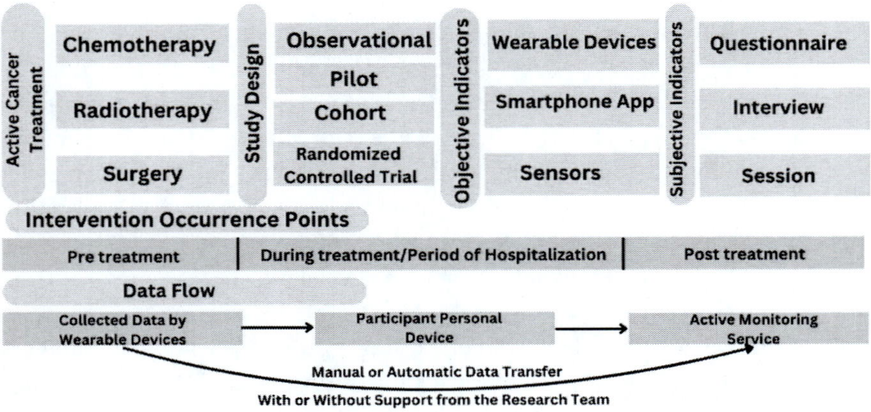

Figure 3. Monitoring system for cancer patients.

1.9. Heart Rate Monitors with Explanations

Wearing devices that monitor heart rates can help identify people who have high blood pressure. Medical practitioners will get access to patient heart monitor data when needed for tests and check-ups. The wearable gadgets can notify medical professionals if a patient experiences a stroke, arrhythmia, palpitations, or heart attack. Thus, prompt ambulance delivery may be the difference between life and death [9]. Increasingly, people in developing nations such as India are seeking alternative methods to consistently monitor their health check-ups. Regular hospital visits for medical consultations have become mandatory, demanding time and financial resources from patients. We provide a design for tracking the patient's health parameters, such as heartbeats sent from an IoT device to a web server, to solve this problem. Recently developed, the Internet of things (IoT) connects all objects and is considered the next big technological breakthrough [10]. Patient monitoring is one of the Internet of Things applications that keeps track of a patient's health. The Internet of Things enables real-time health monitoring, thereby enhancing the effectiveness of medical technology. With IoT, the physician can continuously monitor the patient's condition on his smartphone and access the patient's stored medical history on the web server.

1.10. Systems for Medical Alerts

Individuals may wear items that mimic jewelry, designed to alert friends or family in case of an emergency. For instance, if a person wearing a medical alert bracelet falls out of bed in the middle of the night, their designated emergency contacts immediately receive a smartphone alert [11]. A variety of devices are available for use in setting off alarms.

- Necklace worn around the throat
- Little item fastened to a belt
- Bracelet
- Motion detectors installed in a house
- Radar-based room detectors

Passive systems monitor the user and trigger an alarm based on an algorithm (such as a fall or inactivity), while active devices necessitate an action from the user to initiate an alarm. One drawback of an active gadget is that it requires deliberate input from the user to trigger an alarm. Wearing the gadget is necessary for both passive and active devices. Installed systems can be costly and challenging to use.

1.11. Disposable Sensors

Patients can now ingest devices with sensors that look like tablets. Once ingested, the sensors transmit information to a patient's smartphone app, allowing them to track and follow prescribed medication dosages. Human error or forgetfulness are the main causes of drug abuse. This edible sensor's goal is to ensure that patients are taking the right medications in the right amounts and at the right times [12]. Furthermore, some ingestible sensors are enabling more accurate diagnosis of ailments like colon cancer and irritable bowel syndrome.

1.12. Remote Patient Monitoring

Phones, smartwatches, and monitors automatically collect health data. Remote patient monitoring equipment gathers health information, including blood pressure, body fat percentage, and body temperature. Healthcare providers can view and receive patient data from IoT health devices. A person may be unable to visit a hospital for any of the following reasons. Even when he is accessible for a visit, medical staff might only be able to obtain his biometrics after he arrives at the hospital. Continued patient monitoring is necessary for many conditions that necessitate hospital stays. With data from remote patient tracking, that requirement vanishes. These IoT gadgets for healthcare can issue alarms or suggest treatments based on the data they gather. A sudden increase or decrease in blood pressure could signal a doctor's intervention [13]. Private information is at stake when IoT healthcare devices continuously monitor patients. Their primary worry is this. Hackers might try to get a hold of these medical gadgets.GDPR and HIPAA require healthcare firms to protect patient data. Most devices encrypt their IoT hardware and software to comply with these regulations. As a result, the healthcare sector needs to collaborate with data-secure healthcare organizations.

1.13. Telemedicine and Its Significance

Two important uses of the Internet of Things in healthcare that are revolutionizing the way patients receive care are telemedicine and remote patient monitoring. While remote patient monitoring allows healthcare professionals to remotely and in real-time monitor a patient's health, telemedicine allows patients to receive medical consultations from the comfort of their own homes.

1.13.1. Definition of Telemedicine

Telemedicine is the use of information and communication technology to offer remote treatment. This suggests that patients may have medical consultations in the convenience of their own houses rather than needing to visit a hospital or doctor’s office.

1.13.2. Telemedicine Service Types

Remote monitoring, virtual consultations, and patient education are examples of telemedicine services. Specialized treatments like remote surgery and mental health counseling are also provided by certain telemedicine providers.

1.14. The Benefits of Telemedicine Include

- *Better access to healthcare:* People who live in remote places or have mobility challenges will find that telemedicine makes it easier for them to get treatment. Patients can obtain medical consultations via telemedicine without having to go far.
- *Cost-effectiveness:* By removing the need for in-person appointments and the requirement for patients to travel to see a doctor, telemedicine has the potential to lower healthcare expenses.
- *Enhanced patient satisfaction:* Because telemedicine is more convenient and requires less time than traditional in-person appointments, patients are often happier with it.
- *Enhanced efficiency:* Virtual consultations save more time compared to in-person sessions, hence telemedicine helps doctors to see more patients on a given day.

1.15. The Challenges Associated with Telemedicine Include

- *Reimbursement:* Since some insurance companies do not cover virtual consultations, reimbursement for telemedicine services remains a concern.
- *Technical challenges:* Implementing telemedicine may be challenging due to technical issues such as a bad internet connection or the requirement for specialist equipment.
- *Data security and privacy:* Since sensitive information is sent over the internet in telemedicine, patient data security and privacy are concerns.

1.16. Robotic Surgery

Surgeons can now perform surgeries using IoT medical devices. Surgeons can implant robots with Internet access for surgical tasks. When experts want accuracy, these lessen human mistakes. The primary issue arises from the fact that hand treatments require wider incisions than robotic surgery. People need more room for their hands when doing challenging tasks.

Surgeons can operate more successfully and correctly with the use of IoT robotic equipment. Cuts are less frequent since IoT devices are simple to deploy. Less intrusive therapy and a faster recovery are possible for the patient. For complicated tasks, these gadgets need to be compact and dependable. They must also determine the best surgical procedure and identify the patient's condition [14]. Since surgeons already use these devices for several surgeries, these criteria are doable. Physicians and nurses are already benefiting from the technologies. Technology may lead to an increase in the use of IoT robots in surgery. However, one commonality among all those gadgets is their ability to connect to the Internet. Both users of Internet of Things healthcare devices and online workers prioritize data security. IoT devices might be dangerous even if they make people's lives better because of the security flaws mentioned above.

1.17. Connected Contact Lenses

Unlike regular contact lenses, these connected lenses feature a camera and monitor. These smart glasses enhance vision and identify health issues early on. What constitutes an infection or weakening of the eyes? They might get worse for a while before getting help from a doctor. Certain eye conditions can develop quickly, giving little time for treatment. Connected contacts can detect early eye diseases. Okay, so IoT glasses can detect some general health problems. Tear glucose levels have been identified as a potential precursor to diabetes. Finally, the lenses are equipped with cameras, enabling users to capture images. This is one of the primary reasons non-healthcare companies are developing the technology. Companies are using this technology in a variety of ways. If someone breaches security and gains access to these networked devices, they have the potential to surreptitiously spy on users. The idea that you could see what other people see is unnerving [15]. For this reason, data security should be a top priority for healthcare firms. Those looking for protection should locate reputable businesses whose initiatives align with current safety regulations.

1.18. Parkinson’s Care Monitoring

The idea of treating Parkinson's illness with IoT is intriguing. These health monitors can track the intensity of Parkinson's disease symptoms throughout the day. To prescribe the right medication, doctors need to monitor changes in Parkinson's symptoms and symptoms. Extended hospital stays are necessary for patient monitoring.

IoT devices that collect health data simplify this method. By lowering hospital stays, patient tracking saves money and enables patients to live freely. The most important consideration while looking for signs is the sensitivity of the gadget. The device might misread a sign if it is very sensitive. But a poor device could overlook warnings.

1.19. Mood or Depression Monitoring

One of the most significant issues facing the world's health is mental illness, which is defined by an increasing number of people experiencing anxiety, depression, and other diseases. The World Health Organization (WHO) defines mental health as "a state of well-being in which every individual realizes his or her potential, can cope with the normal stresses of life, can work productively and fruitfully, and can contribute to her or his community." Mental health is essential to overall well-being. The WHO estimates that over 500 million individuals worldwide suffer from mental health illnesses, with depression, schizophrenia, and dementia being the most common. By tracking heart rate, blood pressure, and other biometrics, Internet of Things medical devices can evaluate a patient's emotional state and mental well-being. The newest IoT gadgets can track an individual's eye movements. Monitoring mental health has not always been easy. To diagnose patients, doctors need to understand their feelings, but they are unable to predict when a patient's mood will shift. Another problem is that patients may be misled about how they are feeling. The use of biometrics by IoT devices rather than words is advantageous. These indicators of health that reflect mental health are not under the patient's control [16]. Monitoring may continue even when the patient is asleep. There are still concerns regarding the reliability of this result. These tools don't always pick up on sadness or other problems. But these difficulties also offer an alternative.

1.20. Smart Inhalers to Treat Asthma

For many people, asthma is a chronic illness that causes a tremendous deal of hardship. Non-adherence is one of several factors that contribute to inadequate control of asthma. Thus, there is a critical need for novel approaches that could make monitoring easier and maintain effective asthma management. As a result, intelligent inhalers are starting to play a crucial role in the progression of enhanced treatment [17]. Consequently, in recent years, there has been a notable increase in the value and interest in medical electronic devices. The quantity, quality, and number of sensors and data systems are always growing. Asthma patients can improve and customize their use of smart inhalers by:

- A product for gathering data (Smart inhaler)
- Health condition education
- tracking symptoms and providing comments
- Emergency drug action plan
- Obtaining treatment information
- Lifestyle advice

Patients with asthma can now receive aid when they need it, even in remote areas, thanks to the benefits of IoT technology. Smart inhalers speed up the flow of all the most important data considerably, which shortens the time needed to diagnose and simplifies research.

1.20. Medication Dispensers

Research shows that taking medications can cause memory loss in many people, regardless of age. Elderly people primarily experience this, which increases several other life-threatening risks. Dispensers for medications are useful in this situation. Dispensers come in a variety of forms, all of which work with solid medications. Most dispensers are quite basic and lack any kind of reminder system. This article suggests a medicine dispenser that can dispense liquid and solid medications, and has an app built into it and assists in setting alerts. Medication adherence is one of the major issues facing the healthcare sector. Elderly persons frequently forget to take their medications on time, and the risk of overdosing is significantly higher in those who take many medications. Computer-controlled devices known as automated dispensing systems, or ADS, automate hospital drug dispensing. ADS systems enhance accuracy, operational efficiency, and patient safety. Additionally, they can support hospitals in adhering to drug administration guidelines. Devices implanted in patients can now deliver consistent medication dosages throughout the day. The devices will inform patients when it's time to refill their prescriptions. Patients can also report missed doses to doctors during routine checkups.

1.21. Monitoring of Hand Hygiene

IoT devices for hygiene monitoring have become more popular in hospitals and other healthcare institutions as a way to guarantee appropriate cleaning standards. These medical devices serve as helpful reminders for people to wash their hands frequently or each time they enter a certain space. Critically sick people frequently reside in numerous hospital rooms. Any pathogen introduction could make these patients' situations even worse. Any hospital's operations require following adequate decontamination protocols, even when dealing with generally healthy patients. In addition to reminding users to wash their hands, IoT devices for hand hygiene can also guide how to sanitize items or clean hands. Both patients and medical staff use these gadgets to ensure good hygiene [18]. However, the main issue with these gadgets is their limited functionality, as they only serve to remind users to sanitize their hands. Neither healthcare nor IoT devices can sterilize hospital rooms or make patients sanitize their hands. A simple reminder does make a difference in both situations. The use of these devices results in an approximate 60% decrease in infection rates.

1.22. Wireless Sensors

Wireless sensors ensure constant temperature control for blood samples, cold pharmaceuticals, and other biological materials in labs and hospital refrigerators. Healthcare workers may find and tag items with IoT sensors, such as wheelchairs, scales, defibrillators, nebulizers, pumps, and monitoring equipment. Physical equipment is frequently missing or difficult to find, but workers will always know where everything is thanks to IoT.

1.23. Wearables to Fight Depression

For those suffering from manic depression, Apple has created an app for their Apple Watch that can help them manage their depression. In addition to monitoring cognitive and emotional skills, the app keeps track of a patient's episodes that occur outside of their planned appointments [19].

1.24. Location Services

Medical staff may find and tag items such as wheelchairs, scales, defibrillators, nebulizers, pumps, and monitoring equipment with IoT sensors. Physical equipment is frequently lost or difficult to find, but with IoT, staff members will always know where everything is.

Conclusion

With a multitude of services and copious amounts of data, the Internet of Things (IoT) has recently rendered the vision of a smarter society realistic. The healthcare community, industry, government, and academia are paying close attention to "smart health care" due to the advancements in cloud computing, IoT technologies, and smart Multiple Sensorial Media (MulSeMedia) systems. The current study's goal has been to identify security and privacy concerns related to the AI-driven Internet of Things (AIIoT) and offer recommendations for how to effectively handle them all. We gathered qualitative data for the study using an existing, pertinent secondary source and a qualitative study approach. In the healthcare industry, IoT-based healthcare systems gather a variety of patient data and receive inputs from doctors and medical professionals. Continuous glucose monitoring for insulin pens is the best example of this. All these devices can communicate with each other and take important actions that would provide timely help to save someone's life [20]. An IoT healthcare device collects data and transmits it to the cloud, empowering doctors to take appropriate action. This suggests that the potential application of IoT in healthcare has the potential to enhance patient health, increase the productivity of healthcare employees, and streamline hospital workflow. Furthermore, the adoption of a technology does not always align with its potential. Several factors, including inadequate digital infrastructure, a sizable, diversified, and unregulated private sector, and varying capacities across states and medical experts, anticipate a gradual and highly uneven adoption of artificial intelligence (AI) in India [21, 22, 23]. For similar reasons, well-established private institutions will probably be the first to adopt

AI. That being said, it is unlikely that market forces alone will fully satisfy the dominant narrative, which centers on improving equity and quality regarding the application of AI in healthcare. This is because these solutions are more likely to benefit populations that already have access to high-quality medical care, which is typically the case in urban areas with sophisticated digital infrastructure.

References

[1] Shokrekhodaei, M., Cistola, D. P., Roberts, R. C., Quinones, S. Non-invasive glucose Monitoring Using Optical Sensor and Machine Learning Techniques for Diabetes Applications. *IEEE Access.* 2021;9:73029–73045.

[2] Hashimoto, D. A., Rosman, G., Rus D., Meireles, O. R. Artificial Intelligence in Surgery: Promises and Perils. *Ann. Surg.* 2018; 268:70–76.

[3] Tripathi, P., Kumar, N. Paroha, K. K. Rai, M. Panda, M. K. "Applications of Deep Learning in Healthcare in the Framework of Industry 5.0," *Infrastructure Possibilities and Human-Centered Approaches With Industry 5.0, IGI Global,* 2024, doi: 10.4018/979-8-3693-0782-3.ch005.

[4] Chang, M., Canseco, J. A., Nicholson, K. J., Patel N., Vaccaro, A. R. The Role of Machine Learning in Spine Surgery: The Future Is Now. *Front. Surg.* 2020; 7:54.

[5] Goswami, M., Sebastian, N. J. Performance Analysis of Logistic Regression, K. N. N., S. V. M., Naïve Bayes Classifier for Healthcare Application during COVID-19. In: Raj J. S., Kamel K., Lafata P., editors. *Innovative Data Communication Technologies and Application.* Volume 96. Springer Nature; Singapore: 2022. pp. 645–658.

[6] Kaur, P., Kumar, R., Kumar, M. A healthcare monitoring system using random forest and internet of things (IoT) *Multimed. Tools Appl.* 2019; 78:19905–19916.

[7] Rai, M., Maity, T., Sharma, R. et al. Early detection of foot ulceration in type II diabetic patients using registration method in infrared images and descriptive comparison with deep learning methods. *J Supercomput* 78, 13409–13426 (2022). https://doi.org/10.1007/s11227-022-04380-z.

[8] Ardila, D., Kiraly, A. P., Bharadwaj, S., Choi, B., Reicher, J. J., Peng, L., Tse D., Etemadi, M., Ye, W., Corrado, G. End-to-end lung cancer screening with three-dimensional deep learning on low-dose chest computed tomography. *Nat. Med.* 2019; 25:954–961.

[9] Muhammad, W., Hart, G. R., Nartowt, B., Farrell, J. J., Johung, K., Liang, Y., Deng, J. Pancreatic cancer prediction through an artificial neural network. *Front. Artif. Intell.* 2019;2:2.

[10] Hirschauer, T. J., Adeli, H., Buford, J. A. Computer-Aided Diagnosis of Parkinson's Disease Using Enhanced Probabilistic Neural Network. *J. Med. Syst.* 2015;39:179.

[11] Sarraf, S., DeSouza, D. D., Anderson, J., Tofighi, G. Deep A. D., Alzheimer's Disease Classification via Deep Convolutional Neural Networks using MRI and fMRI. *BioRxiv.* 2017:070441.

[12] Ramzan, F., Khan, M. U. G., Rehmat, A., Iqbal, S., Saba, T., Rehman, A., Mehmood, Z. A deep learning approach for automated diagnosis and multi-class classification of Alzheimer's disease stages using resting-state fMRI and residual neural networks. *J. Med. Syst.* 2020;44:37.

[13] Pang, K., Song, X., Xu, Z., Liu, X., Liu, Y., Zhong, L., Peng, Y., Wang, J., Zhou, J., Meng, F. Hydroplastic foaming of graphene aerogels and artificially intelligent tactile sensors. *Sci. Adv.* 2020;6:eabd4045.

[14] Hayasaka, T., Lin, A., Copa, V. C., Lopez, L. P., Loberternos, R. A., Ballesteros, L. I. M., Kubota, Y., Liu Y., Salvador, A. A., Lin, L. An electronic nose using a single graphene FET and machine learning for water, methanol, and ethanol. *Microsyst. Nanoeng.* 2020;6:50.

[15] Khanam, J. J., Foo, S. Y. A comparison of machine learning algorithms for diabetes prediction. *ICT Express.* 2021;7:432–439.

[16] Rai, M., Yadav, R. K., Husain, A. A., Maity, T., Yadav, D. K., "Extraction of Facial Features for Detection of Human Emotions under Noisy Condition," *International Journal of Engineering and Manufacturing (IJEM),* Vol.8, No.5, pp.49-62, 2018. doi: 10.5815/ijem.2018.05.05.

[17] Kaushik, A. K., Dhau, J. S., Gohel, H., Mishra, Y. K., Kateb, B., Kim, N.-Y., Goswami, D. Y. Electrochemical SARS-CoV-2 Sensing at Point-of-Care and Artificial Intelligence for Intelligent COVID-19 Management. *ACS Appl. Bio Mater.* 2020;3:7306–7325.

[18] Esteva, A., Chou, K., Yeung, S., Naik, N., Madani, A., Mottaghi, A., Liu, Y., Topol, E., Dean, J., Socher, R. Deep learning-enabled medical computer vision. *npj Digit. Med.* 2021;4:5.

[19] Rai, M., Maity, T., Yadav, R. K., Yadav, Shreyash, A Review on Detection of Human Emotions Using Colored and Infrared Images (July 14, 2022). *Proceedings of the Advancement in Electronics & Communication Engineering 2022,* Available at SSRN: http://dx.doi.org/10.2139/ssrn.4161798.

[20] Shen, Y., Li, Y., Zheng, H.-T., Tang, B., Yang, M. Enhancing ontology-driven diagnostic reasoning with a symptom-dependency-aware Naïve Bayes classifier. *BMC Bioinform.* 2019;20:330.

[21] Tkachenko, R. I. Izonin, chopyak, Kryvinska, V. N. and Lotoshynska, N. "Piecewise-linear approach for medical insurance costs prediction using SGTM neural-like structure," *Proc. IDDM,* 2018; 170:179.

[22] Hathaliya, J., Sharma, P., Tanwar, S., and Gupta, R., "Blockchain-based remote patient monitoring in healthcare 4.0," *Proc. IEEE 9th Int. Conf. Adv. Comput.* (IACC), 2019; 87:91.

[23] Ahamed, S., P., Bhatt, S. Sultanuddin, Walia, R., M. Haque, A. and Inayath Ahamed, S. B., "An Intelligent IoT enabled Health Care Surveillance using Machine Learning," *2022 International Conference on Advances in Computing, Communication and Applied Informatics (ACCAI),* Chennai, India, 2022, 1:5.

Chapter 9

Patient Centric Healthcare

Tejasva Maurya[1,*]
Saurabh Kumar[2,†]
Mritunjay Rai[3,‡]
and Abhishek Saxena[4,‖]

[1,2]Department of CSE, Shri Ramswaroop Memorial University, Barabanki, U.P., India
[3,4]Department of EEE, Shri Ramswaroop Memorial University, Barabanki, U.P., India

Abstract

In today's complex healthcare environment, patients often find themselves at a disadvantage due to a lack of transparency and understanding regarding their treatment options, potential outcomes, and associated costs. This gap in knowledge can lead to poor decision-making, unnecessary treatments, and financial exploitation, further complicating the patient's healthcare journey. The rise of healthcare fraud and misguidance exacerbates these issues, leaving patients vulnerable and often misled. In order to address these critical challenges, this research proposes a conceptual framework that develops innovative, AI-driven systems to enhance transparency, empower patients, and detect fraud within the healthcare sector. The proposed framework is made up of several main parts: a Patient Information System (PIS) that collects and customizes medical information for each patient; a Digital Health Literacy System that makes medical terms easier for patients to understand; a Healthcare Provider Transparency Index (HPTI) that rates

* Corresponding Author's Email: mauryatejasva512004@gmail.com
† Corresponding Author's Email: slsaurabh1234567890@gmail.com
‡ Corresponding Author's Email: dr.mritunjayr@gmail.com
‖ Corresponding Author's Email: abhishekec21@gmail.com

In: Harnessing the Power of IoT-Enabled Machine Learning …
Editors: Mritunjay Rai, Ravindra Kumar Yadav, Neha Goel et al.
ISBN: 979-8-89530-626-0

providers based on how open they are, how happy their patients are, and how fair their prices are; an AI-Driven Fraud Detection System that keeps an eye on healthcare transactions and treatment plans for signs of fraud or misinformation; and a Treatment Plan Pricing Chart that shows how much different medical services will cost in a clear and accurate way. Each component leverages advanced AI and machine learning algorithms to deliver clear, accurate, and personalized information, enabling patients to make informed and empowered decisions about their healthcare. The PIS empowers patients by providing a comprehensive guide to their treatment journey, ensuring they have access to clear and personalized information. The Digital Health Literacy System simplifies complex medical terms, making it easier for patients to understand their diagnosis and treatment plans. The HPTI offers a clear, AI-generated transparency score for each provider, helping patients avoid providers with poor communication, unethical billing practices, and low treatment success rates. The AI-Driven Fraud Detection System protects patients from unnecessary procedures and financial exploitation by detecting and flagging suspicious activities in real time. Additionally, the Treatment Plan Pricing Chart provides transparent and personalized cost estimates, enabling patients to make informed decisions based on accurate financial information. While this research remains theoretical due to the current lack of extensive data and resources, it lays the groundwork for future developments by organizations equipped to implement these concepts. The ultimate goal is to transform the patient-provider dynamic into a transparent, equitable, and patient-centered healthcare environment, equipping patients with the necessary knowledge and tools to confidently and effectively navigate their healthcare journey. As the healthcare industry continues to evolve, the integration of AI and patient-centric systems holds significant potential for reducing healthcare-related harm and improving patient outcomes.

Keywords: Patient Information System (PIS), Healthcare Provider Transparency Index (HPTI), healthcare, AI, ML, patient-centric healthcare

1. Introduction

In the intricate and often overwhelming landscape of modern healthcare, patients with limited medical knowledge frequently find themselves at a severe disadvantage. Healthcare providers particularly exploit patients who lack a clear understanding of medical terminology, treatment procedures, and the financial implications of their care. Healthcare providers often leave these patients in the dark about their treatment expectations, the realistic chances of success or failure, and the potential costs involved. This gap in knowledge can lead to poor decision-making, unnecessary treatments, and inflated medical bills, trapping patients in a cycle of uncertainty and financial strain. The lack of transparency not only undermines the trust between patients and healthcare providers but also results in significant physical, emotional [1, 2, 3], and financial consequences.

Globally, the issue of patient safety is a significant concern, with millions of patients experiencing harm due to unsafe healthcare practices. According to the World Health Organization (WHO), about 2.6 million deaths occur annually in low- and middle-income countries alone because of unsafe healthcare practices, most of which are preventable [4]. These adverse events include diagnostic errors, prescription mistakes, and unsafe surgical procedures, leading to substantial financial and social burdens. For instance, the World Health Organization (2019) and Illingworth et al. [5] estimate that medication errors alone incur an annual cost of $42 billion worldwide. The World Health Organization (WHO) emphasizes that primary and ambulatory care harms every four out of ten patients, with diagnostic and medication errors causing the most severe consequences. Surgical care is particularly risky, with complications affecting up to 25% of patients, leading to approximately 1 million deaths annually during or after surgery [4, 5]. The broader context of patient safety reveals that poor communication, lack of transparency, and insufficient patient engagement in their treatment processes significantly contribute to misled or defrauded patients. This is particularly problematic in settings where patients have low medical literacy or where there are significant power imbalances between healthcare providers and patients. Imperial College London developed a data dashboard using Power BI that allows users to visualize and analyze cases of fraud, miscommunication, and other related issues in healthcare. This dashboard provides a powerful tool for researchers, policymakers, and healthcare professionals to understand the extent and impact of these problems on patient care.

1.1. Global Healthcare Fraud Statistics

The statistics of Global Healthcare fraud is show in Figure 1.

2020:

- Healthcare Fraud Incidents: $4.1 billion in healthcare fraud detected globally.
- Misleading Treatment Cases: ~25% of patients reported receiving incomplete or misleading information about their treatment.
- Unnecessary Financial Bills: Around 15% of patients experienced unexpected financial charges [6, 7].

2021:

- Healthcare Fraud Incidents: $4.5 billion in healthcare fraud globally, a 9.8% increase from 2020.
- Misleading Treatment Cases: Reports remained steady at 26% of patients.
- Unnecessary Financial Bills: Increased to 18% of patients [6, 7] .

2022:

- Healthcare Fraud Incidents: $4.8 billion, a 6.7% increase from 2021.
- Misleading Treatment Cases: Increased slightly to 27%.
- Unnecessary Financial Bills: Rose to 20% [6, 7] .

2023:

- Healthcare Fraud Incidents: Projected at $5.1 billion, a 6.3% increase from 2022.
- Misleading Treatment Cases: Expected to increase to 28%.
- Unnecessary Financial Bills: Projected to rise to 22% [6, 7].

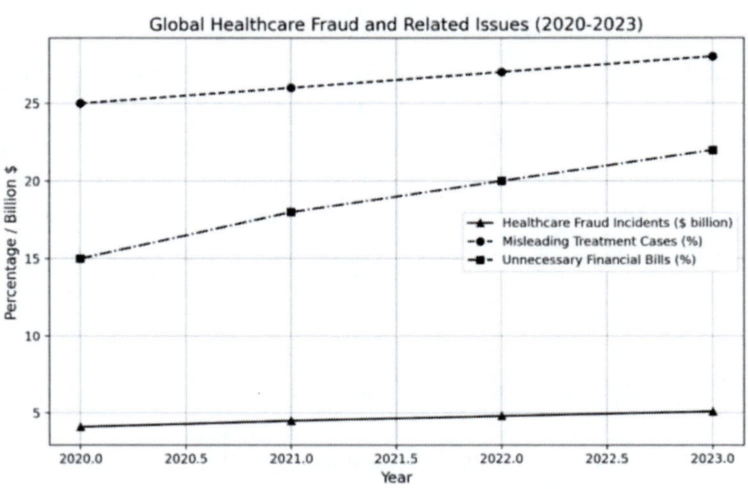

Figure 1. Global healthcare fraud statistics.

The highlights of the chapter are as follows:

- This research introduces a novel conceptual framework that leverages AI and machine learning to enhance transparency and patient empowerment in healthcare, addressing critical issues of healthcare fraud and misguidance.
- The proposed system focuses on providing patients with clear, personalized information about their treatment processes, helping them make informed decisions and avoid unnecessary procedures and financial exploitation.
- While theoretical in nature, this research lays the groundwork for future implementation by organizations with the necessary resources, aiming to revolutionize the patient-provider dynamic and improve overall healthcare outcomes.

In an era where the patient's voice is more vital than ever, the integration of Artificial Intelligence (AI) into healthcare is not just an enhancement; it's a revolution. The conventional healthcare model, often criticized for being provider-centric, is rapidly giving way to a patient-centric paradigm, largely driven by AI. This transformation ensures that patients are no longer passive recipients of care but active participants, empowered with personalized information and guidance. However, as this shift occurs, it becomes crucial to understand how AI is reshaping the landscape, making healthcare more accessible, transparent, and tailored to individual needs.

1.2. AI's Role in Evolving Patient-Centric Healthcare

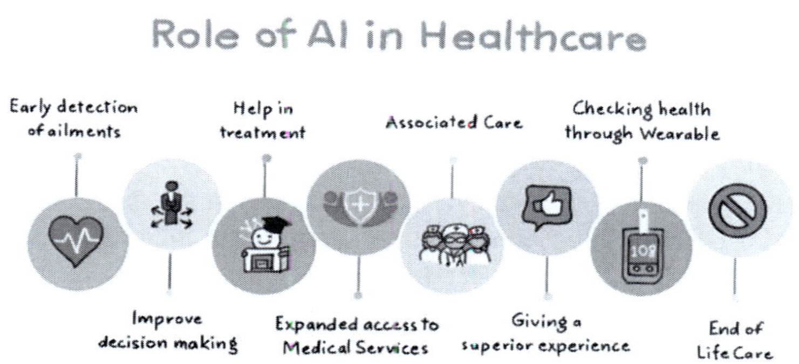

Figure 2. Role of AI in healthcare.

The role of AI in healthcare is shown in Figure 2.

1.2.1. Personalized Treatment Plans

AI analyzes vast amounts of patient data, including medical history, genetic information, and lifestyle factors, to create highly personalized treatment plans. This allows for more accurate diagnoses and treatments that are tailored to the specific needs of each patient, moving away from the one-size-fits-all approach [8, 9].

1.2.2. Predictive Analytics and Early Diagnosis

- AI's ability to process and analyze large datasets enables predictive analytics, which can forecast potential health issues before they become critical. By identifying patterns and trends within patient data, AI tools can suggest preventive measures, leading to early interventions and better outcomes [10].

1.2.3. Enhanced Patient-Doctor Communication

- AI-powered chatbots and virtual assistants are becoming integral in healthcare. These tools provide patients with 24/7 access to information and support, helping them understand their conditions, medications, and treatment options. This continuous engagement fosters a more informed and involved patient, reducing the feeling of isolation and anxiety.

1.2.4. Efficient Healthcare Delivery

- AI optimizes administrative tasks, such as scheduling, billing, and patient record management, allowing healthcare providers to focus more on patient care. This efficiency reduces waiting times and ensures that patients receive timely and accurate information, improving overall patient satisfaction.

1.2.5. Real-Time Monitoring and Remote Care

- AI-powered wearable devices and remote monitoring systems allow for continuous observation of patients' health metrics. This data is analyzed in real-time, alerting healthcare providers to any irregularities that may require immediate attention. This approach is particularly beneficial for managing chronic conditions and reducing hospital readmissions.

1.2.6. Reducing Healthcare Fraud and Enhancing Trust

- AI's advanced algorithms can detect anomalies and potential fraud in real-time, ensuring that patients are not subjected to unnecessary treatments or financial exploitation. By safeguarding patient interests, AI fosters a more trustworthy and transparent healthcare environment.

2. Literature Review

We conducted a literature survey to review the existing works in the field. The following summary presents the key findings from papers related to the proposed research. Emily Hickmann et al. [11] emphasize the critical importance of patient engagement in healthcare systems. It discusses how involving patients in their care processes can significantly improve health outcomes and patient satisfaction. The text highlights various strategies for enhancing patient engagement, such as using digital tools, personalized communication, and collaborative care models. It also addresses the challenges faced in implementing these strategies and suggests that a collective effort from healthcare providers, policymakers, and patients themselves is essential for achieving a more patient-centered healthcare system.

The article "Digital Health Literacy (eHL) in the General Population" by Theresa Sophie Busse et al. [12] discusses various strategies to enhance digital health literacy (eHL) among the general public. It highlights the growing importance of digital health literacy in an increasingly digitalized healthcare environment, where individuals need to effectively use online health information and digital health tools. The document delves into various approaches to enhance eHL, including education and training programs, policy initiatives, and technology design considerations. It also emphasizes the role of healthcare professionals, policymakers, and technology developers in creating an inclusive and supportive environment for improving eHL. The ultimate goal is to ensure that everyone, regardless of their socio-economic background, has the skills and access necessary to benefit from digital health resources.

Liu et al. [13] discuss the integration of AI in patient-centric care, emphasizing how advanced AI technologies can significantly enhance the quality and personalization of healthcare services. It highlights the role of AI in improving diagnostics, treatment plans, and overall patient experience by leveraging data-driven insights. The focus is on the transformative potential of AI to make healthcare more responsive to individual patient needs, leading to better health outcomes and more efficient care delivery systems. The document also suggests that AI can bridge gaps in current healthcare practices, making them more aligned with patient-specific conditions and preferences.

Edgman-Levitan & Schoenbaum [14] emphasize the importance of patient-centered care, where healthcare organizations and professionals must deeply understand what patients value. It argues that patient-centeredness leads to better health outcomes, safer workplaces, and stronger financial performance for healthcare organizations. The article also discusses various strategies to implement patient-centered care, such as actively involving patients in their care decisions, using patient experience surveys, and ensuring continuous feedback. Additionally, it highlights the discrepancies between what healthcare providers think patients value and what patients actually prioritize, underscoring the need for genuine patient engagement to improve healthcare quality.

Minheere et al. [15] explore the dynamics of patient involvement in healthcare settings, particularly in regional health improvement collaborative (RHICs) in the Netherlands. The study highlights the importance of patient empowerment within these collaborative, which consist of healthcare providers, insurers, and patients working together to address healthcare challenges. The article identifies key factors such as mutual trust, information symmetry, and equity as essential for effective collaboration and value co-creation. However, it notes that even when patients feel empowered on a personal level, they often struggle with power imbalances within group dynamics, which can hinder their influence in decision-making processes. To ensure meaningful participation and prevent ineffective involvement, the research highlights the need for further dialogue and inquiry into how these settings facilitate and value patient engagement.

Bhattad & Pacifico [16] discuss the importance of enhancing patient education and health literacy to improve patient care and outcomes. The study emphasizes the need for updated, concise, and accessible patient education materials, integrated into electronic health record (EHR) systems. The authors propose using standardized educational hand-outs, personalized advice, and electronic patient portals to ensure patients receive consistent, evidence-based information. By improving health literacy and encouraging shared decision-making, the approach aims to boost patient satisfaction and adherence to treatment plans. The study also highlights the use of quality improvement techniques, such as the Plan-Do-Study-Act (PDSA) cycle, to optimize the implementation and effectiveness of patient education in clinical settings.

Busch & Rimondini [17] discuss the importance of fostering strong patient-provider relationships and improving the emotional well-being of healthcare providers. It emphasizes that person-centered care, transparent communication, and patient engagement are key to enhancing the quality and safety of healthcare. The COVID-19 pandemic has highlighted the need for a more integrated approach to healthcare, one that supports both patients and providers. The special issue encompasses a variety of studies on these topics, providing valuable insights for enhancing healthcare systems and professional environments.

Kwame & Petrucka [18] explore the critical role of effective communication in achieving patient-centered care within nurse-patient interactions. It highlights various barriers to effective communication, such as institutional constraints, environmental factors, and personal behaviors, which can impede the quality of care. The document also identifies facilitators that can enhance communication, such as active listening, empathy, and patient engagement. A significant portion of the text introduces the Person-Centered Care and Communication Continuum (PC4) Model, which provides a framework for understanding and improving patient-centered communication. Shifting from task-centered to person-centered communication aims to treat patients as active participants in their care, resulting in improved health outcomes and increased patient satisfaction. Fraud and misguidance are increasingly plaguing the healthcare sector, a cornerstone of societal well-being, leaving patients vulnerable and often uninformed. The traditional patient-provider dynamic, where patients rely heavily on the knowledge and ethics of healthcare professionals, has, in some instances, led to exploitation. As healthcare fraud rises globally, there is an urgent need for innovative solutions that ensure transparency and empower patients with the information they need to make informed decisions about their health.

3. Conceptual Approach

Given the current lack of extensive data and resources, this research proposes a conceptual framework that addresses the critical issues of healthcare fraud and patient misguidance. This approach aims to lay the groundwork for future developments by organizations with the necessary resources to turn this vision into reality.

3.1. PIS

The PIS is discussed using block diagram as shown in Figure 3.

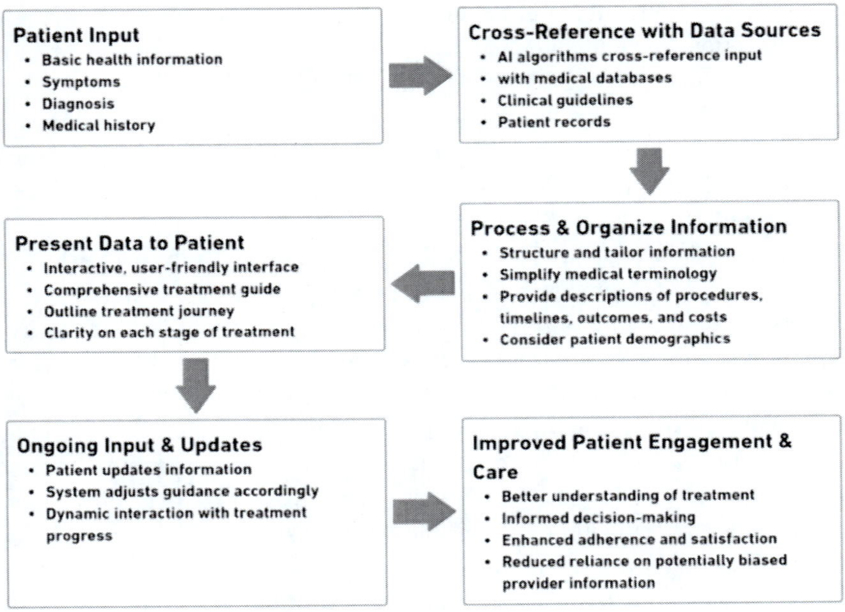

Figure 3. PIS block diagram representing its various processes.

The PIS begins with the patient inputting their basic health information, including symptoms, diagnosis, and medical history, into the system. This data serves as the foundation for personalized information retrieval. The system then uses AI algorithms to cross-reference this input with verified medical databases, clinical guidelines, and patient records to curate relevant data. The AI processes and organizes the identified relevant information into a structured format, tailoring it to the patient's specific needs. This includes breaking down complex medical terminology and presenting it in an understandable way, along with detailed descriptions of expected procedures, timelines, potential outcomes, and associated costs. The system also considers patient demographics, such as age, gender, and pre-existing conditions, to ensure that the information is as relevant and personalized as possible.

An interactive and user-friendly interface then presents the processed data to the patient. The patient receives a comprehensive guide that outlines their treatment journey, providing clarity on what to expect at each stage. This information empowers the patient to make informed decisions about their healthcare, reducing uncertainty and enhancing their understanding of their condition and treatment options. As the patient continues through their treatment, the system allows for ongoing input and updates. If new symptoms arise or treatment outcomes change, the patient can update their information, and the system will adjust the guidance accordingly. This dynamic interaction ensures that the patient remains informed throughout their healthcare journey, continually receiving the most relevant and up-to-date information. The final result is a well-informed patient who is better equipped to navigate their treatment process, leading to improved patient engagement, adherence to treatment plans, and overall satisfaction with their healthcare experience. The PIS effectively reduces the reliance on potentially biased information from healthcare providers and mitigates the risks of miscommunication by providing a transparent and empowering tool for patient care.

3.2. Digital Health Literacy System

The Digital Health Literacy System is discussed below as shown in Figure 4.

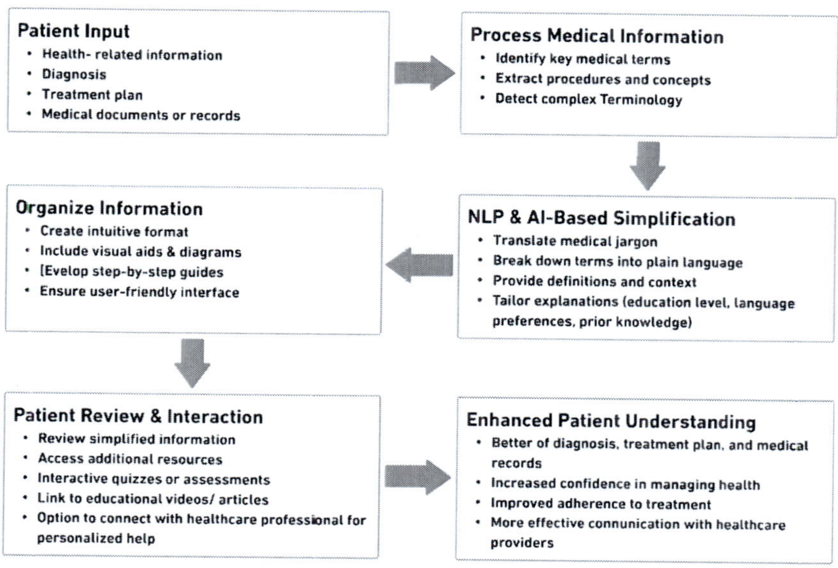

Figure 4. Block diagram of Digital Health Literacy System block diagram representing its various processes.

The Digital Health Literacy system starts with the patient providing their health-related information, including their diagnosis, treatment plan, and any specific medical documents or records they need help understanding. The system initially processes this input to identify key medical terms, procedures, and concepts that require simplification. Using natural language processing (NLP) and AI algorithms, the system then translates complex medical terminology and jargon into plain language. This process involves breaking down medical terms into easy-to-understand explanations, providing definitions, and offering context to ensure the patient fully comprehends the information. Additionally, the system leverages AI to tailor the explanations to the patient's education level, language preferences, and prior knowledge, ensuring the content is both accessible and relevant.

The system organizes the simplified medical information into an intuitive and interactive format. This may include the use of visual aids, diagrams, and step-by-step guides that help the patient understand their condition, treatment plan, and medical records. Patients can easily navigate through the information, ask questions, and access additional resources if needed, thanks to the user-friendly design of the interface. The patient then reviews the simplified information, gaining a clearer understanding of their healthcare situation. If there are still areas of confusion, the system provides options for further clarification, such as linking to educational videos, articles, or connecting with a healthcare professional for a more personalized explanation. The system may also offer interactive quizzes or assessments to reinforce the patient's understanding and ensure they are well-prepared to manage their health.

As a result, the Digital Health Literacy system empowers patients with the knowledge they need to make informed decisions about their healthcare. By demystifying complex medical concepts, the system enhances the patient's confidence in understanding their diagnosis, treatment plan, and medical outcomes. This improved health literacy leads to better adherence to treatment protocols, more effective communication with healthcare providers, and ultimately, better health outcomes. The system also reduces the likelihood of misunderstandings or misinterpretations, contributing to a more transparent and patient-centered healthcare experience.

3.3. HPTI

The HPTI, as shown in Figure 5, begins by collecting data from multiple sources, including patient feedback, independent audits, publicly available healthcare outcomes, and pricing information. This data serves as the foundation for evaluating healthcare providers on various criteria, such as transparency, patient satisfaction, treatment success rates, and pricing fairness. Once gathered, AI algorithms process and analyze the data to identify patterns and trends related to healthcare providers' performance. The AI uses machine learning techniques to assess qualitative and quantitative data, such as patient reviews, treatment outcomes, and pricing structures. It also cross-references these data points with industry benchmarks and standards to ensure accuracy and reliability. The system then aggregates this processed data to generate a transparency score for each healthcare provider. The transparency score is a composite index that reflects the provider's performance across multiple dimensions, including how clearly they communicate with patients, the fairness of their billing practices, and the success rates of their treatments. Patients can easily interpret the score, which offers a clear and concise summary of a provider's overall transparency and trustworthiness.

An accessible and user-friendly interface presents the HPTI to patients. Patients can search for healthcare providers by name, location, or specialty and view their transparency scores along with detailed breakdowns of the factors that contributed to the score. The system also allows patients to compare providers side by side, helping them make informed decisions about where to seek treatment. As patients interact with the HPTI, they can also contribute to the data by providing their own feedback and reviews of healthcare providers they have visited. This feedback loop ensures that the index remains up-to-date and reflective of current patient experiences, continuously improving its accuracy and relevance.

The result of the HPTI is a more informed and empowered patient population. By providing transparent information about healthcare providers, the system helps patients avoid providers with poor records of communication, unfair pricing practices, or low treatment success rates. This transparency fosters greater accountability among healthcare providers, encouraging them to maintain high standards of patient care and fairness. In the end, the HPTI fosters a healthcare system that prioritizes trust and transparency, thereby improving patient outcomes and satisfaction.

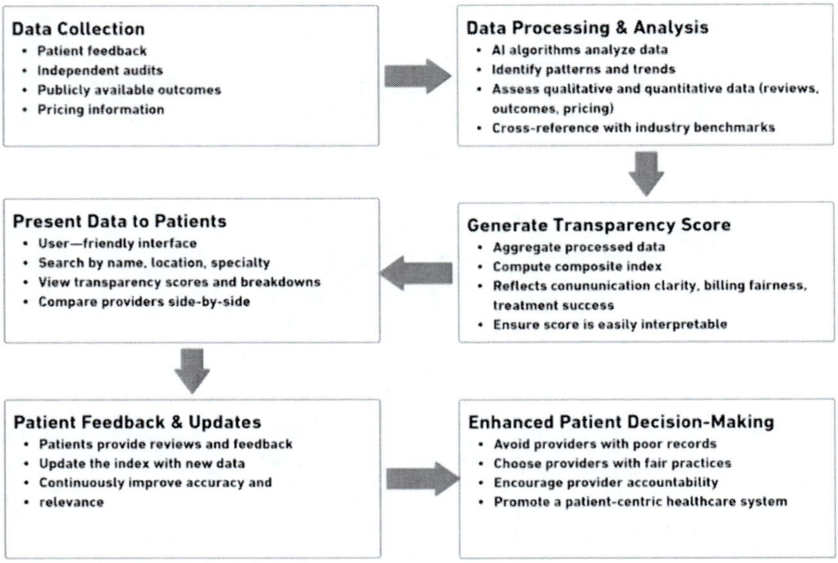

Figure 5. HPTI block diagram representing its various processes.

3.4. AI-Driven Fraud Detection System

The AI-Driven Fraud Detection System, as shown in Figure 6, begins by continuously monitoring healthcare transactions, treatment plans, and patient outcomes across various healthcare providers. The system collects data from billing records, medical procedures, treatment recommendations, and patient histories to build a comprehensive dataset. This data serves as the foundation for detecting fraudulent activities or misguidance in healthcare practices. Using advanced AI algorithms, the system analyzes this dataset to identify patterns and anomalies that could indicate potential fraud [19]. Historical data trains machine learning models to identify common fraud indicators like unusual billing patterns, excessive or unnecessary medical tests, and discrepancies between recommended treatments and patient outcomes. To detect subtle or complex fraud patterns that traditional methods might miss, the system also incorporates deep learning techniques.

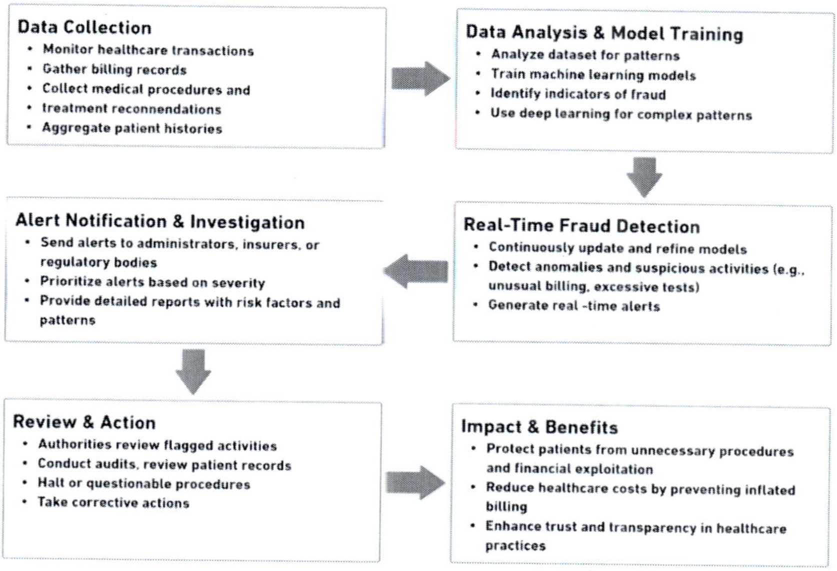

Figure 6. Block diagram of AI-Driven Fraud Detection System representing its various processes.

As the system processes the data, it continuously updates and refines its models based on new information. When the AI identifies a suspicious activity, such as a sudden spike in certain types of procedures or inconsistent billing for similar cases, it generates real-time alerts. Healthcare administrators, insurers, or regulatory bodies receive these alerts for immediate investigation. The system prioritizes alerts based on the severity of the detected anomalies, allowing for efficient resource allocation in investigating potential fraud cases. The relevant authorities can review the flagged transactions or treatment plans in detail once the system generates an alert. The system provides a detailed report of the suspected fraud, including the specific patterns that triggered the alert and the associated risk factors. This information helps investigators quickly assess the legitimacy of the activities and take appropriate action, such as auditing the healthcare provider, reviewing patient records, or halting questionable procedures.

The impact of the AI-Driven Fraud Detection System is significant. By identifying and addressing fraudulent activities early, the system protects patients from unnecessary medical procedures and financial exploitation. By preventing inflated billing practices and ensuring efficient resource allocation, it also aids in reducing overall healthcare costs. Moreover, the system enhances trust in the healthcare system by holding providers accountable for their actions and promoting transparency in medical billing and treatment practices.

Ultimately, the AI-Driven Fraud Detection System contributes to a more ethical and transparent healthcare environment. Patients benefit from receiving only necessary and appropriate treatments, while healthcare providers are encouraged to maintain high standards of integrity in their practices. The system's ability to detect and prevent fraud in real-time helps to safeguard both patients and the healthcare industry as a whole from the negative effects of fraudulent activities.

3.5. Treatment Plan Pricing Chart

The Treatment Plan Pricing Chart, as shown in Figure 7, starts by gathering extensive data on the costs of various medical treatments, procedures, and diagnostic tests from multiple healthcare providers. This data includes historical pricing information, regional cost variations, and pricing trends over time. The system aggregates this information to create a comprehensive database that reflects the true cost landscape of healthcare services. We then apply AI and machine learning algorithms to this dataset to analyze and standardize the pricing information. The system identifies patterns in the data, such as average costs for specific treatments, and adjusts for factors like location, provider type, and complexity of the procedure. The system analyzes these variables to generate an average price range for each treatment and test, which it then uses to create the Treatment Plan Pricing Chart.

Patients will find the pricing chart user-friendly and accessible. When a patient searches for a particular treatment or test, the system provides a detailed breakdown of the expected costs, including the average price, the lowest and highest observed prices, and any factors that may influence the cost, such as additional services or specialized care. The chart also highlights cost-effective alternatives and the potential savings patients can achieve by choosing different providers or locations. Additionally, the system uses AI to personalize the pricing chart for each patient. By inputting their insurance information, location, and specific medical needs, patients receive a tailored chart that reflects their unique situation. The AI also considers any discounts, insurance coverage, or special offers that might apply, providing a more accurate estimate of out-of-pocket expenses.

The impact of the Treatment Plan Pricing Chart is significant. By providing transparent pricing information, the system empowers patients to make informed decisions about their healthcare. Patients can compare prices across providers and choose options that best fit their budget without compromising the quality of care. Transparency helps reduce healthcare costs by encouraging competition among providers and discouraging overpricing. Moreover, the pricing chart fosters fairness in the healthcare industry by mitigating the risk of price gouging and guaranteeing that patients do not incur excessive charges for essential services. It also helps to alleviate financial stress by giving patients a clear understanding of what to expect in terms of medical expenses, allowing them to plan and budget more effectively.

The Treatment Plan Pricing Chart enhances the healthcare experience by making costs more predictable and transparent. Greater financial clarity benefits patients, and it encourages the healthcare industry to adopt more competitive and fair pricing practices, ultimately leading to a more equitable and accessible healthcare system.

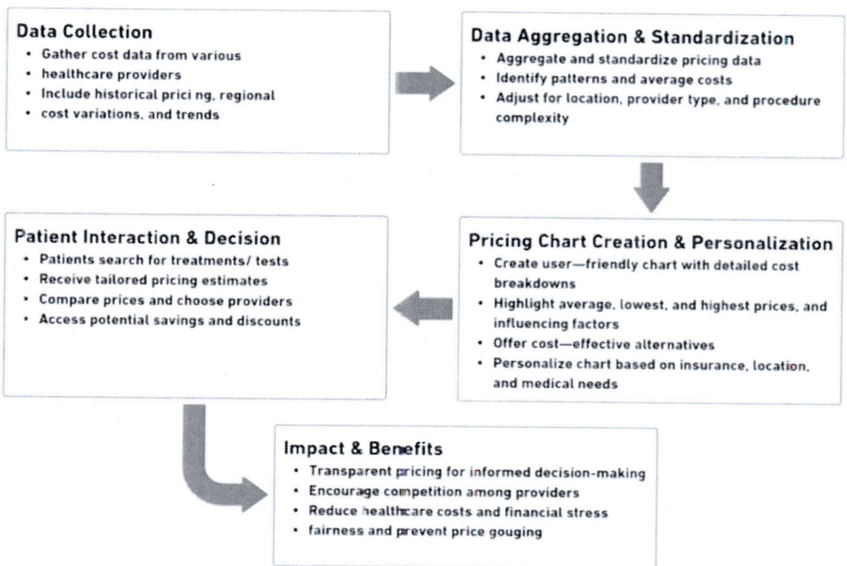

Figure 7. Block diagram of treatment plan pricing chart representing its various processes.

4. Methodology

The methodology introduces a comprehensive healthcare system that leverages AI, machine learning, and deep learning to enhance transparency, empower patients, and prevent fraud.

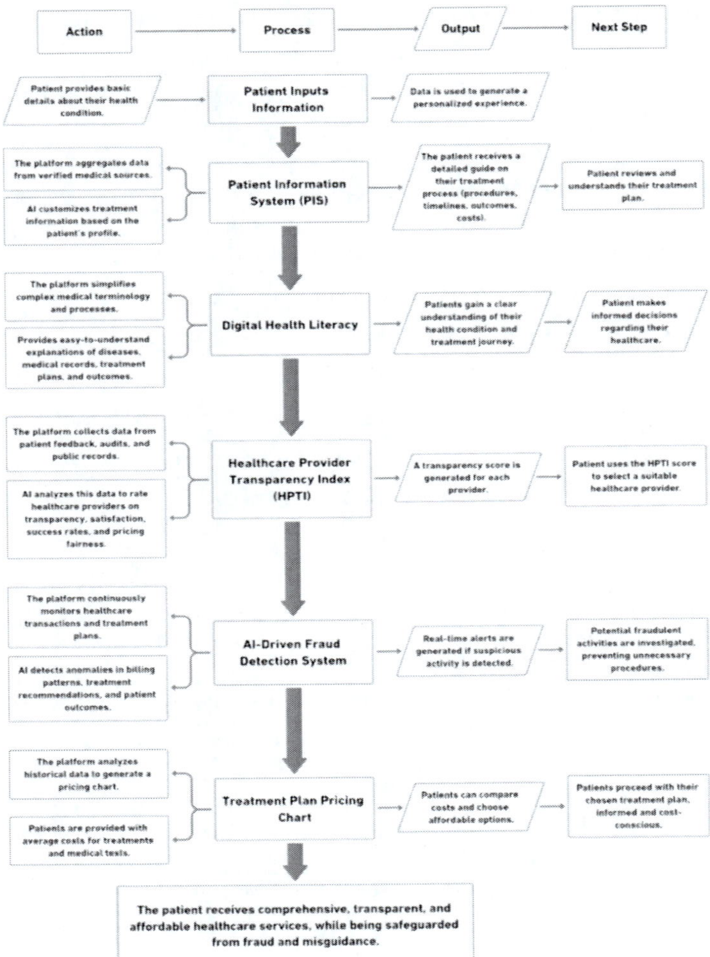

Figure 8. Workflow of methodology the patient centric healthcare system.

The workflow begins with patients inputting their health information into a centralized platform, which then generates personalized treatment plans using AI-driven insights. The system simplifies complex medical terminology, making it accessible through a digital health literacy module, while the HPTI offers a clear rating of providers based on patient feedback and outcomes. The AI-driven fraud detection system consistently scans for suspicious activities, guaranteeing that patients receive accurate information and avoid excessive charges. Additionally, the platform provides a treatment plan pricing chart, helping patients choose cost-effective healthcare options. Together, these features create a seamless, transparent, and affordable healthcare experience for users, as shown in Figure 8.

4.1. Patient Inputs Information

4.1.1. Theoretical Insight & Working

- *User Interface Design:* The platform is designed with an intuitive user interface (UI) that guides patients through the process of entering their health information. This could include dropdown menus for selecting symptoms, text fields for describing conditions, and integrations with wearable devices to automatically upload health data.
- *AI/ML Involvement:* AI algorithms analyze the input data to classify the patient's condition and recommend relevant pathways in real-time. Machine learning (ML) models trained on large datasets can predict which information is most pertinent based on the input provided, ensuring a personalized experience from the start.

4.1.2. Expected Outcome

- *Accurate Classification:* The system quickly and accurately classifies the patient's condition, setting the stage for a customized treatment guide.

4.2. PIS

4.2.1. Theoretical Insight & Working

- *Data Aggregation:* The PIS aggregates data from verified medical databases, electronic health records (EHRs), and peer-reviewed medical journals. This data includes treatment protocols, medication information, success rates, and potential side effects.

- *AI/ML Involvement:* AI processes this vast data using natural language processing (NLP) to extract relevant information. ML models then tailor this information to the patient's profile, considering variables such as age, gender, medical history, and current condition.
- *Deep Learning Integration:* Deep learning models, particularly recurrent neural networks (RNNs) and transformers, can be employed to continuously update and refine the information presented to the patient as new data becomes available.

4.2.2. Expected Outcome

- *Tailored Treatment Plans:* The patient receives a highly personalized and comprehensive treatment plan that considers all aspects of their condition and personal health history.

4.3. Digital Health Literacy

4.3.1. Theoretical Insight & Working

- *Simplification Algorithms:* AI-driven simplification algorithms analyze complex medical information and translate it into plain language. These algorithms can also prioritize information based on the patient's literacy level and preferences.
- *AI/ML Involvement:* NLP and ML models work together to identify key terms and concepts that might be challenging for patients to understand. The system then replaces or explains these terms using simpler language or visual aids.
- *User Interaction:* Interactive AI chatbots or virtual assistants can be integrated to answer patient questions, provide further explanations, and guide them through understanding their condition and treatment plan.

4.3.2. Expected Outcome

- *Improved Understanding:* Patients gain a clearer understanding of their medical situation, leading to better compliance with treatment plans and more effective self-management of their condition.

4.4. HPTI

4.4.1. Theoretical Insight & Working

- *Data Collection & Analysis:* Data is collected from patient reviews, independent audits, and publicly available outcomes data. This data is then fed into the HPTI system for analysis.
- *AI/ML Involvement:* AI algorithms analyze large datasets to assess transparency, patient satisfaction, treatment success rates, and pricing fairness. ML models are used to predict future performance based on historical data, contributing to a dynamic and constantly updated index.
- *Deep Learning Integration:* Convolutional neural networks (CNNs) could be used to analyze visual data such as images of facilities or graphs of patient outcomes, contributing to the transparency score.

4.4.2. Expected Outcome

- *Accurate Ratings:* Patients can access a clear, AI-generated transparency score for each healthcare provider, helping them make informed decisions about where to seek treatment.

4.5. AI-Driven Fraud Detection System

4.5.1. Theoretical Insight & Working

- *Pattern Recognition:* The fraud detection system continuously monitors transactions, treatment plans, and patient outcomes to identify patterns that deviate from the norm.
- *AI/ML Involvement:* ML models trained on historical fraud data identify suspicious activities, such as unusual billing patterns or treatment recommendations that do not align with established medical protocols.
- *Deep Learning Integration:* Deep learning models, such as autoencoders or deep belief networks, could be used to detect complex, nonlinear patterns that traditional ML models might miss. These models can analyze the relationships between different data points to flag potential fraud.

4.5.2. Expected Outcome

- *Fraud Prevention:* Real-time alerts are generated when potential fraud is detected, allowing for immediate investigation. This system protects patients from unnecessary procedures and financial exploitation.

4.6. Treatment Plan Pricing Chart

4.6.1. Theoretical Insight & Working

- *Cost Analysis:* The platform compiles historical data on treatment costs from various providers and geographical regions. It then analyzes this data to create a pricing chart that reflects average costs and cost variations.
- *AI/ML Involvement:* AI models analyze pricing data to identify trends and patterns. ML algorithms can suggest cost-effective alternatives for tests or treatments, considering factors like location, provider reputation, and patient preferences.
- *Deep Learning Integration:* Deep learning models could be employed to forecast pricing trends over time, helping patients and providers anticipate future costs and plan accordingly.

4.6.2. Expected Outcome

- *Cost Savings:* Patients are equipped with detailed, transparent pricing information, enabling them to choose cost-effective healthcare solutions without compromising quality.

4.7. End of Workflow: Transparent, Affordable Healthcare

4.7.1. Theoretical Insight & Working

- *System Integration:* The entire platform integrates AI, ML, and deep learning across various modules to ensure that patients receive accurate, personalized, and transparent healthcare services. Each component interacts with the others to provide a seamless experience, with AI constantly learning from new data to improve system performance.

- *AI/ML Involvement:* AI acts as the backbone of the platform, enabling data-driven decisions at every step. ML models continuously learn from patient interactions, fraud detection patterns, and treatment outcomes to enhance the platform's accuracy and efficiency over time.
- *Deep Learning Integration:* Deep learning models, with their ability to process and learn from complex, high-dimensional data, are crucial in refining the accuracy of the system's predictions and recommendations.

4.7.2. Expected Outcome

- *Optimal Patient Experience:* The final outcome is a healthcare platform that offers patients transparent, affordable, and high-quality care, tailored to their unique needs and preferences. The system's use of advanced AI, ML, and deep learning ensures that patients are empowered with the information and tools they need to navigate their healthcare journey confidently.

5. Comparison of Proposed Model with the Existing Models

Table 1 shows the comparison of proposed model with the existing models.

Table 1. Comparison between the proposed model and previous models

Aspect	Proposed Model (Patient-Centric Framework)	Previous Models
Patient Engagement	Focuses on active patient involvement via a PIS and HPTI to empower decision-making.	Hickmann et al. [11] emphasize the importance of patient engagement but focus more on digital tools and collaborative care models without specific mechanisms for transparency and fraud prevention.
Fraud Detection	Incorporates an AI-Driven Fraud Detection System to minimize financial exploitation and misguidance in healthcare practices.	No previous models specifically address fraud detection in healthcare. Previous models focus on improving care quality and patient satisfaction but overlook the issue of financial exploitation and misguidance.

Table 1. (Continued)

Aspect	Proposed Model (Patient-Centric Framework)	Previous Models
Digital Health Literacy	Enhances patient understanding through a PIS and digital resources integrated into the framework.	Busse et al. [12] discuss enhancing digital health literacy through education and training programs but do not provide specific patient-driven systems for digital literacy improvement within healthcare environments.
AI Integration	Leverages AI in the Fraud Detection System and improves personalized care by enabling patients to access transparent information and make better decisions.	Liu & Xiao [13] focus on AI's role in diagnostics and treatment personalization, but without an emphasis on patient-driven transparency or fraud detection.
Transparency	Introduces a HPTI to reduce misguidance and provide clear, accessible treatment options for patients.	Edgman-Levitan & Schoenbaum [14] highlights the importance of understanding patient values but lack specific tools like HPTI to enhance transparency between healthcare providers and patients.
Patient Empowerment	Prioritizes patient empowerment through transparent systems, fraud detection, and comprehensive health information accessibility.	Minheere et al. [15] address patient empowerment within collaborative healthcare settings but emphasize issues like power imbalances, without offering AI-driven solutions for transparency and empowerment on an individual patient level.
Healthcare Professional's Role	Healthcare professionals are supported by AI systems for fraud detection and patient data transparency, shifting their role towards guiding patients with accurate and transparent data.	Busch & Rimondini [17] focus on enhancing patient-provider relationships and provider well-being, but without integrating technology like AI to facilitate transparency and fraud prevention in patient interactions.
Communication & Decision Making	Facilitates better communication between patients and healthcare providers by providing accessible, transparent data on treatment plans and healthcare practices.	Kwame & Petrucka [18] introduce a communication framework (PC4) focused on person-centered care, enhancing communication but not addressing structural transparency or fraud prevention as in the proposed model.
Patient-Centered Care	The proposed framework emphasizes patient-centered care by integrating tools that ensure transparency, empower decision-making, and protect patients from fraud.	Various studies (e.g., Edgman-Levitan & Schoenbaum [14]) discuss patient-centered care but mainly focus on enhancing patient satisfaction and care experience, lacking the AI-driven tools for fraud detection and transparency found in the proposed model.

Aspect	Proposed Model (Patient-Centric Framework)	Previous Models
Implementation	The proposed framework is conceptual and serves as a foundation for future practical implementation in healthcare systems.	Existing models, such as [11, 12, 14] have explored patient engagement and care improvement but have not proposed comprehensive frameworks integrating fraud detection and AI.

Conclusion and Future Scopes

This paper delves into the challenges faced by patients in navigating the complex healthcare system, where limited medical knowledge often leaves them vulnerable to misguidance, financial exploitation, and a lack of transparency. The initial exploration of these issues reveals a concerning gap between patients' understanding of their treatment options and the realities of medical care, leading to poor decision-making and inflated costs. We proposed a conceptual framework to address these challenges, which focuses on developing a PIS, Digital Health Literacy System, HPTI, AI-Driven Fraud Detection System, and Treatment Plan Pricing Chart. We have designed each of these components to empower patients, enhance transparency, and lower the risks of fraud and miscommunication. The current progress in this area has been primarily theoretical, laying the groundwork for future implementation by organizations with the necessary resources. As the healthcare industry continues to evolve, the integration of AI and patient-centric systems holds enormous promise for creating a more informed, equitable, and trustworthy healthcare environment. This research underscores the need for ongoing efforts to refine and realize these concepts, ultimately leading to a significant shift in the patient-provider dynamic and a reduction in healthcare-related harm.

References

[1] Singh, S. Pandey, J. K. Rai, M. Saxena, A. K. "Advancements in Facial Expression Recognition Using Machine and Deep Learning Techniques," *Machine and Deep Learning Techniques for Emotion Detection, IGI Global,* 2024, doi: 10.4018/979-8-3693-4143-8.ch007.

[2] Arora et al. (2024) "Importance of Industry 5.0 in Understanding Emotional intelligence," *Human-Machine Collaboration and Emotional Intelligence in*

Industry 5.0, IGI Global, 2024, doi: 10.4018/979-8-3693-6806-0 ISBN13: 9798369368060.

[3] Tyagi, N., Rai, M., Sahw, P., Tripathi, P., & Kumar, N. "Methods for the Recognition of Human Emotions Based on Physiological Response: Facial Expressions." *Smart Healthcare for Sustainable Urban Development,* edited by Rosy Madaan, et al., IGI Global, 2022, pp. 183-202. https://doi.org/10.4018/978-1-6684-2508-4.ch013

[4] World Health Organization (2019). "WHO calls for urgent action to reduce patient harm in healthcare." Retrieved September 13, 2019, from https://www.who.int/news/item/13-09-2019-who-calls-for-urgent-action-to-reduce-patient-harm-in-healthcare. Accessed August 28, 2024.

[5] Illingworth et al. (2023). "Global State of Patient Safety 2023." Imperial College London. Retrieved from https://www.imperial.ac.uk/Stories/global-state-of-patient-safety/. Accessed August 28, 2024.

[6] Office of Inspector General (2023). "2023 Nationwide Health Care Fraud Enforcement Action." U.S. Department of Health and Human Services. Retrieved from https://oig.hhs.gov/newsroom/media-materials/2023-nationwide-health-care-fraud-enforcement-action/. Accessed August 28, 2024.

[7] Peck & McKenna (n.d.). "Fraud in healthcare: A worldwide concern." HealthManagement. Retrieved from https://healthmanagement.org/c/health management/issuearticle/fraud-in-healthcare-a-worldwide-concern. Accessed August 28, 2024.

[8] Johnson et al. (2021). "Precision Medicine, AI, and the Future of Personalized Health Care." *Clinical and Translational Science,* 14(1), 86–93. https://doi.org/10.1111/cts.12884. Accessed August 31, 2024.

[9] Khosravi et al. (2024). "Artificial Intelligence and Decision-Making in Healthcare: A Thematic Analysis of a Systematic Review of Reviews." *Health Services Research and Managerial Epidemiology,* 11, 23333928241234863. https://doi.org/10.1177/23333928241234863. Accessed August 31, 2024.

[10] Alowais et al. (2023). "Revolutionizing healthcare: the role of artificial intelligence in clinical practice." *BMC Medical Education,* 23(1), 689. https://doi.org/10.1186/s12909-023-04698-z. Accessed August 31, 2024.

[11] Hickmann, Richter & Schlieter (2022). "All together now – patient engagement, patient empowerment, and associated terms in personal healthcare." *BMC Health Services Research,* 22, 1116. https://doi.org/10.1186/s12913-022-08501-5. Accessed August 28, 2024.

[12] Busse et al. (2022). "Approaches to Improvement of Digital Health Literacy (eHL) in the Context of Person-Centered Care." *International Journal of Environmental Research and Public Health,* 19(14), 8309. doi: 10.3390/ijerph19148309. PMID: 35886158; PMCID: PMC9316109. Accessed August 28, 2024.

[13] Liu & Xiao (2021). "A framework of AI-based approaches to improving eHealth literacy and combating infodemic." *Frontiers in Public Health,* 9, 755808. https://doi.org/10.3389/fpubh.2021.755808. Accessed August 28, 2024.

[14] Edgman-Levitan & Schoenbaum (2021). "Patient-centered care: Achieving higher quality by designing care through the patient's eyes." *Israel Journal of Health Policy Research,* 10(1), 21. https://doi.org/10.1186/s13584-021-00459-9. Accessed August 28, 2024.

[15] Minheere et al. (2023). "Patient power and empowerment: Mitigating elements of valuable patient participation in healthcare collaboratives." *Behavioral Sciences,* 13(4), 347. https://doi.org/10.3390/bs13040347. Accessed August 28, 2024.

[16] Bhattad & Pacifico (2022). "Empowering patients: Promoting patient education and health literacy." *Cureus,* 14(7), e27336. https://doi.org/10.7759/cureus.27336. Accessed August 28, 2024.

[17] Busch & Rimondini (2021). "Empowering patients and supporting health care providers—New avenues for high quality care and safety." *International Journal of Environmental Research and Public Health,* 18(18), 9438. https://doi.org/10.3390/ijerph18189438. Accessed August 28, 2024.

[18] Kwame & Petrucka (2021). "A literature-based study of patient-centered care and communication in nurse-patient interactions: Barriers, facilitators, and the way forward." *BMC Nursing,* 20(1), 158. https://doi.org/10.1186/s12912-021-00684-2. Accessed August 28, 2024.

[19] Johnson & Khoshgoftaar (2023). "Data-Centric AI for Healthcare Fraud Detection." *SN Computer Science,* 4(4), 389. doi: 10.1007/s42979-023-01809-x. Epub May 11, 2023. PMID: 37200563; PMCID: PMC10173919. Accessed August 28, 2024.

Chapter 10

IoT-Driven Machine Learning in Modern Healthcare

Reeta Mishra[1,*]
Padmesh Tripathi[2,†]
Krishna Kumar Paroha[3,‡]
Mritunjay Rai[4,‖]
and Sonia Arora[5,¶]

[1]School of Computer Science and Engineering, IILM University, Greater Noida, UP, India
[2]Delhi Technical Campus, Greater Noida, UP, India
[3]Gyan Ganga College of Technology, Jabalpur, MP, India
[4]Shri Ramswaroop Memorial University, Barabanki, UP, India
[5]Noida Institute of Engineering and Technology, Greater Noida, UP, India

Abstract

Modern healthcare is undergoing a revolution towards the cutting-edge technologies that the Internet of Things (IoT) and machine learning (ML). By gathering enormous volumes of data from sensors, wearable technology, and medical equipment, IoT devices allow for ongoing, real-time patient monitoring. This data can be examined to find trends, offer prognostic information, and assist healthcare practitioners in making decisions by combining it with sophisticated machine learning

* Corresponding Author's Email: ree76shok@gmail.com
† Corresponding Author's Email: padmesh01@rediffmail.com
‡ Corresponding Author's Email: kkparoha@ggct.ac.in
‖ Corresponding Author's Email: er.mritunjayrai@gmail.com
¶ Corresponding Author's Email: soniasitm@gmail.com

In: Harnessing the Power of IoT-Enabled Machine Learning …
Editors: Mritunjay Rai, Ravindra Kumar Yadav, Neha Goel et al.
ISBN: 979-8-89530-626-0

techniques. With a focus on the revolutionary effects of these technologies on patient care, illness management, and healthcare operations, this review paper examines the state of IoT-driven machine learning in the healthcare industry. Through the use of predictive analytics, IoT-driven machine learning applications are improving preventative care by facilitating the early detection of diseases including cancer, diabetes, and cardiovascular disorders. Wearable technology with Internet of Things (IoT) sensors, for example, may continually track vital signs and send out alerts when aberrant patterns are detected, enabling fast interventions. Improved patient outcomes and tailored treatment strategies are made possible by using ML models to process this real-time data stream. Reduced hospital readmissions and enhanced patient quality of life have been two major benefits of remote patient monitoring, especially in the management of chronic diseases. Along with improving workflow efficiency and resource allocation, IoT and ML are revolutionising hospital operations. IoT-enabled smart healthcare solutions facilitate patient flow management, asset tracking, and even the early detection of equipment malfunctions. When ML algorithms are combined with these systems, the results can be better service delivery, shorter wait times, and patient admission forecasts. IoT-driven machine learning in healthcare still faces a number of obstacles, despite these developments. The ongoing gathering and sharing of private medical information expose patients to potential cyber-attacks, thus data security and privacy continue to be top priorities. To protect patient information, it is essential to ensure compliance with laws like the General Data Protection Regulation (GDPR) and the Health Insurance Portability and Accountability Act (HIPAA). Integration is further hampered by the heterogeneity of IoT devices and the absence of defined protocols, which prevents data from flowing seamlessly between platforms and systems. To prevent incorrect conclusions, rigorous data pre-treatment and validation techniques are necessary to ensure that IoT data is reliable and of a high enough quality for machine learning predictions to be made. IoT-driven machine learning's promise for personalized medicine and drug development is also covered in the paper. To create personalized treatment regimens, ML algorithms may analyze patient-specific data gathered from IoT devices. IoT data and machine learning (ML) can be used in drug research to speed clinical trials, find new biomarkers, and predict drug responses. This will lead to more precise and effective treatments. In short, IoT and ML combined provide a great deal of promise for modern healthcare: more precise diagnosis, tailored therapies, and effective resource allocation. Still, major issues including data privacy, device interoperability, and data quality must be resolved if these technologies are to reach their full potential. Growing patient outcomes and lower healthcare costs are anticipated as IoT and ML technologies are integrated into healthcare systems and continue to develop. This will make healthcare more proactive and predictive. A roadmap for next research and implementation techniques is provided in this review article, which also addresses the opportunities and obstacles in IoT-driven machine learning in the healthcare sector.

Keywords: Internet of Things (IoT), machine learning, remote patient monitoring, personalized medicine, smart healthcare

1. Introduction

The integration of the IoT and ML is ushering in a new era of healthcare, characterized by real-time data analysis, personalized treatment, and proactive care. IoT refers to a network of interconnected devices that collect, transmit, and analyze data in real-time, enabling continuous monitoring of patients and seamless communication between healthcare providers. These devices, including wearable sensors, smart medical equipment, and remote monitoring systems, generate massive amounts of health-related data that can be analysed to provide actionable insights. When combined with ML, a branch of artificial intelligence (AI) that allows computers to learn from data and improve over time, IoT can significantly enhance the quality of healthcare services. Yousefnezhad et al. [1] said that cutting-edge advancements in the field of item lifecycle security are used to investigate IoT security, particularly the product lifecycle. Handling long-term conditions like diabetes is a fascinating real-time illustration of IoT-driven machine learning in the healthcare industry. IoT-based Continuous Glucose Monitoring (CGM) systems constantly monitor blood glucose levels and send the information to a cloud-based platform or a smartphone app. In order to detect trends and forecast future glucose levels, machine learning algorithms evaluate the incoming data. This enables patients and healthcare professionals to take preventive action before a notable variation happens. Patients with diabetes have better results, a lower chance of complications, and a higher quality of life as a result of this proactive strategy [2].

Remote patient monitoring for cardiac conditions is another example. Heart rate, electrocardiogram, and other vital indicators of a patient are continuously monitored by wearable technology, such smart watches and sensor-equipped chest straps. A platform powered by machine learning receives this data and uses it to analyze it in real time, looking for anomalies or abnormalities that could point to a cardiac event. A user who had atrial fibrillation (AFib) in 2019 was effectively diagnosed by the Apple Watch's built-in ECG capability; the user sought medical assistance and received treatment on time. In recognizing health hazards before they become critical, this case shows how IoT-driven machine learning can offer actions that could save lives.

Predictive maintenance of medical equipment is one area in which IoT-driven machine learning is very important in hospitals. Examples of essential equipment that need routine maintenance to perform at their best are ventilators and MRI machines. These devices are equipped with Internet of Things (IoT) sensors that are constantly monitoring their operational characteristics and performance. Hospitals are able to plan repairs ahead of time when ML algorithms evaluate this data to forecast when a machine is likely to break down or need maintenance. The total effectiveness of healthcare service is increased by predictive maintenance, which not only avoids expensive downtime but also guarantees the availability of vital medical equipment when needed. There are obstacles in the way of IoT and ML integration in healthcare. Securing and protecting data is one of the main issues. Cyberattacks could target the enormous volumes of data produced by IoT devices, which frequently contain private patient information. In 2017, for instance, the WannaCry ransomware attack hit multiple hospitals globally, causing service disruptions and drawing attention to the vulnerabilities in medical devices that are connected. Protecting patient data and upholding confidence in these technologies depend critically on the security of IoT-driven healthcare systems.

Still another major obstacle is interoperability. A common cause of problems with data interoperability and integration in the healthcare ecosystem is the variety of platforms and devices that come from different manufacturers. As an illustration, a patient may utilize a glucose monitor from one firm, a hospital system from another, and wearable technology from still another. Integrated and multi-source data analysis can be challenging in the absence of common protocols for data communication. The full promise of IoT-driven machine learning to deliver all-encompassing and well-coordinated care is hampered by this fragmentation.

The advantages of IoT-driven machine learning in healthcare are significant, notwithstanding these obstacles. These technologies not only improve results and patient care, but they also lower costs. IoT devices can lessen the requirement for recurrent hospital admissions and extended hospital stays by enabling remote monitoring and early health concern identification. Based on real-time data analysis, studies have demonstrated that remote monitoring of patients with chronic heart failure can lower the risk of readmissions to hospitals by enabling timely interventions. Along with greatly reducing healthcare expenses, this also enhances the patient's quality of life. Furthermore, personalized medicine—in which treatment regimens are customized for each patient based on their particular health data—is made possible by IoT-driven ML. One well-known instance is oncology, where ML models are used to deliver individualized cancer treatment by analyzing data from IoT devices—such as wearable sensors that monitor a patient's vital signs—along with genomic data. A patient diagnosed with metastatic cancer in 2020 received treatment based on a customized treatment plan created by analyzing real-time data from genomic sequencing and wearable technology. The course of treatment was extremely successful in prolonging the patient's life and showing how IoT-driven machine learning may be used to provide personalized medication.

Additionally important are the ethical issues raised by the application of ML and IoT in healthcare. There can be major repercussions from problems like algorithmic bias, in which machine learning algorithms may generate biased outcomes because of the data they are trained on. A hospital's emergency department may provide biased treatment recommendations if an ML model was trained on data that under-represented specific demographic groups. Thorough evaluation of the data used to train machine learning models, together with openness and responsibility in the models' application in healthcare environments, are necessary to address these ethical issues.

Regulatory frameworks and standards are crucial in guiding the ethical and safe use of IoT-driven ML in healthcare. In the United States, the Food and Drug Administration (FDA) has started to develop guidelines for the use of AI and ML in medical devices, focusing on aspects such as algorithm transparency, performance monitoring, and patient safety. Similarly, the European Union's General Data Protection Regulation (GDPR) sets strict standards for data privacy, which apply to the use of IoT devices in healthcare. These regulations are essential in ensuring that the integration of IoT and ML in healthcare is conducted in a manner that safeguards patient rights and promotes trust in these technologies. Looking to the future, the integration of IoT and ML in healthcare is poised to become even more sophisticated with advancements in technology. Emerging trends such as AI-driven wearables, which not only monitor health metrics but also provide real-time analysis and feedback, are set to revolutionize patient care. For instance, wearable devices that monitor blood pressure, oxygen levels, and other vital signs can be combined with ML algorithms to provide real-time health alerts to both patients and healthcare providers, enabling immediate interventions. These advancements are expected to improve the management of chronic diseases, enhance preventive care, and reduce the burden on healthcare systems. Another promising development is the use of edge computing in IoT-driven healthcare, where data processing occurs locally on the device rather than in a centralized cloud. This approach reduces latency, allowing for faster analysis and decision-making, which is crucial in emergency situations. For example, in the case of a stroke patient, every minute counts, and edge computing can enable immediate analysis of vital signs and brain activity, leading to quicker diagnosis and treatment.

This review aims to provide a comprehensive analysis of IoT-driven machine learning in modern healthcare. It will explore the current applications of these technologies, examine the benefits and challenges associated with their integration, and discuss the ethical and regulatory considerations that arise. Additionally, the review will highlight emerging trends and future directions, offering insights into how IoT and ML are likely to continue shaping the healthcare landscape in the coming years.

2. IoT in Modern Healthcare

2.1. Overview of IoT Technology

The Internet of Things (IoT) is fundamentally transforming the landscape of modern healthcare by enabling a more connected, efficient, and patient-centered approach. IoT technology refers to a network of interconnected devices embedded with sensors, software, and other technologies that enable them to collect, transmit, and exchange data over the internet. In the context of healthcare, these devices range from wearable fitness trackers and implantable medical devices to remote monitoring systems and smart hospital infrastructure. The integration of IoT in healthcare facilitates real-time data collection and analysis, improves patient outcomes, and supports a more proactive approach to disease management. Krishnamoorthy et al. [3] suggested examining various architectural implementations' benefits, drawbacks and needs for quality of service. In conclusion, emphasize the importance of building security and privacy in future healthcare systems. Duodu et al. [4] proposed a real-time intelligent IoT-based EHR system that uses contactless sensors (such as the Raspberry Pi Noir Camera and rPPG camera) and contacted wearable sensors made of immunogens, enzymatic sensors, and nanosensors to generate students' vital signs while they are in an educational setting in order to detect cancer (leukaemia). With an accuracy of 99.66% and an error rate of 0.34%, the random forest algorithm emerged as the top-performing model among the others.

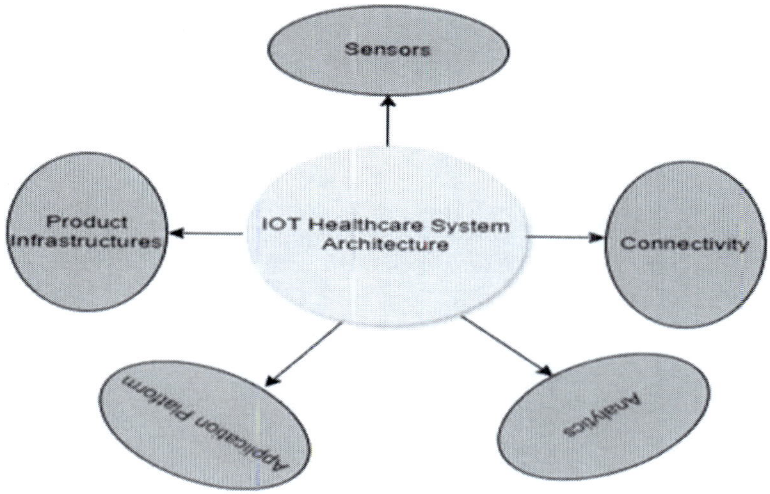

Figure 1. IoT healthcare system.

2.2. IoT Devices and Applications in Healthcare

IoT devices in healthcare are diverse and serve a wide range of purposes. They can be broadly categorized into the following groups:

2.2.1. Wearable Devices

These include smart watches, fitness trackers, and wearable biosensors that monitor various health metrics such as heart rate, blood pressure, physical activity, and sleep patterns. It can be further elaborated under different categories such as:

2.2.1.1. Wearable Diagnostic Devices

One of the most significant applications of IoT in diagnostics is the development of wearable devices that continuously monitor physiological parameters and provide real-time data to healthcare providers. These devices can detect early signs of medical conditions, allowing for timely intervention.

2.2.1.1.1. Continuous Glucose Monitors (CGMs)

For patients with diabetes, IoT-enabled CGMs are a game-changer. These devices continuously monitor blood glucose levels through sensors placed under the skin and transmit the data to a smartphone or a cloud-based platform. Healthcare providers can access this data remotely, analyze glucose trends, and adjust treatment plans accordingly. Early detection of glucose fluctuations can prevent severe hypoglycemia or hyperglycemia, reducing the risk of complications and hospitalizations.

2.2.1.1.2. Smartwatches with ECG Functionality

Devices like the Apple Watch, equipped with electrocardiogram (ECG) sensors, allow users to monitor their heart rhythms in real-time. These wearable can detect irregular heartbeats, such as atrial fibrillation, and alert the user to seek medical attention. The ECG data can be shared with healthcare providers, aiding in the early diagnosis and management of cardiovascular diseases.

2.2.1.2. Point-of-Care Diagnostic Devices

IoT technology has enabled the development of portable, point-of-care diagnostic devices that can be used in remote or resource-limited settings. These devices are connected to healthcare networks, allowing for rapid diagnosis and treatment, even in areas where access to traditional laboratory facilities is limited.

2.2.1.2.1. IoT-Enabled Ultrasound Machines

Portable ultrasound devices connected to smartphones or tablets can be used in point-of-care settings to diagnose conditions such as pregnancy complications, liver disease, or kidney stones. These devices are particularly useful in remote areas where access to large, traditional ultrasound machines is not feasible. The images and data captured can be transmitted to specialists in real-time for further analysis and diagnosis.

2.2.1.2.2. Smart Diagnostic Kits

IoT-enabled diagnostic kits for conditions like infectious diseases (e.g., COVID-19, malaria) allow for rapid testing and result transmission. For instance, smart diagnostic kits can be used to test for COVID-19 at home, with the results automatically sent to a healthcare provider. This enables timely diagnosis, quarantine, and treatment, helping to contain the spread of the virus.

2.2.1.3. Remote Diagnostics and Telemedicine

IoT has greatly expanded the capabilities of remote diagnostics and telemedicine, enabling healthcare providers to diagnose and monitor patients from afar. This is particularly valuable for patients in rural or underserved areas, as well as those with chronic conditions requiring ongoing monitoring.

2.2.1.3.1. Remote ECG Monitoring

Patients with cardiovascular conditions can use IoT-enabled ECG monitors at home to record their heart rhythms. These monitors are connected to a telemedicine platform, where the data is analyzed in real-time by healthcare professionals. Any abnormalities, such as arrhythmias or ischemic changes, are immediately flagged, and the patient can be advised on the next steps, such as medication adjustments or hospital visits.

2.2.1.3.2. Remote Imaging Diagnostics

IoT technology is also being used in imaging diagnostics, where portable imaging devices, such as X-ray or MRI machines, are connected to cloud-based platforms. The images captured can be uploaded to the cloud and analyzed by radiologists located anywhere in the world. This application is particularly beneficial in areas with a shortage of radiologists, ensuring that patients receive timely and accurate diagnoses.

2.2.1.3.3. Remote Patient Monitoring (RPM) Systems

These systems allow healthcare providers to monitor patients' vital signs and health status remotely, often from the comfort of the patient's home. For instance, patients with chronic conditions like heart disease or diabetes can use RPM devices that continuously monitor vital signs, blood glucose levels, or weight, sending this data to healthcare providers in real time. This allows for early detection of potential health issues and timely interventions, reducing the need for hospital visits and improving the overall quality of care.

2.2.1.3.4. Smart Medical Devices

These are advanced devices used in clinical settings, such as smart inhalers for asthma patients, insulin pumps for diabetes management, and connected imaging devices like MRI and CT scanners. These devices are integrated with IoT technology to collect and transmit data, enabling more precise and personalized treatment plans.

2.2.1.3.5. Implantable Devices

These include pacemakers, defibrillators, and other devices implanted within the body to monitor and regulate specific bodily functions. IoT-enabled implantable devices can send real-time data to healthcare providers, allowing for continuous monitoring and immediate response in case of abnormalities.

2.2.1.3.6. Smart Hospital Infrastructure

IoT technology extends beyond individual devices to encompass entire hospital systems. Smart hospitals utilize IoT to optimize various operational aspects, such as patient flow, asset tracking, and environmental monitoring. For example, IoT sensors can monitor the temperature and humidity in operating rooms, ensuring optimal conditions for surgeries. Additionally, RFID tags and IoT-enabled inventory systems help manage medical supplies and equipment, reducing waste and improving efficiency.

2.3. Benefits of IoT in Healthcare

The adoption of IoT technology in healthcare offers numerous benefits, enhancing the quality of care, improving patient outcomes, and reducing costs. According to Ranjan et al. [5], data analytics and networked devices improve operational effectiveness, individualized patient care, and the efficiency of medical operations.

2.3.1. Real-Time Monitoring and Early Intervention

One of the most significant advantages of IoT in healthcare is the ability to monitor patients in real-time. Continuous data collection from wearable devices and RPM systems allows healthcare providers to detect early signs of health deterioration and intervene promptly. This proactive approach can prevent complications, reduce hospital admissions, and improve patient outcomes. For example, in cases of heart failure, IoT-enabled devices can detect changes in vital signs that precede a heart attack, allowing for immediate medical attention.

2.3.2. *Enhanced Patient Engagement and Self-Management*

IoT devices empower patients to take an active role in managing their health. Wearable devices and mobile health apps provide patients with valuable insights into their health metrics, encouraging healthier lifestyle choices and better adherence to treatment plans. For instance, patients with diabetes can use IoT-enabled glucose monitors to track their blood sugar levels and receive personalized recommendations on diet and medication.

2.3.3. *Personalized Healthcare*

IoT technology facilitates the collection of large amounts of personalized health data, which can be analyzed to develop tailored treatment plans. This shift towards personalized medicine enables more accurate diagnoses, targeted therapies, and improved patient outcomes. For example, IoT-enabled devices can continuously monitor a patient's response to a specific treatment and adjust dosages in real time, optimizing therapeutic outcomes.

2.3.4. *Operational Efficiency in Healthcare Facilities*

IoT plays a crucial role in improving the operational efficiency of healthcare facilities. Smart hospital systems equipped with IoT sensors and automation technology can streamline workflows, reduce wait times, and optimize resource allocation. For example, IoT-enabled patient tracking systems can help manage patient flow in emergency departments, ensuring that critical cases receive timely attention. Additionally, IoT-based inventory management systems help track the usage of medical supplies, reducing waste and ensuring that essential items are always in stock.

2.3.5. *Cost Reduction*

By enabling remote monitoring and early detection of health issues, IoT technology can significantly reduce healthcare costs. Patients with chronic conditions can be monitored remotely, reducing the need for frequent hospital visits and minimizing the risk of costly complications. Additionally, IoT-enabled predictive maintenance of medical equipment helps prevent unexpected breakdowns, reducing downtime and repair costs.

3. Machine Learning in Healthcare

Machine Learning (ML) is a subset of artificial intelligence (AI) widely used in different fields [6, 7, 8, 9] that empowers systems to learn from data, improve their performance, and make decisions without explicit programming. ML algorithms are designed to identify patterns, predict outcomes, and enhance decision-making processes by analyzing large datasets. In the context of healthcare, ML plays a transformative role in improving diagnostics, personalizing treatments, and optimizing operational efficiencies. To understand its applications, it is essential to grasp the core concepts of ML, including its types and how ML models are trained and refined. Predictive analytics is a machine learning approach that Jain et al. [10] suggested should be added to the current system to raise the general standard of healthcare services rendered. There are more opportunities to improve patient care and treatment outcomes when cutting-edge technologies are combined with real-time patient-doctor contact. Kumar, et al. [11] observed several applications of machine learning in healthcare.

3.1. Core Concepts of Machine Learning

ML refers to algorithms and statistical models that enable computers to perform specific tasks without explicit instructions. Instead, ML systems use data and learn from it to make decisions or predictions. The primary goal of ML is to enable systems to recognize patterns and adapt their behavior based on new information.

ML models are trained using historical data, which includes input features and corresponding outcomes. During training, the model adjusts its parameters to minimize errors in its predictions or classifications. This process involves iteratively refining the model based on feedback from the data. Once trained, ML models can make predictions or classifications on new, unseen data. The performance of these models is evaluated using metrics such as accuracy, precision, recall, and F1 score, depending on the type of problem being addressed.

3.2. Types of Machine Learning

3.2.1. Supervised Learning

In supervised learning, the model is trained on a labeled dataset, where each training example is paired with an output label. The model learns to map inputs to outputs based on this labeled data. Supervised learning is commonly used for classification and regression tasks. Predicting the likelihood of a patient developing a specific disease based on historical health records. The model learns from examples with known outcomes (e.g., patients with or without the disease) and makes predictions for new patients.

3.2.2. Unsupervised Learning

Unlike supervised learning, unsupervised learning deals with unlabeled data. The model tries to identify hidden patterns or structures within the data without prior knowledge of the outcomes. It is often used for clustering, dimensionality reduction, and anomaly detection. Grouping patients with similar symptoms or genetic profiles to discover previously unknown subtypes of a disease or to identify patterns in patient data that might indicate emerging health trends.

3.2.3. Reinforcement Learning

Reinforcement learning involves training a model to make decisions by rewarding or penalizing actions based on their outcomes. The model learns to take actions that maximize cumulative rewards over time. This type of learning is particularly useful for sequential decision-making problems. Developing treatment strategies or optimizing scheduling in a way that maximizes patient outcomes or resource utilization. For instance, a reinforcement learning algorithm could be used to determine the optimal dosage and timing of medication for a chronic condition.

3.3. Training Machine Learning Models

3.3.1. Data Collection and Preparation

3.3.1.1. Data Collection

The first step in training an ML model is to gather relevant data. In healthcare, this can include electronic health records (EHRs), medical imaging, genomic data, or patient surveys. High-quality, diverse datasets are crucial for building effective ML models.

3.3.1.2. Data Preparation

Once collected, the data must be cleaned and preprocessed. This involves de-noising, handling missing values, normalizing or scaling features, and encoding categorical variables. Data preparation ensures that the input data is in a format suitable for the ML algorithms. De-noising the data is vital in analysis of data [12, 13, 14, 15].

3.3.2. Model Selection and Training

3.3.2.1. Choosing a Model

Depending on the task, different ML algorithms are selected. For classification tasks, algorithms like logistic regression, decision trees, and support vector machines might be used. For regression, linear regression or more complex models like gradient boosting might be chosen. In healthcare, deep learning models such as convolutional neural networks (CNNs) are often used for analyzing medical images.

3.3.2.2. Training the Model

During training, the ML algorithm iterates over the dataset, adjusting its parameters to minimize the difference between its predictions and the actual outcomes. This process involves splitting the data into training and validation sets to tune the model and avoid overfitting.

3.3.3. Model Evaluation and Tuning

3.3.3.1. Evaluation

After training, the model's performance is evaluated using metrics such as accuracy, precision, recall, F1 score, or mean squared error, depending on the task. Evaluation on a separate test set ensures that the model generalizes well to new data.

3.3.3.2. Hyperparameter Tuning

ML models have hyperparameters that control their behavior (e.g., learning rate, number of layers). Hyperparameter tuning involves experimenting with different values to find the optimal settings for the model.

3.3.4. Deployment and Monitoring

3.3.4.1. Deployment
Once trained and evaluated, the ML model is deployed into production environments where it can make predictions or provide insights based on new data. In healthcare, this could involve integrating the model into clinical decision support systems or patient management platforms.

3.3.4.2. Monitoring and Maintenance
Continuous monitoring is essential to ensure that the model performs well over time. As new data becomes available, the model may need to be retrained or updated to maintain its accuracy and relevance.

3.4. Applications of Machine Learning in Healthcare

ML has a wide range of applications in healthcare, including but not limited to:

3.4.1. Predictive Analytics
Forecasting patient outcomes, disease progression, and healthcare resource needs based on historical data.

3.4.2. Personalized Medicine
Tailoring treatments to individual patients based on their genetic makeup, lifestyle, and medical history.

3.4.3. Medical Imaging
Analyzing medical images to detect and diagnose conditions such as tumors, fractures, and neurological disorders.

3.4.4. Drug Discovery
Accelerating the process of discovering new drugs by analyzing biological data and predicting how different compounds will interact with targets.

3.4.5. Disease Prediction
Discuss how ML models are used to predict the likelihood of diseases like diabetes, cancer, and heart disease based on patient data.

3.4.6. Personalized Medicine

Explain how ML helps in tailoring treatments to individual patients based on their genetic makeup, lifestyle, and other factors.

3.4.7. Image Analysis

Describe the use of ML in analyzing medical images for the detection of abnormalities such as tumors, fractures, and other conditions.

3.4.8. Natural Language Processing (NLP)

Discuss the role of NLP in extracting meaningful insights from clinical notes, research papers, and patient records.

3.5. ML Algorithms Commonly Used in Healthcare

3.5.1. Neural Networks

Explain how neural networks, particularly deep learning models, are used in image recognition, diagnostics, and genomics.

3.5.2. Decision Trees and Random Forests

Describe their application in making clinical decisions, such as predicting treatment outcomes.

3.5.3. Support Vector Machines (SVM)

Discuss how SVMs are used in classifying medical data, such as differentiating between healthy and diseased tissues.

3.5.4. Reinforcement Learning

Explore how reinforcement learning is applied in optimizing treatment plans and robotic surgery.

4. Integration of IoT and Machine Learning in Healthcare

The integration of the Internet of Things (IoT) with healthcare systems has revolutionized how data is collected, processed, and utilized. IoT devices, such as wearable sensors, remote monitoring systems, and smart medical devices, continuously generate vast amounts of real-time data, which is invaluable for

Machine Learning (ML) applications in healthcare. In order to enhance prediction accuracy, Alzakari et al. [16] presented a methodology that makes use of the Extreme Gradient Boosting (XGBoost) algorithm to efficiently analyze large datasets and extract key features. Further improving prediction abilities to uncover intricate temporal patterns from patient data is done with the deep learning model Bidirectional Long Short-Term Memory (Bi-LSTM). It achieved a higher prediction accuracy of 99.4%, outperforming Naïve Bayes, decision trees, and random forests utilizing the method.

This data serves as the foundation for training ML models that can predict patient outcomes, enhance diagnostics, optimize treatment plans, and improve overall healthcare management. Below is a detailed exploration of how IoT generates data for ML in healthcare. According to Tenepalli et al. (2024), with the help of IOT and machine learning technologies, healthcare professionals would be able to monitor their patients more closely and communicate with them more proactively. Machine learning technology can be used to anticipate and diagnose diseases by feeding data gathered from IoT devices.

According to Aghalya et al. [18], the suggested method offers a viable way to monitor and forecast respiratory disorders on a continuous basis. This can give patients and medical professionals important information and guidance for managing respiratory diseases. While addressing heterogeneity, Saravanan et al. [19] suggested an automated strategy integrating AI and IoT. With a particular emphasis on breast cancer patients, this system, which combines AI, IoT, and sophisticated neural networks, makes real-time health monitoring easier. The paradigm, which incorporates pre-, in-, and post-treatment phases, strives for precise diagnosis, increased cost-effectiveness, and longer hospital stays. The assessment highlights the framework's scalability, enhances its trustworthiness, and confirms its effectiveness in changing healthcare procedures.

4.1. Continuous Monitoring and Data Collection

IoT devices are designed to continuously monitor various physiological and environmental parameters of patients, generating large volumes of data over time.

These devices can be worn by patients, embedded in medical equipment, or placed in healthcare environments to track vital signs, patient activities, and environmental conditions.

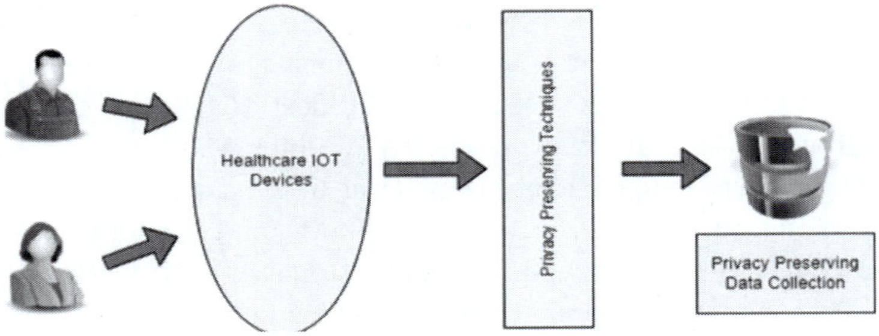

Figure 2. Patient data collection and monitoring.

4.1.1. Wearable Devices

Wearables such as smartwatches, fitness trackers, and health monitoring patches collect data on heart rate, blood pressure, glucose levels, sleep patterns, physical activity, and more. This real-time data is crucial for monitoring chronic conditions, detecting anomalies, and assessing patient well-being. For instance, continuous glucose monitors (CGMs) provide a stream of glucose level data that can be used to train ML models to predict hypo- or hyperglycemic events.

4.1.2. Remote Monitoring Systems

IoT-enabled devices used in remote patient monitoring, such as blood pressure monitors, ECG devices, and pulse oximeters, collect and transmit data from patients' homes to healthcare providers. This data helps in managing chronic conditions, post-operative care, and monitoring elderly patients, and it provides a rich dataset for ML algorithms to detect trends and predict health outcomes.

4.1.3. Smart Medical Devices

Devices like smart inhalers, connected insulin pumps, and IoT-enabled imaging devices generate data on medication usage, dosage administration, and imaging results. This data can be used to personalize treatment plans and monitor the effectiveness of treatments.

4.2. Data Variety and Volume

The diversity of data generated by IoT devices is a significant advantage for ML in healthcare. IoT devices capture a wide range of data types, including structured data (e.g., vital signs, medication doses), unstructured data (e.g., patient notes, audio recordings), and semi-structured data (e.g., sensor readings). The high volume of data generated over time enables the development of robust ML models.

4.2.1. Sensor Data

IoT sensors measure various physiological parameters such as temperature, heart rate, oxygen levels, and motion. This sensor data is often generated in high frequency and large volumes, making it ideal for ML models that require extensive training data to learn complex patterns.

4.2.2. Environmental Data

IoT devices can also collect environmental data, such as air quality, temperature, and humidity in patient care environments. This data is valuable for ML models that aim to assess and predict the impact of environmental factors on patient health, such as respiratory conditions or skin allergies.

4.2.3. Behavioral Data

Wearable and other IoT devices track patients' daily activities, sleep patterns, and lifestyle habits. This behavioral data is crucial for ML models that seek to understand the relationship between lifestyle factors and health outcomes, such as the impact of physical activity on cardiovascular health.

4.3. Real-Time Data Transmission and Storage

One of the key benefits of IoT in healthcare is the ability to transmit data in real-time to centralized databases or cloud platforms. This real-time transmission enables immediate analysis and decision-making, which is essential for critical healthcare scenarios. It also ensures that ML models are trained on the most up-to-date information, leading to more accurate predictions and insights.

4.3.1. Cloud Integration

IoT devices are often connected to cloud platforms where data is stored, processed, and analysed. Cloud-based storage solutions can handle the large volumes of data generated by IoT devices and provide the computational resources necessary for training ML models. For example, data from multiple patients' wearable devices can be aggregated in the cloud, providing a comprehensive dataset for developing predictive models.

4.3.2. Edge Computing

In some cases, IoT devices utilize edge computing to process data locally before transmitting it to the cloud. This approach reduces latency and allows for faster decision-making, which is critical in emergency situations. For instance, an IoT-enabled ECG monitor may process the data locally to detect an arrhythmia and alert the patient or healthcare provider immediately, while also transmitting the data to the cloud for further analysis.

4.4. Data Labeling and Annotation

For supervised ML models, labeled data is essential. IoT devices contribute to this process by generating labeled datasets through user input, device interactions, or automated processes. For example, when a patient uses a smart inhaler, the device can record the time and dosage of each use, creating a labeled dataset that correlates with the patient's respiratory health outcomes.

4.4.1. Patient-Generated Labels

In some cases, patients provide labels for the data collected by IoT devices. For example, a patient might label a specific time period when they experience symptoms, which can then be correlated with the data collected by wearable or other monitoring devices.

4.4.2. Automated Labeling

IoT devices can also automatically generate labels based on predefined thresholds or events. For instance, a smart glucose monitor might automatically label data as "normal," "low," or "high" based on glucose levels, providing a labeled dataset for training ML models.

4.5. Data Integration and Interoperability

IoT in healthcare often involves the integration of data from multiple devices and sources, creating a comprehensive dataset that can be used to train more effective ML models.

Interoperability between different IoT devices and healthcare systems is crucial for this integration.

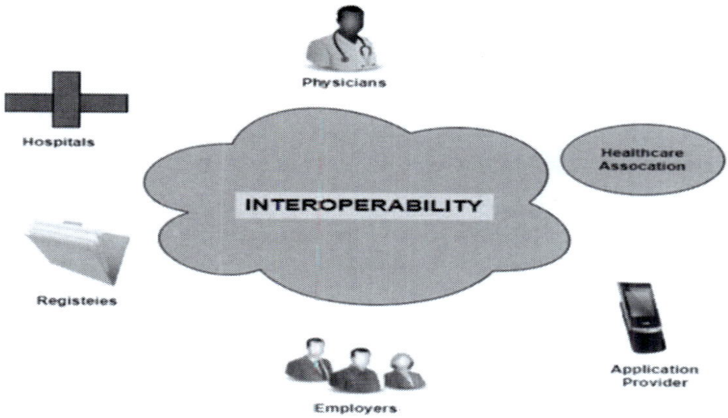

Figure 3. Data integration and interoperability.

4.5.1. Integration with Electronic Health Records (EHRs)

IoT-generated data can be integrated with EHRs to provide a complete picture of a patient's health. This integrated data is invaluable for training ML models that consider both real-time monitoring data and historical health records to make predictions and recommendations.

4.5.2. Interoperability Standards

Standards such as HL7 FHIR (Fast Healthcare Interoperability Resources) facilitate the seamless exchange of data between IoT devices and healthcare systems. This interoperability ensures that data from different sources can be aggregated and used to train ML models effectively.

5. ML Algorithms for IoT Data

The synergy between IoT and machine learning (ML) in healthcare has revolutionized how data is analyzed and utilized to improve patient outcomes, optimize treatment plans, and streamline healthcare operations. The logistic reversion model was proposed by Madanan et al. [20] as an improvement to the ongoing efforts to improve the early diagnosis, disease, and therapy reaction involved in respiratory ailments. IoT devices generate vast amounts of data, and choosing the right ML algorithms to process and interpret this data is critical for extracting actionable insights. Below is a detailed exploration of the ML algorithms commonly used to analyze IoT data in healthcare. In 2024, Ferdous et al. [21] proposed a CNN model that is based on feature selection and a stacking classifier of ensemble methods. Several machine learning algorithms, including K-Nearest Neighbor's classifier, Gaussian Naïve Bayes, Bernoulli Naïve Bayes, Decision Tree Classifier, Support vector machine, Random Forest classifier, and CNN [22], were applied after a comparison of the results obtained from training and testing periods in terms of stroke probability prediction. Results indicate that the highest accuracy, 99.89% for testing and 100% for training, is obtained by stacking six algorithms. The table 1 shows different ML techniques with different algorithms along with purpose and example.

Table 1. ML based algorithms for various healthcare system

S.No	ML Techniques	Algorithms	Purpose	Example
1	Supervised Learning Algorithms	Logistic Regression	To predict the presence of a disease or condition based on sensor data	Predicting whether a patient will develop a heart condition based on IoT data.
		Support Vector Machines	Work well with high-dimensional data	Classifying different stages of a disease.
		Decision Trees and Random Forests	Dealing with complex IoT data with multiple variables.	Using IoT data to predict patient outcomes.
		K-Nearest Neighbours (KNN)	Instance-based learning algorithm	Classifying patients into risk categories based on IoT data
		Artificial Neural Networks (ANNs)	Data is large and unstructured, such as medical images or continuous sensor data.	Analyzing IoT data from wearable ECG monitors to detect abnormal heart process.
2	Unsupervised Learning Algorithms	K-Means Clustering	Clustering algorithm that partitions data into k clusters based on similarity	Clustering patients with similar sleep patterns and activity levels using data from wearable's device.
		Hierarchical Clustering	To explore the relationships between different patient groups and identify hierarchical structures	Grouping patients with similar vital signs from IoT data.

S.No	ML Techniques	Algorithms	Purpose	Example
		Principal Component Analysis (PCA)	Convert high-dimensional data into a lower-dimensional space	Reducing the dimensionality of IoT sensor data
		Autoencoders	For processing complex IoT data, such as time-series data or images.	Detecting anomalies in continuous monitoring data
3	Reinforcement Learning Algorithms	Q-Learning	To learn the optimal action policy by maximizing cumulative rewards	Optimizing insulin dosage for diabetes patients by analyzing IoT data
		Deep Q-Networks (DQN)	To handle high-dimensional state spaces.	Managing chronic conditions like hypertension by continuously adjusting medication dosage based on IoT data.
		Policy Gradient Methods	Dynamic decision-making processes	Personalizing physical therapy regimens for stroke patients by continuously monitoring their progress through IoT devices.
4	Deep Learning Algorithms	Convolutional Neural Networks (CNNs)	To analyze medical images, detect abnormalities, and assist in diagnostics.	Analyzing X-ray or MRI images captured by IoT-enabled imaging devices
		Recurrent Neural Networks (RNNs)	For sequential data and are widely used for analyzing time-series data generated by IoT devices.	Predicting future glucose levels in diabetes patients
		Long Short-Term Memory Networks (LSTMs)	Effective at capturing long-term dependencies in sequential data.	Monitoring and predicting the progression of chronic conditions like epilepsy by analyzing time-series data
		Generative Adversarial Networks (GANs)	To generate synthetic data that resembles real data	Generating synthetic medical images for training diagnostic models

5.1. Supervised Learning Algorithms

Supervised learning algorithms are widely used in healthcare IoT applications, where the data is labeled, and the objective is to predict specific outcomes based on input features. These algorithms learn from historical data and use it to make predictions on new, unseen data.

5.1.1. Logistic Regression

Logistic regression is a simple, yet powerful algorithm used for binary classification tasks. In healthcare IoT, it is often used to predict the presence or absence of a disease or condition based on sensor data. Predicting whether a patient will develop a heart condition based on IoT data such as heart rate, blood pressure, and activity levels collected by wearable devices.

5.1.2. Support Vector Machines (SVM)

SVMs are effective for both binary and multi-class classification problems. They work well with high-dimensional data, making them suitable for IoT-generated data that may include numerous features. Classifying different stages of a disease based on data from IoT-enabled diagnostic devices, such as continuous glucose monitors or ECG sensors.

5.1.3. Decision Trees and Random Forests

Decision trees and their ensemble version, random forests, are popular for their interpretability and ability to handle both classification and regression tasks. They are particularly useful when dealing with complex IoT data with multiple variables. Using IoT data to predict patient outcomes, such as the likelihood of hospital readmission, by analyzing factors like vital signs, medication adherence, and environmental conditions.

5.1.4. Nearest Neighbors (KNN)

KNN is a simple, instance-based learning algorithm that can be used for both classification and regression. It works by comparing a new data point to the k-nearest data points in the training set and predicting the outcome based on the majority class or average outcome. Classifying patients into risk categories based on IoT data such as physical activity levels, diet, and sleep patterns collected from wearable.

5.1.5. Artificial Neural Networks (ANNs)

ANNs, particularly deep learning models, are powerful tools for modeling complex relationships in data. They are used in healthcare IoT applications where the data is large and unstructured, such as medical images or continuous sensor data. Analyzing IoT data from wearable ECG monitors to detect abnormal heart rhythms or early signs of atrial fibrillation.

5.2. Unsupervised Learning Algorithms

Unsupervised learning algorithms are used when the data is unlabeled, and the goal is to discover hidden patterns, groupings, or anomalies within the data. These algorithms are particularly useful for exploratory analysis and identifying previously unknown correlations in IoT data.

5.2.1. K-Means Clustering

K-means is a popular clustering algorithm that partitions data into k clusters based on similarity. It is used to group patients with similar characteristics or symptoms based on IoT data. Clustering patients with similar sleep patterns and activity levels using data from wearable to identify potential health risks associated with different lifestyle patterns.

5.2.2. Hierarchical Clustering

Hierarchical clustering builds a tree-like structure of nested clusters. It is used in healthcare IoT to explore the relationships between different patient groups and identify hierarchical structures within the data. Grouping patients with similar vital signs (e.g., heart rate, blood pressure) from IoT data to identify clusters of patients who may require similar treatment plans.

5.2.3. Principal Component Analysis (PCA)

PCA is a dimensionality reduction technique that transforms high-dimensional data into a lower-dimensional space while preserving the most important information. It is often used as a preprocessing step before applying other ML algorithms to IoT data. Reducing the dimensionality of IoT sensor data (e.g., from wearable or remote monitoring devices) to focus on the most significant variables that influence patient outcomes, such as specific vital signs or environmental factors.

5.2.4. Autoencoders

Auto encoders are neural networks used for unsupervised learning tasks, such as dimensionality reduction and anomaly detection. They are particularly useful for processing complex IoT data, such as time-series data or images. Detecting anomalies in continuous glucose monitoring data by learning the normal patterns and identifying deviations that may indicate a potential health issue.

5.3. Reinforcement Learning Algorithms

Reinforcement learning (RL) algorithms are used in scenarios where an agent learns to make decisions by interacting with an environment and receiving feedback in the form of rewards or penalties. In healthcare, RL is applied to optimize treatment strategies, resource allocation, and patient management.

5.3.1. Q-Learning

Q-learning is a model-free RL algorithm used to learn the optimal action policy by maximizing cumulative rewards. It is applied in healthcare IoT to develop personalized treatment plans and optimize patient outcomes. Optimizing insulin dosage for diabetes patients by analyzing IoT data from continuous glucose monitors and adjusting treatment plans based on real-time feedback.

5.3.2. Deep Q-Networks (DQN)

DQN is an extension of Q-learning that uses deep neural networks to approximate the Q-value function, enabling it to handle high-dimensional state spaces. It is used in healthcare IoT applications where decision-making involves complex, continuous data streams. Managing chronic conditions like hypertension by continuously adjusting medication dosage based on IoT data, such as blood pressure readings and patient behavior, to achieve optimal blood pressure control.

5.3.3. Policy Gradient Methods

Policy gradient methods are a class of RL algorithms that directly optimize the policy (the decision-making strategy) by adjusting the parameters to maximize expected rewards. These methods are used in healthcare IoT for dynamic decision-making processes. Personalizing physical therapy regimens for stroke patients by continuously monitoring their progress through IoT devices and adapting the exercises and intensity based on real-time data.

5.4. Deep Learning Algorithms

Deep learning algorithms, a subset of machine learning, are particularly effective in handling large and complex IoT datasets, such as those involving images, time-series data, and natural language.

5.4.1. Convolutional Neural Networks (CNNs)

CNNs are specialized neural networks designed for processing grid-like data, such as images. In healthcare IoT, CNNs are used to analyze medical images, detect abnormalities, and assist in diagnostics. Analyzing X-ray or MRI images captured by IoT-enabled imaging devices to detect conditions like tumors, fractures, or other abnormalities.

5.4.2. Recurrent Neural Networks (RNNs)

RNNs are designed for sequential data and are widely used for analyzing time-series data generated by IoT devices. They are particularly useful for making predictions based on historical data. Predicting future glucose levels in diabetes patients using continuous glucose monitoring data by analyzing past trends and patterns.

5.4.3. Long Short-Term Memory Networks (LSTMs)

LSTMs are a type of RNN that are effective at capturing long-term dependencies in sequential data. They are used in healthcare IoT for tasks where the data has temporal dependencies. Monitoring and predicting the progression of chronic conditions like epilepsy by analyzing time-series data from IoT-enabled devices over extended periods.

5.4.4. Generative Adversarial Networks (GANs)

GANs are used to generate synthetic data that resembles real data, which can be particularly useful for augmenting training datasets in healthcare. This is especially valuable in cases where labeled data is scarce. Generating synthetic medical images for training diagnostic models when there is a lack of real patient data due to privacy concerns or limited availability.

6. Benefits of Integration

6.1. Real-Time Monitoring

Explain how IoT-driven ML enables real-time monitoring of patients, leading to quicker interventions and better outcomes.

6.2. Improved Diagnostics

Discuss how the integration of IoT and ML enhances diagnostic accuracy by analyzing large datasets and identifying patterns that might be missed by humans.

6.3. Personalized Treatment

Explore how IoT data combined with ML algorithms can provide personalized treatment plans, improving patient outcomes.

6.4. Impact on Healthcare Delivery

6.4.1. Enhanced Patient Care and Outcomes

6.4.1.1. Improved Monitoring

Discuss how continuous monitoring via IoT devices and real-time analysis through ML improves patient care by enabling timely interventions.

6.4.1.2. Early Detection

Explore how predictive analytics and early warning systems lead to the early detection of diseases, reducing mortality rates.

6.4.1.3. Reduced Hospital Admissions

Explain how remote monitoring and telemedicine reduce the need for hospital visits, allowing patients to receive care at home.

6.5. Cost Reduction and Efficiency Improvements

6.5.1. Operational Efficiency

Discuss how IoT and ML optimize hospital operations, such as resource management, patient flow, and equipment maintenance, leading to cost savings. According to Bano et al. [23] machine learning is crucial to the Internet of Things (IoT) since it handles massive data sets, powers IoT functions in smart cities, and looks at how the IoT affects healthcare facilities.

6.5.2. Preventive Care

Explain how predictive analytics allows for preventive care measures, reducing the overall cost of healthcare by avoiding expensive treatments.

6.6. Personalized Medicine

6.5.3. Tailored Treatment Plans

Explore how ML-driven analysis of IoT data leads to personalized treatment plans, improving patient outcomes and reducing adverse reactions.

6.5.4. Pharmacogenomics

Discuss how ML models analyze genetic data to predict how patients will respond to different medications, enabling personalized drug prescriptions.

6.6. Remote Patient Monitoring and Telemedicine

6.6.1. Telehealth Platforms

Describe how IoT devices and ML models power telehealth platforms, enabling remote consultations, diagnostics, and treatment.

6.6.2. Chronic Disease Management

Discuss how remote monitoring and data analysis help in managing chronic diseases, allowing for adjustments in treatment without the need for frequent hospital visits.

6.7. Impact on Rural and Underserved Areas

Highlight how telemedicine and remote monitoring are bridging the gap in healthcare access for rural and underserved populations.

7. Ethical and Legal Considerations

7.1. Data Privacy and Security Issues

7.1.1. Patient Data Protection

Discuss the ethical concerns regarding the collection, storage, and sharing of patient data from IoT devices.

7.1.2. Cybersecurity Risks

Explore the vulnerabilities in IoT systems that could be exploited by cybercriminals, risking patient data and potentially compromising patient safety. Savanović et al. [24] presented an approach for identifying and acting quickly to address the sustainability issues in healthcare. The SHapley Additive exPlanations (SHAP) model is used to identify the contributing reasons to difficulties that arise. Its tests and comparisons show that the problem formulation has significantly improved.

7.1.3. Anonymization and Data Sharing

Discuss the challenges of anonymizing IoT data and the ethical considerations around data sharing among healthcare providers, researchers, and third parties.

7.2. Ethical Concerns in AI/ML-Driven Healthcare

7.2.1. Bias in Algorithms

Address the ethical implications of bias in ML algorithms, which could lead to disparities in healthcare outcomes.

7.2.2. Autonomy and Informed Consent

Discuss the importance of patient autonomy and informed consent, especially when AI and ML systems are used in decision-making processes.

7.2.3. Transparency and Accountability

Explore the need for transparency in how ML models make decisions and the importance of accountability in cases where AI-driven decisions lead to adverse outcomes.

7.3. Regulatory Frameworks and Standards

7.3.1. Existing Regulations

Provide an overview of the current regulatory frameworks governing the use of IoT and ML in healthcare, such as HIPAA in the U.S. and GDPR in Europe.

7.3.2. Need for New Regulations

Discuss the need for updated or new regulations to address the unique challenges posed by IoT-driven ML in healthcare, including data governance, algorithm transparency, and patient safety.

7.4. Patient Consent and Data Ownership

7.4.1. Ownership of IoT Data

Explore the debate around data ownership—whether patients, healthcare providers, or device manufacturers own the data generated by IoT devices.

7.4.2. Informed Consent for Data Use

Discuss the importance of obtaining informed consent from patients for the use of their data in ML models, especially for secondary uses such as research or commercial purposes.

7.4.3. Ethical Use of Data

Address the ethical considerations around the use of patient data, including issues related to data commodification and the potential exploitation of vulnerable populations.

8. Future Directions

8.1. Emerging Trends in IoT and ML in Healthcare

8.1.1. AI-Driven Wearables

Discuss the future of AI-driven wearables that not only monitor health but also provide real-time analysis and personalized recommendations.

8.1.2. Smart Implants

Explore the potential of smart implants that can monitor internal health metrics and provide real-time data to healthcare providers.

8.1.3. Edge Computing

Explain how edge computing could enhance IoT-driven ML by processing data locally on devices, reducing latency, and improving real-time decision-making.

8.2. Potential Advancements in IoT and ML Technologies

8.2.1. Improved Data Integration

Discuss advancements in data integration technologies that could allow for seamless aggregation of data from multiple IoT devices.

8.2.2. Quantum Computing

Explore how quantum computing could revolutionize ML by providing the computational power needed to analyze vast amounts of IoT data quickly and accurately.

8.2.3. Federated Learning

Describe how federated learning allows ML models to be trained on decentralized data from IoT devices without sharing sensitive information, enhancing privacy.

8.3. The Future of Personalized Medicine and Smart Healthcare

8.3.1. Genomics and IoT

Discuss the integration of genomics data with IoT and ML to create highly personalized treatment plans.

8.3.2. AI-Powered Diagnostics

Explore the potential for AI-powered diagnostic tools that could analyze data from IoT devices to diagnose diseases with high accuracy.

8.3.3. Smart Hospitals

Discuss the concept of smart hospitals where IoT and ML are used to optimize every aspect of healthcare delivery, from patient care to operational efficiency. To oversee the healthcare supply chain and guard against access violations and tampering with medical information, Rizzardi et al. (2024) [25] have proposed an IoT-driven blockchain-based architecture. Because the data collected is secret and sensitive, permission-based blockchains like Hyperledger Fabric have gained traction.

8.4. Challenges and Opportunities for Future Research

8.4.1. Data Privacy and Security

Highlight the need for research into more secure and privacy-preserving technologies in IoT and ML.

8.4.2. Algorithm Fairness

Discuss the importance of researching and developing algorithms that are fair, transparent, and free from bias.

8.4.3. Scalability and Cost

Address the challenges related to scaling IoT-driven ML solutions and the need for cost-effective technologies that can be deployed across various healthcare settings.

8.4.4. Collaboration Across Disciplines

Explore the importance of interdisciplinary research involving healthcare professionals, data scientists, ethicists, and policymakers to address the complex challenges of IoT-driven ML in healthcare.

Conclusion

Modern healthcare is undergoing a change thanks to the creative solutions that IoT-driven machine learning (ML) is bringing to the table. These solutions optimise treatment plans, improve patient care, and simplify healthcare operations. Internet of Things (IoT) devices, such as wearable sensors, smart medical devices, and remote monitoring systems, generate massive volumes of real-time data. ML algorithms can process this data to deliver predictive analytics and continuous monitoring. This real-time data greatly reduces the likelihood of complications and hospital stays by enabling early diagnosis of illnesses, prompt therapies, and better management of chronic diseases. For example, gadgets like smartwatches with electrocardiogram (ECG) sensors and continuous glucose monitors (CGMs) enable the early detection and treatment of diabetes and cardiovascular disorders, thereby improving patient outcomes. Furthermore, through processing and analyzing big datasets, finding patterns, and generating predictions that aid medical practitioners in making decisions, IoT-driven machine learning improves diagnostic accuracy. This has prompted the creation of sophisticated diagnostic tools that are able to evaluate data and medical images from IoT-enabled devices, enabling early diagnosis and individualized treatment regimens catered to the requirements of each patient. Beyond providing personalized care, IoT-driven machine learning enhances the effectiveness of the healthcare system by streamlining patient flow, inventory control, and resource allocation in hospitals. While machine learning (ML) algorithms forecast future requirements and optimize supply chains to cut waste and guarantee that essential supplies are available when needed, Internet of Things (IoT) sensors track medical supplies in real time. In addition, these technologies help with hospital operations management and patient admission prediction, which results in more effective and efficient healthcare delivery. However, we need to resolve issues like data privacy, security, and interoperability to ensure the safe and efficient application of IoT-driven ML in healthcare. Despite these difficulties, IoT-driven machine learning has enormous promise to improve healthcare by being more proactive, individualized, and patient-centered. IoT-driven ML holds the potential to revolutionize healthcare by making it more accessible and efficient, thereby improving patient care and maximizing resources for the healthcare sector as a whole. Besides enhancing current procedures, the combined application of IoT and ML in healthcare is paving the way for a future where healthcare will be more accessible, efficient, and effective, ultimately improving patient outcomes and quality of life for individuals worldwide.

References

[1] Yousefnezhad, N., Malhi, A. Främling, K. (2020). Security in product lifecycle of IoT devices: A survey. *Journal of Network and Computer Applications,* 171, 102779, ISSN 1084-8045.

[2] Tyagi, N., Rai, M., Sahw, P., Tripathi, P., Kumar, N. (2022) *Methods for the Recognition of Human Emotions Based on Physiological Response: Facial Expressions in Smart Healthcare for Sustainable Urban Development,* pp 183-202, IGI Global, USA.

[3] Krishnamoorthy, S., Dua, A., & Gupta, S. (2023). Role of emerging technologies in future IoT-driven Healthcare 4.0 technologies: A survey, current challenges and future directions. *Journal of Ambient Intelligence and Humanized Computing*, *14*(1), 361-407.

[4] Duodu, N. Y., Patel, W. D., Koyuncu, H., Nartey, F., & Torgby, W. (2024). Empowering Health and Well-being: IoT-Driven Vital Signs Monitoring in Educational Institutions and Elderly Homes Using Machine Learning. *International Journal of Electrical and Electronics Research*, *12*(Special issue), 40-47.

[5] Ranjan, R., & Sahana B. C. (2024). A Comprehensive Roadmap for Transforming Healthcare from Hospital-Centric to Patient-Centric through Healthcare Internet of Things (IoT). *Engineered Science*. 30, 1175.

[6] Nain, V., Shyam, H. S., Kumar, N., Tripathi, P., Rai, M. (2024). Study on Object Detection Using Artificial Intelligence and Image Processing-Based Methods. In Tripathi, et al. (Eds.), *Mathematical Models Using Artificial Intelligence for Surveillance Systems,* Wiley-Scrivener, USA.

[7] Joshi, A., Amrita, Mathur, R. S., Kumar, N., Tripathi, P. (2024). Study of Traditional, Artificial Intelligence and Machine Learning Based Approaches for Moving Object Detection. In Tripathi, et al. (Eds.), *Mathematical Models Using Artificial Intelligence for Surveillance Systems,* Wiley-Scrivener, USA.

[8] Mishra, R., Tripathi, P., Kumar, N. (2024a). Application of Emotional Intelligence in improvement of Human-Robot Collaboration. In, Kumar, et al., (Eds.), *Human-Machine Collaboration and Emotional Intelligence in Industry 5.0,* pp. 251-267, IGI, Global, USA.

[9] Mishra, R., Tripathi, P., Kumar, N. (2024b). Future Directions in the Applications of Machine Learning and Intelligent Optimization in Business Analytics. In Bansal, S., Kumar, N., Agarwal, P. (Eds.), *Intelligent Optimization Techniques for Business Analytics,* pp. 49-76, IGI, Global, USA.

[10] Jain, A., & Rakesh, S. K. (2024). IoT-driven predictive healthcare system for proactive treatment and improved patient management. In *AIP Conference Proceedings* (Vol. 3111, No. 1). AIP Publishing.

[11] Kumar, N., Tripathi, P., Nanda, R. P., Tiwari, S., Sharma, S. (2024). Machine Learning for Smart Health Services in the Framework of Industry 5.0. In M. Khan, R. Khan, P. Praveen, A. R. Verma & M. K. Panda (Eds.), *Infrastructure Possibilities and Human-Centered Approaches With Industry 5.0* (pp. 215-230). IGI Global.

[12] Tripathi, P., Siddiqi, A. H. (2016). Denoising Raman spectra using a non-Convex regularizer in Total Variation, *Indian Journal of Science and Technology*, 9(48), 1-5.

[13] Tripathi, P., Siddiqi, A. H. (2017). De-noising EEG signal using iterative clipping algorithm, *Biosciences and Biotechnology Research Asia*, 14(1), 497- 502.

[14] Tripathi, P. (2020). Electroencephalpgram Signal Quality Enhancement by Total Variation Denoising Using Non-convex Regulariser, *Int. J. Biomedical Engineering and Technology*, 33(2), 134-145.

[15] Tripathi, P., Kumar, N., Siddiqi, A. H. (2020). De-noising Raman spectra using total variation de-noising with iterative clipping algorithm in Computational Science and its Applications, Taylor and Francis Group, CRC Press, USA, pp 225-231.

[16] Alzakari, S. A., Menaem, A. A., Omer, N., Abozeid, A., Hussein, L. F., Abass, I. A. M., ... & Elhadad, A. (2024). Enhanced heart disease prediction in remote healthcare monitoring using IoT-enabled cloud-based XGBoost and Bi-LSTM. *Alexandria Engineering Journal*, *105*, 280-291.

[17] Tenepalli, D., & TM, N. (2024). A systematic review on IoT and machine learning algorithms in e-healthcare. *International Journal of Computing and Digital Systems,* 16(1), 279-294.

[18] Aghalya, S., Rao, N. V., Roy, R. R., Srinivasan, C.,& Premi, G. "Real-time Monitoring and Prediction of Respiratory Diseases Using IoT and Machine Learning," *2023 Second International Conference on Smart Technologies for Smart Nation (SmartTechCon)*, Singapore, Singapore, 2023, pp. 635-640.

[19] Saravanan, M. S., & Thisin, S. Integrating AI and IoT for Enhanced Predictive Healthcare Monitoring: A Comprehensive Study on Breast Cancer Patient-Centric Approach. In *2024 International Conference on Advances in Data Engineering and Intelligent Computing Systems (ADICS)* (pp. 1-5). IEEE.

[20] Madanan, M. (2024). Analysis of IoT-Driven Machine Learning Algorithms for Predicting Respiratory Diseases. In *2024 4th International Conference on Innovative Practices in Technology and Management (ICIPTM)* (pp. 1-6). IEEE.

[21] Ferdous, M. J. & Shahriyar, R. A. Comparative Analysis for Stroke Risk Prediction Using Machine Learning Algorithms and Convolutional Neural Network Model. *2023 International Conference on Electrical, Computer and Communication Engineering (ECCE)*, Chittagong, Bangladesh, 2023, pp. 1-6, doi: 10.1109/ECCE57851.2023.10101567.

[22] Naik, S. B., Sreedevi, M., Rafick, S., Ravivarman, G., Rajendiran, M., & Maranan, R. (2024). Machine Learning and MANET-Driven 5G Technology for Smart Healthcare: Enhanced Patient Diagnosis and Treatment. In *2024 International Conference on Expert Clouds and Applications (ICOECA)* (pp. 700-705). IEEE.

[23] Bano, S., Hussain, A., Arif, A., Khursheed, S., & Arif, M. A. (2024). Data-Driven Internet of Things: Role in Smart Cities. *The Asian Bulletin of Big Data Management*, *4*(02), Science-4.

[24] Savanović, N., Toskovic, A., Petrovic, A., Zivkovic, M., Damaševičius, R., Jovanovic, L., & Nikolic, B. (2023). Intrusion detection in healthcare 4.0 internet of things systems via metaheuristics optimized machine learning. *Sustainability*, *15*(16), 12563.

[25] Rizzardi, A., Sicari, S., & Coen-Porisini, A. (2024). IoT-driven blockchain to manage the healthcare supply chain and protect medical records. *Future Generation Computer Systems*.

Conclusion

As this volume draws to a close, it is evident that the integration of IoT-enabled machine learning in healthcare represents more than just a technological evolution—it marks a profound shift in how we perceive, deliver, and experience healthcare itself. The chapters presented throughout this book reflect a growing body of interdisciplinary knowledge and innovation that is shaping the next generation of medical systems.

We have explored the transformation of healthcare through real-time data collection, predictive analytics, personalized treatment pathways, remote monitoring, and the rise of smart hospitals. From algorithmic diagnosis to proactive care models, the potential of this synergy between IoT and ML is immense. It enables systems that are not only smarter, but also more responsive, scalable, and patient-centered.

However, this transformation also brings with it critical challenges—ensuring data privacy and security, achieving device interoperability, maintaining clinical accuracy, and addressing ethical concerns regarding automated decision-making. These challenges are not mere obstacles but vital checkpoints in our collective journey toward sustainable, intelligent healthcare ecosystems.

This book has aimed to strike a balance between celebrating the technological advancements and acknowledging the complexities that accompany them. It is our hope that readers come away with a deeper appreciation of the possibilities, a clear understanding of the responsibilities, and a renewed motivation to pursue responsible innovation in the healthcare domain.

As we look ahead, the future of healthcare lies in collaboration—among technologists, clinicians, researchers, policy-makers, and patients. Only through such collective effort can we ensure that the promise of IoT-enabled machine learning translates into equitable, ethical, and effective health solutions for all.

Let this volume serve not as a conclusion, but as a beginning—a stepping stone for further exploration, invention, and impact in the rapidly evolving landscape of digital health.

Index

A

B

C

D

K

L

M

N

O

P

R